5. 6. , 13. 14 , 18 , 19, 20, 21.

INTRODUCTION TO TRAVEL AND TOURISM

INTRODUCTION TO TRAVEL AND TOURISM

An International Approach

Michael M. Coltman

Van Nostrand Reinhold
_____NEW YORK

Copyright © 1989 by Van Nostrand Reinhold
Library of Congress Catalog Card Number 88-34629
ISBN 0-442-20652-6

All chapter opening photographs are used by permission of The Image Bank®:
pages 1 and 133 © Marcel Isy-Schwart; page 19 © 1988 Grant V. Faint; page
31 © 1988 Richard and Mary Magruder; page 41 © K. Bhatia; page 57 ©
Elyse Lewin; page 71 © Guido Alberto Rossi; page 87 © Giuliano Colliva;
page 101 © 1981 Louis Jawitz; page 113 © 1985 Daniel Weinberg and
Miriam Clark; page 123 © Faustino; page 143 © Aran Gesae; page 161 ©
1987 Jeff Smith; page 181 © 1985 Walter Bibikow; pages 191 and 345 ©
George Obremski; page 203 © 1982 Steve Dunwell; page 219 © 1985 Geoff
Gove; page 235 © David W. Hamilton; page 249 © Eric Meola; page 265 ©
1988 Robert Kristofik; page 285 © 1981 Lou Jones; page 297 © 1988 Alan
Becker; page 323 © 1988 Romilly Lockyer; page 333 copyright © 1985
Colin Molyneux

Printed in the United States of America

Designed by M. R. P. Design

Van Nostrand Reinhold
115 Fifth Avenue
New York, New York 10003

Van Nostrand Reinhold International Company Limited
11 New Fetter Lane
London EC4P 4EE, England

Van Nostrand Reinhold
480 La Trobe Street
Melbourne, Victoria 3000, Australia

Macmillan of Canada
Division of Canada Publishing Corporation
164 Commander Boulevard
Agincourt, Ontario M1S 3C7, Canada

16   15   14   13   12   11   10   9   8   7   6   5   4   3   2   1

Library of Congress Cataloging-in-Publication Data
Coltman, Michael M., 1930–
  Introduction to travel and tourism: an international approach/
  Michael M. Coltman.
    p. cm.
    Bibliography: p.
    Includes index.
    ISBN 0-442-20652-6
    1. Tourist trade. I. Title.
  G155.A1C533 1989
  380.1′4591—dc19   88-34629
                                            CIP

Contents

Introduction:
A Trip Through Time

People have always traveled, in search of food or animal skins for clothing, or for territorial expansion. Travel in these early days was time-consuming and dangerous. Indeed, our word *travel* comes from the French word *travail*, which means work, and that is what it was, hard work. Most early travel was on foot, but later donkeys began to be used. Waterways and seaways also frequently became paths for trade and commerce.

THE GREAT EMPIRES_____

Organized travel in the West probably began during the great empires of the Persians, Assyrians, Greeks, Egyptians, and Romans. This period began several millennia B.C. and continued for several hundred years A.D. During the empire period, travel developed for military, trade, and government reasons, as well as for communication from the central government to its distant territories.

Travel was also necessary for the artisans and architects "imported" to design and construct the great palaces and tombs, many of which today's tourists travel to see. Travel led, as well, to an infrastructure of roads, canals, mileage markers, sentinel posts, wells, hostelries (crude as they were), and eating spots.

In ancient Greece, people traveled to the Olympic Games, an event that required accommodations and food services for both the participants and the spectators. The same demands are made today by people flocking to major sporting events.

Travel Methods

For overland travel, ordinary people used donkeys or camels, but for military and government purposes, horses were used, along with wagons and chariots. Goods also had to be transported. For example, the Egyptians had to bring in needed minerals from abroad, and the Assyrians had a monopoly on the Lebanese cedar that they exported abroad. In Persia between 500 and 400 B.C., all the provinces were connected with the capital, Susa, by roads, and one of them was fifteen hundred miles long. The Greeks, on the other hand, constructed few roads.

Sea travel also thrived. The first great system of sea transportation was established by the Phoenicians and connected the early inland camel caravan routes with seaports around the Mediterranean. The Phoenicians' ships carried goods of high value and little bulk, such as gems, spices, perfume, and fine handiwork. The Phoenicians also explored the Atlantic and West African coasts. Water travel was necessary to expand the markets for commercial goods, and the Greeks, and then the Romans, became dominant sea powers. Sea travel was also important to the Chinese and Japanese.

Money

The first coins are thought to have been used in Lydia (a gold-producing country in Asia Minor) in about 700 B.C. At first, for reasons of security, people often carried small coins in their mouths. Ordinary people, however, continued to trade by barter. Indeed, when one considers the unavailability of small coins or other means of payment for goods or services, it is easy to understand how difficult, if not impossible, private travel was in those days. But by the height of the Roman Empire, money had become common. A cash and credit system had been developed, and money played a role similar to that played today. One can imagine how difficult and complex travel would be today if each phase of a trip had to be arranged by barter instead of paid for in cash or by credit card.

The Romans

The Romans used their own coins, and Latin was the common language of an empire that, at its peak, stretched from Scotland in the north to the Euphrates River in southeast Europe. The Romans introduced a legal system that crossed boundaries, and they also were great road builders. One of their most famous, well-marked, and well-built roads was the Appian Way, which stretched for 350 miles from Rome to Brundisium and was the main highway to Greece and the East. The Romans could travel from the 73-mile-long Hadrian's Wall (built in the second century, A.D. and still visited today by tourists) in Great Britain to the Euphrates River without crossing a hostile border. Their lines of communication were excellent, and their inns housed traveling traders and government employees. Indeed, the

Romans had what today would be called a good tourist infrastructure (transportation/communication system).

In the government system of inns along the roads, travelers knew by their signs what amenities each inn offered: A square within a square (symbolizing a courtyard) signified a first-class inn; two triangles surmounting a rectangle (symbolizing a country house) was less fancy; and a triangle atop a square indicated a rudimentary hostelry with just shelter and water. We use the same kind of pictographs today. For example, a hotel sign accompanied by a fork, knife, and plate symbol indicates that it has a restaurant.

Even for the Romans, however, distant travel still was slow. For most people, therefore, leisure travel had to be confined to places close to home, such as the Bay of Naples, about a hundred miles from Rome. Vacation villas were first built on this bay two centuries before Christ. Two hundred years later, construction had peaked, with dense development reminiscent of the type seen today in Waikiki, Florida, or Costa del Sol in Spain. One of the more luxurious villas was that of Emperor Hadrian near Tivoli, of which extensive ruins remain today. In its original form it is said to have covered more than seven square miles.

Although the Romans were not the first people to visit other places for pleasure, as Feifer (1985, p. 8) states, "the first culture genuinely to produce mass tourism, in both the letter and the spirit of the term, was Imperial Rome. In the second century A.D., it was at its peak."

Sea Voyages

For those who could afford the time (and the money), sea trips were quite common. Greece, rich in treasures, was close to Italy and was a popular destination. Passenger ships—as we know them today with regular schedules—did not appear until after steamships were invented in the mid-1800s. Instead, tourists simply went to the nearest port and waited for a ship going in their direction. Because these vessels had no passenger accommodations, the passengers slept on deck in small tents that they brought with them. They also had to bring along their own food, cooking utensils, and wine for drinking. Their own servants prepared their meals.

At their destination the tourists camped or stayed at any available inn, or with friends of friends if they had any there. Even if one arrived unannounced, the custom of the day required extending hospitality to unknown travelers.

The Romans often crossed the Mediterranean from Italy and then sailed up the Nile to see Egypt's speaking statue, a favorite sightseeing monument. Egypt's weather also was an attraction, as it was hot, sunny, and dry, and Alexandria in those days was thus a cosmopolitan city of various nationalities such as Egyptians, Greeks, Jews, Ethiopians, Indians, and Syrians. The tourists came to shop, to look, and to travel inland. Local restaurants featured such ethnic specialties as smoked fish with garlic, snails, giblet stews, and barley beer. When the tourists returned home weighed down with purchased goods, they paid heavily on passing through customs, for there was a 25 percent duty on imported items. The governments of the day knew then how to raise money, just as they do today.

Early Religious and Other Travel

Early travel was not limited to government needs and to the very rich; religious festivals and the theater also attracted travelers. Drama, poetry, art, architecture, and philosophy flourished and brought in their share of tourists. Indeed, the Olympic Games (first held in 776 B.C.) were founded in Greece during this time and encouraged travelers to witness them. Gladiator spectacles also attracted large crowds.

This period also saw the growth of cities, which acted as magnets to travelers. Travel for health began also as mineral springs were sought out by those who could afford to visit them. There is some evidence, as well, of health sea cruises during this period.

During the latter part of the Roman Empire the establishment of Christianity led to religious travel to the cities of Jerusalem and Bethlehem.

Early Sightseeing

Sightseeing was popular in the empire period, and many of the monuments still standing today reveal the travelers' names or marks scratched on the stone to show that they had been there.

Indeed, the Seven Wonders of the World were built with an eye to attracting tourists, particularly those of an aristocratic, scholastic, or artistic bent. These Seven Wonders were

1. Great Pyramid of Khufu
2. Pharos Lighthouse at Alexandria
3. Hanging Gardens of Babylon
4. Colossus of Rhodes
5. Statue of Zeus at Olympus
6. Temple of Artemis at Ephesus
7. Tomb of Mausolus at Halicarnassus

Unfortunately, only the Great Pyramid remains for modern-day tourists to marvel at.

The early sightseeing tourists also went to Egypt and Greece to baths, shrines, and seaside resorts and to see where Alexander the Great slept, Socrates lived, Ajax committed suicide, and Achilles was buried, and to see the Pyramids, the Sphinx, and the Valley of the Kings.

The End of the Empires

The ancient empires became large and unwieldy and difficult to administer, and as they did so, they crumbled. The established political and economic structures were destroyed, and travel became unsafe, as there were no soldiers to provide protection. Bandits were a menace. Travel diminished. The roads, communication systems, and inns that the Romans had built fell apart. It was hazardous to travel and difficult to find what a tourist might want to travel to see, anyway. A look back at this early history of tourism is quite revealing. During the time of the Roman Empire, people traveled much more freely than in the period to follow. One of the main reasons for this was that the tourists felt safe and free from terrorism. The situation is no different today. Terrorism, where it is likely, is still a deterrent to tourism.

THE MIDDLE AGES_____

During the Middle Ages, from about A.D. 500 to 1400, much of the middle class disappeared, and trade declined as people returned to the land. The shadow of what is sometimes referred to as the Dark Ages began to lift in about A.D. 1000 when the Church began to do a great deal of building, particularly in France where the new churches and cathedrals became, and still are today, tourist attractions.

Pilgrimages

The monasteries were also acquiring wealth, and the monks educated the public about miracles and other holy matters and encouraged them to go on pilgrimages, which vast numbers of people did. By the fourteenth century, pilgrimages were an organized mass phenomenon served by a growing network of charitable hospices. Pilgrims came from all social classes, except the very poor who were still tied to the land.

In the later part of this period the Christian Crusades freed the Holy Land, and peaceful pilgrimages by Muslims to Mecca, and Christians to Jerusalem and Rome, began. These pilgrimages had a religious basis, but they were also social and recreational events. In England, pilgrimages to Canterbury were made popular through Geoffrey Chaucer's *Canterbury Tales*. Other favorite destinations were Santiago de Compostela in Spain and Rome in Italy. It took the average horseback rider almost two months to travel the twelve hundred miles from London to Rome—and twice that long if the pilgrim were on foot. The journey to Rome was particularly arduous, as it meant crossing the treacherous Alps.

Travel Books

With the advent of the printing press in the fifteenth century, books began to appear and, in particular, travel books that gave those who could read the desire to travel to the faraway places they described. One of the best-known early books, translated into many foreign languages, was Sir John Mandeville's *Travels*, printed in 1357. Mandeville's travels took him as far away as southeast Asia.

Package Tours

By this time, package tours (probably the first ever available) from Venice to the Holy Land were offered. The trip's cost included passage, meals and wine, accommodations, donkey rides, and bribe money, in order, as Feifer (1985, p. 48) explained, "to prevent confiscation of baggage, endless delays over red tape, or mischief from the camel drivers." There were always local hustlers who found the neophyte tourists easy to exploit, but these travelers also had for their convenience accommodation bureaus, travel agencies, guidebooks, souvenir shops, and many other aspects of travel familiar to us today. Even if people did not travel in a formal group, they tended to stick together, because solitary pilgrimage was too dangerous. As Feifer (1985, pp. 34–35) commented about this era:

> Tourism was big business: innkeepers and souvenir manufacturers prospered, and the Church benefited most of all, by the spectacular offerings of wealthy pilgrims. Competition between shrines could be fierce.... When pilgrim traffic was heavy, roadside "victuallers" appeared, selling from their tents wine, fruit, fish, meats, pastries, bread, and cake—the prototypical "fast-food" stand.

By the fifteenth century, Rome boasted over a thousand hostelries, varying from charitable hospices to luxurious inns. Tourist guidebooks were available in a dozen different languages and were often altered to highlight the foreigners' preferences, much as do today's tourist brochures.

Marco Polo

In the latter part of the thirteenth century a native of Venice, Marco Polo, explored the land routes from Europe to China and other parts of Asia. The Chinese had a fairly well developed road system; indeed, the first was built during the Chou dynasty (1122–221 B.C.). Polo's book on his travels was the West's main source of information about life in the East, and it described, among other things, the use of paper money, which at that time was unheard of in the West.

Sea Travel

Wherever people encountered rivers and oceans, they used them as a medium for travel. The sea was particularly challenging, but nonetheless some remarkable voyages were made. For example, some fifteen hundred years ago the Polynesians traveled a distance of about two thousand miles from their home islands to Hawaii, overcoming major problems of water and food availability for such a long journey.

There is also evidence that the Vikings arrived in North America as early as A.D. 1000. The Spanish also traveled by sea, and Christopher Columbus brought trade to North America as early as 1492. Indeed, Marco Polo's book is said to have inspired Christopher Columbus to travel west from Genoa, Italy, across the Atlantic to try to reach Asia. At that time the North American continent was not known to exist. When Columbus first reached land in 1492, he thus thought he had arrived in India, and so he named the islands he had reached the West Indies (today known as the Caribbean). The Portuguese were also great sailors and went on voyages to the Azores, Africa, and Asia, settling Macao (an island off Hong Kong) in 1557.

Revival of the Cities

During the Middle Ages Christendom became a unifying force, and most travel was for religious reasons. Agricultural innovations and a rise in productivity improved the well-being of individuals, and the cities in Europe also prospered. This improvement in trade and manufacturing was paralleled by an increase in population and a growing middle class. Political and commercial organizations and universities such as Oxford and Cambridge (twelfth century), Salamanca (thirteenth century), Vienna and Prague (fourteenth century), Uppsala (fifteenth century), and Leiden (sixteenth century) also proliferated.

A pivotal point was the ascendancy of Queen Elizabeth I to the throne in England in the sixteenth century and the resultant growth in England's trade and commerce spearheaded by the Royal Navy. This set the stage for the Renaissance, which lasted from the fourteenth to the seventeenth century.

THE RENAISSANCE

The Renaissance, or rebirth, introduced the view that truth lay outside the mind and spirit. It thus created a desire to explore, discover, and understand and encouraged historic and scientific investigations. At the same time that explorers were bringing back tales about distant lands, the aristocracy and wealthy were traveling extensively in Europe.

The Renaissance began in Italy, where relative political stability, economic expansion, a flourishing urban civilization, and wide contact with other cultures provided a new view of the world and the concept that people could master their environment and control their future. From Italy the Renaissance spread throughout the rest of Europe.

The Elizabethan traveler was described by Francis Bacon as the "merchant of light." This new type of tourist traveled to broaden his or her experience and knowledge, whereas the pilgrim had traveled to experience the mystery of the

Church. The pilgrim was guided by the Church, whereas the new traveler was an individual. Queen Elizabeth sanctioned this form of travel, and the crown often paid for part of it, especially for future diplomats. Universities also began giving travel fellowships.

Travel Licenses

In order to leave England in those days, travelers first had to obtain a license, which indicated how long they could stay away (usually two or three years), where they must not go, and how much money and how many horses and servants (usually three) they could take. Tourists also had a passport but surrendered it, along with an exit fee, when they left England; they picked up a new passport en route for each country they visited.

"Student" tourists were also given discounts on fares, entry fees, and tolls for bridges or highways. They carried very little cash, instead using letters of credit (a letter from a banker or other person to his agent in another country authorizing the bearer to receive money from the agent) which, like today's travelers' checks, generally could not be used by others if lost or stolen.

The First Trade Show

The main destination of this Elizabethan Renaissance tourist was the undisputed apex of culture at that time: Italy. For the Elizabethans, ancient Rome was the greatest civilization the world had ever had. A popular stop on the way to Rome was the Frankfurt book fair where publications were displayed that imbued the travelers with the right spirit of discovery and enterprise. Besides the book fair there was a vast merchandise exposition where visitors could gather ideas about manufacture and commerce, the major issues of the day. The Frankfurt fair was one of the earliest trade shows that attracted tourists, and it is still a major annual international event today.

Another major stop on the way to Italy was Paris, where the future diplomats could observe French court life. From there they would travel south to Lyons and then cross the Alps to Italy. The Alps were no less frightening to these tourists than they had been to the pilgrims and could be far more dangerous, as the tourists usually traveled alone on horseback.

The Fork

One of the early Elizabethan travelers to Italy, Thomas Coryate, brought back the first table fork to England. Even the cultured French did not have forks at the turn of the seventeenth century. The fork's introduction into England did not, however, discourage for some time even aristocratic diners from eating with their hands. Elizabethan travelers were also exposed to banking systems and mercantilism, which up to that time the English aristocracy had disdained.

These early travelers, both personally and through their writings, brought back a new way of looking at things to a population deeply curious about what was "out there." Soon, the loosely organized Elizabethan tour became the much more highly structured event known as the Grand Tour.

The Grand Tour

The Grand Tour was developed some 150 years after the peak of the Elizabethan tour. By the mid-eighteenth century it had been pared down to a quite specific itinerary. Instead of a complete immersion in whatever one encountered, the Grand Tourist's objective was to visit only the best of places. Italy was still the major destination, as it was where one could explore the ancient classical ruins and see and buy art, which became an important aspect of the Grand Tour.

The Grand Tour became a necessary part of the training of future administrators and political leaders. Its focus was Italy because of its culture and language, but the tour could also encompass Germany and France and even Vienna.

Because it could last for as long as three years the Grand Tour was available only to the aristocracy. The typical Grand Tourist was a recent university graduate. The more affluent brought along their tutors, valets, coachmen, and footmen, as well as portrait painters to copy monuments and statues and landscape painters to paint the scenery.

The Grand Tour was not easy. Passports were required to get out of the country (that is, to pass through the port), and there were money exchange problems, although the introduction of bills of exchange helped resolve that difficulty. Linen and bedding frequently had to be taken along, as well as an inflatable bathtub, a medicine chest, and other accoutrements. Grand Tour travels could be dangerous, and so travelers carried guns.

The Italian part of the Grand Tour started in Turin, and from there travelers went on to Milan, Venice (which by this time had slowly begun sinking into the mud), Florence, Naples, and finally Rome where they stayed for several weeks. Rome catered mainly to English tourists and offered English types of inns and restaurants and even coffee houses where London newspapers were available.

England was growing steadily more prosperous, and the Grand Tour became more and more popular. It was interrupted by the Seven Years' War (1756–1763) but became even more popular after that. At its peak an estimated forty thousand Britons were traveling on the Continent.

In 1778, the first travel guidebook for the Grand Tour travelers was published: Thomas Nugent's *The Grand Tour*.

It was during the Grand Tour epoch that tourists—much as they feared the trip —began to admire the Alps for their own scenic beauty, and in 1765 the first tourist inn was opened at Chamonix, the foundation for what was to become a major tourist influx to Switzerland. The Grand Tourist produced a real revolution in British taste in many matters, including Renaissance architecture, and many "noble houses" such as Blenheim Palace and Burlington House became showpieces of this style, as did the White House in Washington, for Thomas Jefferson was himself a Grand Tourist.

In 1789 the Grand Tour possibilities were severely disrupted by the French Revolution, followed by the Napoleonic Wars, and so travel to the Continent from England virtually came to a halt until 1814. When tourism resurfaced in the early nineteenth century it was reinspired by poets such as Byron and Shelley who romanticized countries such as Switzerland where they stayed. These poets turned the Alps into something to be appreciated rather than feared. Tourists thus began to turn their sights upward into the mountains and to become nature tourists. In addition, the male-dominated Grand Tour began to become a family affair.

But during the epoch of the Grand Tour something else was happening that had a far greater impact on mass tourism than did the Grand Tour: the Industrial Revolution. It laid the foundation for millions to do later their own three-week version of the Grand Tour, or "packaged tour."

THE INDUSTRIAL REVOLUTION AND TOURISM TODAY

The Industrial Revolution, which lasted from about 1750 to 1850 in Europe, created the base for mass tourism as we know it today. This period brought profound economic and social changes and turned most workers away from basic agriculture into the town/factory and urban way of life that we have today.

Wells (1961, p. 766) contrasted the Industrial Revolution with the expansionary period of the Roman Empire:

> The economic revolution of the Roman republic had never been clearly apprehended by the common people of Rome. The ordinary Roman citizen never saw the changes through which he lived clearly and comprehensively as we see them. But the industrial revolution, as it went on towards the end of the nineteenth century, was more and more distinctly seen as one whole process by the common people it was affecting, because presently they could read and discuss and communicate, and because they went about and saw things as no commonality had ever done before.

The Industrial Revolution introduced machinery that vastly increased productivity. New kinds of power to move vehicles (such as trains and ships) were invented, as were new methods of mineral extraction. Raw materials were required from the New World, and a new wave of imperial expansion began. All of these developments required scientific learning and exchange. Many new occupations led to a rapid expansion in the middle class's wealth and education, as well as an increase in leisure time and a demand for recreation travel activities; the elitist Grand Tour declined in popularity.

Initially, recreational tourist trips were generally only day trips, because most people still had only limited discretionary income, and even weekends "off" had only just become the norm. Later, workers began to take annual vacations and to escape from the rapidly growing urban areas in which most of them had to earn their income. They turned to the spas and seasides for these holidays and set the tone for much of the tourist industry base today. Some destinations—up until then visited primarily by the rich—expanded, and others were newly established to capture this growing middle-class market. To the destinations the middle class was a huge market compared with the small number of the earlier aristocratic visitors. What the new tourists did not have in large amounts of money to spend, they more than made up in numbers.

The Birth of the Spa and the Seaside

When their empire collapsed, the Romans stopped going to their Riviera, the Bay of Naples, and to their baths (or spas), and so this mode of recreation fell out of fashion. Then in the Middle Ages the former Roman baths became sacred springs and later health spas. The aristocracy began to travel for health reasons, and hence the health spa (named after a Belgian town famous for its mineral springs) was born. These spas gradually turned into pleasure resorts.

Some of the better-known European spas were Bath (England), Baden-Baden (Germany), Baden (Austria), Bains-les-Bains (France), and Lucca (Italy). In North America, White Sulphur Springs and Saratoga Springs were fashionable spas. By 1900 there were some 750 spas in Europe, many in resort and entertainment areas. Spas have declined in popularity today, but many of them are still extensively used in Eastern Europe. Some of these spa cities have become tourist attractions in their own right. For example, any tourist to Bath will have missed a major attraction if he or she does not see the magnificent Regency Terraces built to house the early aristocrats who used Bath as a health spa.

The aristocracy initially paved the way to the spas (for example, Charles II made Tunbridge Wells, near London, fashionable), but where the aristocracy went the masses soon followed, and then the aristocracy moved on. In fact, it moved on to the seaside and by 1800 had made places like Scarborough, Margate, and Brighton (in England) popular with the rich, who also built luxurious vacation villas in Nice and Cannes on the Mediterranean coast.

Surprisingly, even though seaside destinations were popular, it was not until the eighteenth century that the English turned to saltwater bathing. As with the spas, the seaside was first visited for health reasons. At the popular seaside resorts, as Feifer (1985, p. 204) described it, one

> took one's place in an enclosed wooden cart mounted on large wheels, which was drawn into the ocean by a horse, whereupon a sturdy individual called the "dipper" would hold one in the icy water for hours at a time—the women in big, tentlike bathing dresses, the men naked, quite out of each other's sight, of course.

By the 1820s, Brighton on the south coast of England had become accessible to day trippers, and the long amusement pier, typical of those at many seaside resorts, was built in 1824.

Although the spas and seaside resorts were originally opened for health reasons, they soon became—because of rail access—destinations for recreation and entertainment. Indeed, tourist destinations frequently become successful as a result of a number of factors, rather than one factor alone.

Rail Travel

Transportation improved the development of railways in the 1800s, making travel cheap, fast, and safe. With the advent of rail travel the middle classes in Europe flocked to the seaside resorts. Hotels, restaurants, shops, and other tourist attractions sprang up to cope with this flood. Access to the rail system was a major consideration governing where the tourist destinations would expand or appear.

The railway also revolutionized thoughts about where people could go. A factory worker could now travel as quickly as an aristocrat. In other words, the train became an agent of democracy. Another agent who helped this along was the travel agent, who first appeared in the form of Thomas Cook, who organized the first train tour trip in England in 1841. Also in 1841, Henry Wells in the United States started in the travel business with what became Wells Fargo and later American Express.

By 1863 the railway had reached Cannes in France, and once again the middle class arrived and began to crowd out the aristocracy. They moved on to Monte Carlo, in Monaco, where the gambling casino was built in 1868. Its profits were so great that the citizens of Monte Carlo no longer had to pay taxes, and Monaco became the first "underdeveloped" nation to solve its economic problems through tourism.

North American Travel

North America was first explored in the sixteenth century by the Spanish, who settled primarily in the southwest and in what is now known as Florida. The Spanish are credited with introducing horses here, which were unknown to the native Americans.

With the aid of horses the North American settlers became great travelers. The pioneering spirit that inspired them to leave Europe to go to North America in the first place continued to encourage them to move ever westward across the vast continent.

As in Europe, the great rivers of North America induced travel. For example, riverboats on the Mississippi played their part in commerce and also hosted tourists by providing gambling and other entertainment on trips from St. Louis in the north to New Orleans in the south. The foundation for New Orleans's Mardi Gras was laid in the mid-nineteenth century. Other great rivers such as the Ohio, the Delaware, and the Hudson also encouraged travel.

A network of roadways was established along the eastern seaboard in the early 1800s, and later in that century the railroads made mountain and lakeside resorts popular and travel through the western mountains much easier.

Tourism started in the Catskills area of New York State in the 1820s with the construction of a large first-class resort hotel on a bluff above the Hudson River valley. In those early years its patrons were the aristocrats of the large cities of New York and Philadelphia who reached the resort after a day-long steamboat ride along the Hudson and a stagecoach trip of several more hours. The railroad did not reach the Catskills until 1868. But once the railroad was built, many new resort hotels, catering primarily to summer tourists, opened along its route. Tourism in this area mushroomed as people wanted to escape the cities and enjoy the natural beauty of the mountains.

As this happened, what had once been a relatively remote resort area catering to the elite became open to the middle-class business and professional people, and so its social character changed, and as was the case with tourist destinations popular with the aristocracy in Europe, the elite moved on. They often moved south and west as the railroads extended in those directions.

Many of the new resorts opened by the railways had as their attraction the natural settings in which they were built. But although this railroad expansion made travel easier, it also affected other types of transportation. For example, until the arrival of the railroads, most people traveled along and across the Ohio and Mississippi rivers by boat. Crossing the rivers in any other way was impossible. Then the railways built their own bridges across the rivers and began to open up the south and west. In turn, this put out of business many of the riverboat operators, as it was now faster and more comfortable for most people to travel by rail rather than by boat.

The *Nouveaux Riches*

World War I (1914–1918) saw the disappearance of much of the European aristocracy and ruling families. These people were soon replaced by the *nouveaux riches* (newly rich) from North America who became the new seekers of fashionable recreation/vacation destinations in Europe. The *nouveaux riches* made popular these destinations which soon had to cater to the golden hordes who followed.

The infrastructure to take Americans to Europe in style had been created in World War I. Transatlantic troop ships were converted into modern ocean liners. Even though good passenger steamships had been around since the mid-1800s, nothing before the war could equal the luxury liners that crossed the Atlantic in the 1920s. From 1919 to 1933 America was in the grip of Prohibition, and sea travel to Europe was thus quite popular, as the ship's bars opened twelve miles out from New York. There were many competitive liners, but one of the favorites was the Cunard Line's *Aquitania* which crossed the Atlantic from New York to London.

Paid holidays became the norm in Britain and France in the 1930s, and the Riviera in the summertime became more popular than ever with middle-class tourists from not only North America but also all Europe.

Up to this time, suntanning as a recreational endeavor was not known. White skins were far more fashionable, for they indicated that their owners were part of the aristocracy, who did not work outdoors. But during the 1920s and 1930s this changed—no doubt to the great satisfaction of the manufacturers of suntan lotions and related products.

The Automobile

In the last fifty years the automobile has had an immense impact on tourism. Although it was invented in the 1890s it was not until twenty or thirty years later that its mass production gave society a mobility never before possible.

In the 1930s the automobile became such a common and cheap form of highway travel in North America that it gave birth to highway "autocourts" or "motor-courts," the forerunner of what we know as motor hotels and motels today.

One of the problems of the automobile as a means of travel is that it has led to the construction of major road networks which in turn have encouraged more automobile traffic, which in turn demands even better highways. It is difficult to know where this might end.

World War II

Soon after the Great Depression of the 1930s World War II (1939–1945) began. As was the case with previous wars this one eliminated one version of the good life but created a new infrastructure for more tourists than ever to enjoy their version of another good life. After World War II, tourism, restrained as it had been for several years, began to burst out again as the optimism of peace, along with prosperity, blossomed. More people than ever now belonged to the middle class.

World War II put hundreds of thousands of North American military personnel into contact with other cultures, environments, and peoples in both Europe and Asia. The war was also the impetus for dramatic improvements in communication and air transportation that have made travel so rapid and easy today. Indeed, more people today travel between North America and Europe than between any other two distant areas in the world, and it was cheap, mass air travel that allowed that to happen.

SUMMARY

This quick trip through history shows us that tourism is founded on various phenomena: As the production of goods and services increases, it creates both more money and more available leisure time. At the same time, a better-educated population will want to travel and improve their knowledge and education. Improved transportation makes travel cheap, rapid, easy, and relatively secure. Finally, improved communication through print, radio, and television makes the marketing of tourism much easier today than in earlier times. As Murphy (1985, p. 21) explained:

> Although the dramatic changes in mobility after the Second World War may have had the most visible impact, other forces were at work which permitted the growth and proletarianization of tourism. More people found they had the leisure time and discretionary income that are necessary prerequisites for a vacation. Thanks to labor negotiations and social legislation the length of official and paid holidays has been steadily increasing. Governments have created more vacation time by incorporating isolated public holidays into the now familiar "long weekends" throughout the year. In addition, the post-war economic recovery provided a major increase in real income, which many people converted into increased recreation and travel.

DISCUSSION QUESTIONS

1. Discuss how the Roman Empire affected early travel.
2. Which of the Seven Wonders of the World is still a tourist attraction today?
3. What happened in the early Middle Ages to cause travel to decline?
4. Explain how pilgrimages contributed to travel in the late Middle Ages.
5. Who was Marco Polo, and what did he do?
6. What was the Renaissance, and how and when did it begin?
7. Describe the Grand Tour.
8. Discuss the effect of the Industrial Revolution on society and thus on early tourism.
9. Describe the role of the spa in travel.
10. Describe the effect of early rail travel on tourist destinations.
11. Explain how seaside resorts became popular and why suntanning was not popular with early tourists to these resorts.
12. Who were the *nouveaux riches*? To where did they usually travel and by what method(s)?
13. Describe the effect of the automobile on travel.
14. How did World War II affect today's mass tourism?
15. Explain the factors that have led to mass tourism as we know it today.

REFERENCES

Feifer, Maxine. 1985. *Going Places: The Ways of the Tourist from Imperial Rome to the Present Day*. London: Macmillan.

Murphy, Peter E. 1985. *Tourism—A Community Approach*. New York: Methuen.

Wells, H. G. 1961. *The Outline of History*. New York: Doubleday.

SUGGESTED READINGS

Balsdon, J. P. V. D. 1969. *Life and Leisure in Ancient Rome*. London: Bodley Head.

Bathe, Basil W. 1972. *Seven Centuries of Sea Travel*. London: Barrie & Jenkins.

Beebe, Lucius. 1966. *The Big Spenders*. London: Hutchinson.

Burgess, Anthony, and Frances Haskell. 1967. *The Age of the Grand Tour*. London: Paul Elek.

Burkart, A. J., and S. Medlik. 1974. *Tourism: Past, Present and Future*. London: Heinemann.

Casson, Lionel. 1974. *Travel in the Ancient World*. London: Allen & Unwin.

D'Arms, John. 1970. *Romans on the Bay of Naples*. Cambridge, Mass.: Harvard University Press.

Feifer, Maxine. 1985. *Going Places: The Ways of the Tourist from Imperial Rome to the Present Day*. London: Macmillan.

Hibbert, Christopher. 1974. *The Grand Tour*. London: Spring Books.

Lochsberg, Winifred. 1979. *History of Travel*. Leipzig: Edition Leipzig.

Murphy, Peter E. 1985. *Tourism—A Community Approach*. New York: Methuen, pp. 17–26.

Nash, D. 1979. "The Rise and Fall of an Aristocratic Tourist Culture: Nice, 1763–1936." *Annals of Tourism Research* 6:61–76.

Owen, Charles. 1979. *The Grand Days of Travel*. Exeter, England: Webb & Bower.

Rosenow, John E., and Gerald L. Pulsipher. 1979. *Tourism: The Good, the Bad, and the Ugly*. Lincoln, Neb.: Three Century Press.

Rowling, Marjorie. 1971. *Everyday Life of Medieval Travellers*. London: Batsford.

Rugof, Milton. 1960. *The Great Travelers*. New York: Simon & Schuster.

Turner, Louis, and John Ashe. 1975. *The Golden Hordes*. London: Constable.

Twain, Mark. 1869. *The Innocents Abroad*. New York: Harper.

Woon, Basil. 1927. *The Frantic Atlantic*. New York: Knopf.

Young, Sir George. 1973. *Tourism, Blessing or Blight?* Harmondsworth, England: Penguin.

Travel Patterns and Trends

DOMESTIC TOURISM_____

When we use the word *tourism*, we usually think of international travel—people from one country visiting another. However, for most developed nations by far the greatest amount of tourism is generated by people traveling within their own country. This is commonly known as *domestic tourism*. According to Lundberg (1976, p. 9) domestic travel—although it is more difficult to quantify than is international tourism, because there are no national borders to be crossed at which tourists can be counted—is estimated to be 75 to 80 percent of all tourism activity.

Most domestic tourism is a natural offshoot of changes in life-styles and particularly in the use of the automobile as a means of transport. First came a move away from rural living to urbanization. This urbanization led to families' moving to the suburbs from where they were able to commute to and from work. The growth in incomes also meant more visits to relatives and friends. People increasingly came to perceive vacations as an intrinsic part of their life rather than as a luxury. Finally, the automobile is estimated to be the chosen mode of transportation for more than 75 percent of domestic tourism.

Most governments try to encourage domestic tourism and discourage their own citizens—often through advertising, although sometimes by other means such as currency controls—from going abroad. But sometimes these controls are not necessary, as world economic forces can change monetary values. For example, when world economic conditions force the dollar to drop in regard to foreign currencies, this makes the purchase of those foreign currencies (and thus the cost of foreign tourist vacations that must be paid for in those foreign currencies) more expensive.

Travel Deficit

Residents of a country who take a holiday abroad need the currency of the foreign country they plan to visit. In order to buy foreign currency they must spend their own money. From a financial point of view, this is the equivalent of importing goods from abroad. The more money that flows out of a country as a result of its citizens' traveling abroad, the more probable it is that that country will have a travel deficit.

A *travel deficit* occurs when more of a country's money is spent abroad by its own citizens than is earned by that country from foreigners visiting it. A travel deficit is the same as spending more money on imported goods than is earned from exported goods. Thus, it is important for most countries not only to encourage domestic tourism but also to discourage its own citizens from traveling abroad. Economists define this as *import substitution*.

Some people find it difficult to visualize tourists coming into a country as an export for that country; they usually consider exports to be goods going out of a country. However, tourists coming into a country can be conceptualized as an export by thinking about who receives the money from selling the product. In other words, who is the seller in tourism? The answer is the host country or region. Tourism differs from many other types of export only in that the purchaser "consumes" the goods and services on the seller's premises!

Balance of Trade

For both political and currency reasons, some countries impose severe restrictions on their citizens' traveling abroad, while still welcoming foreign travelers into their country. This helps ensure that they do not have a travel deficit and also that they have what economists refer to as a *positive balance of trade*. This positive balance of trade occurs when the total earnings from exports of goods and services (which includes foreign travelers coming into the country) are higher than the cost of imported goods and services (which includes its own citizens' going abroad).

Travel Restrictions

Most of the Eastern bloc countries in Europe have a rigid system of foreign currency and passport controls so that its traveling citizens have no choice but to be domestic tourists. Although some Western European countries may have some currency controls, their citizens usually are free to travel without restrictions. The United States and Canada currently have neither controls nor restrictions, and their governments generally use advertising only to maximize domestic tourism and minimize travel abroad.

Local Tourism

Even within a country, cities and regions vie with one another to keep their own tourism "local." They also try to increase their share of the total domestic tourism pie, as well as maximize the number of foreign tourists coming to that city, area, or region.

Cities and regions do this by investing in tourism research, planning, and promotion. For example, many cities have tourism and convention bureaus. Conventions, in particular, can be a major generator of tourism if they are national or international in scope. They bring a great deal of new money into an area to be spent in hotels, restaurants, shops, and attractions and on many other goods and services. This money filters through many levels and greatly benefits the local economy.

Domestic Transportation

Transportation companies (airlines, railways, and bus lines) profit from international tourism, but less so from domestic tourism. Studies show that most domestic travel in North America and Europe is by automobile, as it is a relatively inexpensive form of travel, regardless of the trip's purpose, such as visiting friends and relatives (the main purpose of most domestic tourism) or for some other reason.

To the automobile traveler, the use of the auto has other advantages besides cost. For example, an automobile allows more flexibility in the specific start and stop of a day's travel, and the ability to take side trips to visit attractions on the way to a destination. Automobile travel also benefits motels, gas stations, restaurants, and similar businesses on travel routes. As the travel distances increase, automobiles become less common as a travel mode: For business and convention travel of more than a few hundred miles, the airplane is the dominant mode of transportation.

INTERNATIONAL TOURISM

Most international travelers come from countries with a relatively high standard of living combined with a high rate of economic growth in which industry and commerce form the base of the economy. Such countries have a high rate of urbanization, in which equality of incomes is part of their social system. The international tourism market is primarily composed of middle-income people who have managerial or professional positions or work in supervisory and skilled jobs.

Exporting goods is one way to earn foreign currency. Another way that is becoming more and more important to most countries is to attract foreign tourists. This form of export is often referred to as an *invisible export.*

Developing Countries

Invisible exports are also critical to many Third World or developing countries who have no tangible goods to export. These developing countries must rely solely on exporting their tourism to earn the foreign currency they need to import goods to help raise the economic well-being of their citizens. These developing countries generally have few or no domestic tourists and so must depend on foreign tourists to occupy their hotels, eat in their restaurants, and spend money in their shops and on their attractions.

International Tourism Patterns

International tourism has risen steadily since the end of World War II, except for a slight decline during the oil crisis of the early 1970s. According to the International Union of Official Travel Organizations (IUOTO), there were 25 million international tourist arrivals in 1950. A *tourist arrival* is a person from one country arriving in another. In 1970 this number had grown to 183 million, an increase of 158 million in twenty years, or a compound growth rate of over 10 percent per year. In the early 1970s the world oil price crisis caused dramatic increases in the costs of most products, including tourism. As a result the World Tourism Organization (WTO—formerly the IUOTO) estimated that international tourist arrivals grew to 280 million in 1982, an increase of 97 million since 1970, or a compound growth rate of about 4 percent per year. Since that time tourism has continued to increase at about the same rate.

International tourism is dominated by travel between Europe and North America. The European Travel Commission (ETC), made up of twenty-three member countries, recently reported that Europe receives almost 60 percent of all international tourist arrivals. By contrast, North America currently accounts for only a little more than 10 percent of international arrivals. In Europe about 6 million a year of those arrivals are from the United States, 1 million from Canada, and 500,000 from Japan. There are fewer arrivals in Europe from Latin America, but Latin Americans spend more money. One reason that the largest number of arrivals in Europe are from North America is the historical link between most North Americans and their ancestors in Europe. In addition, the hundreds of thousands of military people who spent time in Europe during World War II helped reinforce this tie and create new ties. The airlines also have encouraged mass travel between the two continents by offering relatively low fares.

North America Verus Europe

The number of international arrivals to North America is increasing in absolute terms (even if not as a proportion of total world arrivals). This is so because of the increasing affluence of the residents of other nations (particularly the Europeans and Japanese) relative to that of North Americans, combined with fluctuating currency levels which have seen the value of the dollar decline severely in recent years (making it cheaper for foreign tourists to buy it).

The absolute number of people traveling from North America to Europe still forms a relatively low percentage (less than 3 percent) of all North Americans traveling abroad. For most European countries, a higher percentage of their citizens travels abroad each year, but these figures must be interpreted with care. For example, most European countries are geographically very small compared with the United States and Canada. Many of them are bordered by several other countries, and the time to reach another country, even by car, is often only a few hours. There are few border-crossing restrictions in Western Europe, and most of these countries are industrialized, with populations with a high standard of living and mobility. For these reasons, a greater percentage of Europeans are international tourists. On the other hand, many states and provinces in North America are larger than most European countries. Geographically speaking, what is international travel in Europe is domestic travel in North America.

Intra–North American Travel

Intra–North American travel is in many ways far greater and more significant than is North American travel to Europe. For example, Canadians and Mexicans are first and second in their contributions to tourist inflows to the United States, and the United States is Canada's biggest international travel market. In addition, the United States and Canada are Mexico's biggest sources of tourists.

Generators of Tourists

A curious fact in analyzing international tourism statistics is that some of the smallest countries in Europe (for example, Switzerland, Holland, and Austria) are high generators of international tourists. One reason for this (apart from the geographic factors discussed earlier) is that these countries have a sound economic base that creates wealth, thereby allowing their citizens to travel. In addition, the small size of their countries and the limited number of attractions at home give them incentives to travel abroad.

On the other hand, the United States and Canada are relatively isolated, and travel distances—even to nearby countries such as Mexico—necessitate considerable travel time compared with that for Europeans traveling to other European countries. In addition, North America contains many varied attractions that domestic tourists can visit.

TRAVEL PATTERNS

A destination's accessibility is often based on a sequence of transportation methods. For example, roads that led to seaports or connected major cities were later supplemented by railroads which reinforced the travel patterns. Air travel often connected cities across oceans that were previously crossed only by ocean liners.

Generally, however, for tourists to travel between two regions, there must be a supply of tourist services (such as hotels, restaurants, and attractions) in one and a desire to travel there in the other. The area must also be easily accessible. For example, Florida in the winter attracts more Canadian tourists from Quebec and Ontario than does California. The main reason is that for them, Florida is generally easier to reach than is California. Also, for most of those tourists, Florida is a traditional winter destination, implying that a tourist destination must look beyond simple transportation linkages in order to see what types of tourists it will attract by means of available routes and methods.

Established Patterns

Travel patterns between countries, and even between regions within a country, are constantly shifting. Sometimes a new tourist opportunity will open up, depriving a traditional destination of some of its market. Nevertheless, some consistencies and general trends can be determined. For example, business travel is most common in countries that have had consistently strong trade ties, which in turn generate other types of tourist travel, as do international connections for military and political reasons. Many countries have a traditional source of visitors, such as Spain and Portugal have in the British, Mexico has in U.S. residents, and the United States has in Canadians.

Cost also is important. One reason that there is so much travel between North America and Europe is the relatively low travel cost. But which comes first, low cost or travelers?

The national character of the host and the source countries is also a factor. Some nationalities just seem to get along better with each other or else simply appear to get along with each other for their mutual benefit. For example, the Spanish and the British do not generally have similar temperaments, but tourists from Britain flock to Spain because the Spanish seem to be able to provide the environment and services that British vacationers seek (including fish and chips just like those at home). For the same reason, citizens of northern Europe also flock to Spain and Portugal during their long dark winters. They even stay in hotels that are known to be "Swedish," "Norwegian," or "Danish," knowing that they will have familiar surroundings and atmosphere.

When most people travel abroad for the first time, they tend to be more comfortable with what is familiar than with what is new. They appreciate the host country residents' speaking the visitors' language and finding familiar foods and customs. When they discover this type of environment and enjoy their vacation there, they often return to it several more times before seeking a more different experience. This is one reason that Western Europe has remained such a magnet to most North Americans.

Once travel patterns, both domestic and international, are firmly established, they tend to become self-perpetuating. For this reason it seems likely that there will be little or no shift in most prevailing international travel patterns.

International Trends

For several decades, Western Europe has been a popular destination for international tourist arrivals and will probably remain so for the foreseeable future. But tourists from North America, Western Europe, and other parts of the world are now traveling more often to Eastern Europe. In turn, the Eastern European countries (as well as other countries such as China) are removing their travel restrictions and making it easier to visit them, as their governments recognize the economic benefits of tourism. Also, as travelers become used to visiting Western Europe, they become curious about less "explored" parts of the world, including Eastern Europe and less developed parts of the world such as Africa.

In general, there seems to be a slow shift of tourist arrivals from the economically advanced countries to the less developed ones. People and their attitudes change over time along with demographics, and thus some tourist destinations increase in popularity while others decline. Improvements in communication (particularly television) can also broaden and influence people's desire to travel. McIntosh and Goeldner (1984, p. 142) summarized this as follows:

> Rising standards of living, changes in the population age composition, the increasing levels of educational attainment, better communication, increased social consciousness of people relating to the welfare and activities of other people throughout the world, and the psychological shrinking of the world by the jet plane have combined to produce an interest among nations in all other nations.

However, it must be noted that there will always be many travelers who do not want to distance themselves culturally from the familiar.

The Future

Some observers of tourism have suggested that without continued economic growth there cannot be continued growth in tourism. In the short run this is probably true.

But tourism has always rebounded, or has found new ways to cope with adversity. In this regard tourism is really a reflection of society at large. For example, if we look at the record for the 1970s, we will find that the tourism industry, despite the setbacks caused by the oil crisis, was quite resilient and still managed to grow, even if at a slower rate. One of the ways that people coped in this situation was to attempt to lower their vacation costs. For example, many people turned to self-catering by buying or renting recreation vehicles (RVs), leading to a dramatic upturn in the RV industry during this period. People were not willing to give up their vacations, but they were willing to change.

The industry also responded with innovation, particularly the tour package type of vacation. Today there are tour packages to suit every taste and income level. These vacations' low costs are a result of economies of scale in such things as the block booking by tour wholesalers of airplane seats and hotel rooms. The savings are then passed on to the consumer, the traveling vacationer. In some cases costs are held down by vertically linking airlines to tour wholesalers and hotels so as to ensure high traffic volumes through all parts of the system. The airlines have also adapted by reducing the number of flights in some cases and rescheduling to produce more occupied seats per flight.

There also have been some temporary traffic pattern upheavals in relation to tourism. For example, in the mid-1980s, the number of tourists from North America to Europe fell sharply as a result of terrorism at certain spots in Europe. But in most cases such setbacks were relatively temporary. Business fell back for one year but the following year bounced back to its previous, if not a higher, level.

For these reasons, such as people's flexibility in their travel habits and the adaptability of the industry to cope rapidly with change, there should be no major shifts in travel patterns in the short and medium run, and possibly even in the long run.

DISCUSSION QUESTIONS

1. Explain why domestic tourism in North America occupies such a high proportion of its overall tourism.
2. Explain the term *travel deficit* and why tourism is an export.
3. Define *import substitution*.
4. What is a positive balance of trade, and how does tourism affect it?
5. Why are conventions considered important to the tourism industry?
6. Why is the automobile the dominant form of tourist transportation in North America?
7. Why is international tourism important to developing countries, and why do they have little or no domestic tourism?
8. Why are North Americans the largest group of international arrivals in Europe?

9. Only about 3 percent of all North Americans are international tourists to Europe each year. Why are the percentages of international tourists higher for most European countries?

10. What is intra–North American travel? Explain its significance.

11. Why are small countries with low populations such as Switzerland, Holland, and Austria large generators of international tourists?

12. Explain the importance of accessibility in determining travel patterns.

13. Discuss three reasons that international travel patterns become relatively firmly established.

14. Discuss two ways in which tourism has recently rebounded from setbacks in established travel patterns.

PROBLEM

In order to boost its domestic tourism and reduce its balance of trade, Israel has imposed a "restriction" on its citizens who travel abroad. This restriction is a travel tax that each Israeli citizen must pay on leaving the country. This tax is approximately $120 per person in the off-season and $300 per person in the peak season. This tax obviously encourages the Israelis to stay and vacation in their own country, but it also has a negative effect. Before the imposition of the tax in the early 1980s, as many as eighty thousand of its citizens who lived abroad visited Israel each year. That number has now been reduced to less than half, because even though they are no longer residents of the country, they still are citizens and so must pay the tax on leaving. Obviously, there are pros and cons to this tax.

Assume that you are the minister responsible for this tax and are debating whether to maintain it or eliminate it. What other information would you like to have about domestic tourism in Israel and about international tourism by its citizens living abroad? Or assume that you have all the information you want and use figures of your own choosing to show how you would calculate whether the tax was an advantage or disadvantage, based on the net tourism balance of trade.

REFERENCES

Lundberg, Donald E. 1976. *The Tourist Business*. Boston: CBI.

McIntosh, Robert W., and Charles R. Goeldner. 1984. *Tourism: Principles, Practices, Philosophies*. New York: Wiley.

SUGGESTED READINGS

D'Amore, L. J. 1983. *Monitoring Report on Tourism Trends.* Montreal: L. J. D'Amore Associates.

Doxey, G. V. 1983. "Leisure, Tourism, and Canada's Aging Population." In *Tourism in Canada: Selected Issues and Options,* ed. P. E. Murphy. Victoria: University of Victoria Western Geographical Series 21, pp. 57–72.

Goeldner, C. R., and Karen P. Dicke. 1981. *Travel Trends in the United States and Canada.* Boulder: University of Colorado Press.

Gomes, Albert J. 1985. *Hospitality in Transition.* Houston: Pannell Kerr Forster.

Gray, H. Peter. 1971. *International Tourism: International Trade.* Lexington, Mass.: Heath.

Hawkins, Donald E., Elwood L. Shafer, and James M. Rovelstad. 1980. *Summary and Recommendations International Symposium on Tourism and the Next Decade.* Washington, D.C.: George Washington University Press.

Hotel and Travel Index. 1982. *The U.S. Resort Travel Market: A Perspective on Trends and Forecasts for U.S. Resort Travel: 1982–83.* New York: Ziff-Davis, pp. 63–71.

Jakle, John A. 1985. *The Tourist—Travel in Twentieth Century North America.* Lincoln: University of Nebraska Press.

Organization of Economic Cooperation and Development. 1984. *Tourism Policy and International Tourism in OECD Member Countries.* Paris: OECD.

Pannell Kerr Forster. 1986. *Trends in the Hotel Industry.* Houston: Pannell Kerr Forster.

Pannell Kerr Forster. 1986. *Trends in the Hotel Industry, International Edition.* Houston: Pannell Kerr Forster.

Pepson, S. 1979. "Tourism: World's Biggest Industry in the Twenty-First Century?" *The Futurist* 12: 249–257.

Sunday, Alexander A. 1978. "Foreign Travel and Tourism Prices." *Annals of Tourism Research* 5(2): 268–273.

Turner, L., and J. Ash. 1975. *The Golden Hordes: International Tourism and the Pleasure Periphery.* London: Constable.

U.S. Travel Data Center. 1984. *Economic Review of Travel in America, 1983–1984.* Washington, D.C.: U.S. Travel Data Center.

Van Doren, Carlton S. 1981. "Outdoor Recreation Trends in the 1980s: Implications for Society." *Journal of Travel Research* 19(3): 3–10.

World Tourism Organization. 1986. *Yearbook of Tourism Statistics.* Madrid: WTO.

Leisure Time and Tourism

A little more than a hundred years ago the average workweek was seventy hours, or ten hours a day seven days a week. The weekend (with freedom from work) was unknown. Today the average workweek is about thirty-five hours, providing considerably more leisure hours. In fact, the word *leisure* means freedom from an occupation or business.

ATTITUDES AND LEISURE_____

However, in many ways, our attitudes toward leisure time still have ingrained in them the idea that the time should be used constructively. For example, for many of us the weekend is the time to do household work, such as cutting the grass or washing the car. In other words, we feel guilty if we are not occupied during our leisure time.

Vacation Time

The word *vacation* stems from the word *vacare*, which means "empty" or time free from work. It is sometimes referred to as recreation time or time to recreate the mind and body for the next round of work. It is time that we have earned, but nevertheless, we often fill it with activity because we do not like the idea of empty time.

Many people also feel guilty about taking a vacation and doing nothing. Indeed, those not going away on vacation often schedule that time for doing things at home (such as painting the house) that they do not have time for during the rest of the working year. To relieve this guilt, much tourism advertising tells us that to take a vacation is to go somewhere and do something, to use this time constructively. To stay home and do nothing is practically immoral and may indicate a lower status in life! Travel has thus become "the thing to do" during our vacations, even if it is only visiting friends and relatives (VFR).

But as recently as fifty years ago, to travel during a vacation period was quite uncommon for the ordinary person. The reasons were primarily financial: Employers did not pay employees while they were on vacation, and so most people could not afford to travel. They just stayed home.

When mass travel began between the two world wars, there was still a sharp distinction between work and leisure. For most workers at that time, including the middle class, work was still tedious and tiring, and vacations concentrated on the three R's: rest, relaxation, and recuperation for the next year's struggle ahead. But after World War II, because of rapidly growing incomes and the fact that for many people the workweek was considerably shorter and less arduous, rest, recreation, and relaxation have been possible for most of the year, and vacations today have lost that *raison d'être*.

Growth of Unions

The growth of the labor unions in the 1930s and 1940s reduced the number of working hours per week (providing more leisure time) and increased the levels of pay and the amount of paid vacation time. Indeed, in some Eastern European countries, such as the Soviet Union, the state frequently pays the cost of the holiday (travel, hotel, meals). We have not yet reached that level of largesse in Western Europe and North America, but it could happen if the unions negotiate such benefit packages as part of a contract.

Income Levels

In the last thirty years some other factors have also helped raise families' disposable income, thereby allowing for more travel. Families have generally grown smaller; more women are now working and earning an income; and in real terms the costs of travel have fallen. There is no question that both real and disposable incomes and increased leisure time have contributed greatly to the dramatic increases in tourism over the past fifty years.

Two-Income Families

The trend toward women's participating in the work force grew stronger during World War II when women were asked to work in the factories to replace the men called up for military service. This movement never was reversed and was in fact part of the reason for the sudden growth in mass travel from 1945 on. Today, many more women than ever before now have careers. In addition, when they marry, they often postpone having a family, or when they do have a family, they often choose to return to work, thus creating lifelong two-income families and increasing the possibility of having more disposable income, of which some can be spent on travel.

Mobility

We have also become far more mobile as the rigidity of train schedules gave way to the flexibility of automobiles, and along with automobiles came better highways. For example, even though the *autobahns* in Germany were built in the 1930s primarily for military purposes, they also were used by civilian automobile travelers.

Since the end of World War II these same kinds of superbly engineered highways have spread throughout Europe as well as North America. It is now possible to drive from one coast to the other in the United States without having to stop for a single traffic light. With these great highways have come the other factors that make the auto traveler's life easier—the motels, restaurants, campgrounds, attractions, entertainment centers, and souvenir and gift shops.

More recently, airplanes (although their fixed schedules do impose the same rigidity as does train travel) have cut travel times.

CONTINUED TOURISM GROWTH

Can we assume that the growth in tourism over the past few decades will continue? The answer is that we probably can. Some of the reasons for this are the following.

Greater Disposable Income

People's continuing greater affluence, and thus the availability of disposable income for travel, should mean no decline in tourism growth as long as the industry can persuade people to spend some or all of that disposable income on travel.

Declining Relative Costs of Travel

As long as the relative costs of travel continue to decline, the tourism industry should be able to continue to attract its share of disposable income. There is a distinct correlation between costs and people's travel destinations. For example, in the early 1970s when oil costs shot up and travel costs also rose, people still traveled but, to stay within their disposable income budgets, they went shorter distances or switched from air travel to automobile travel which meant that they stayed closer to home.

One factor that might help lower travel costs is improved transportation technology. We are witnessing this with air travel, in which more efficient aircraft engines have cut fuel costs, a saving reflected in reduced fares.

Higher Education Levels

As the general population becomes better educated, they want even more education or knowledge, and travel is one way to satisfy that desire.

Changing Demographics

Those born in the post–World War II baby boom are now in their thirties and forties. Many are parents whose own children are grown up and leaving home. At the same time these "baby boomers" may well have paid off the mortgage on their house. All these factors add up to more people with more flexibility and more money to travel.

Increased Urbanization of Society

Over the past forty or fifty years, cities have grown, and the population has become more urban and more mobile. At the same time, this has meant that families do not stay together as family units in the same dwelling, or even in the same town, as used to be the case. Families are geographically today far more spread out. This, of course, generates a great deal of VFR travel.

Growth of Government Security Programs and Employment Benefits

The growth in government security programs means that more families may have long-term financial security and so may be more willing to spend money now on vacations. That, along with larger employment benefits, such as longer vacation periods, means both more money and time for vacations.

Earlier Retirement Ages

People now tend to retire earlier, with their pensions arranged to allow a constant income during their retirement years. Because demographics show that a steadily increasing percentage of the population is moving into their retirement years, there is now a vast untapped pool of tourists.

The elderly, however, have a problem. Statistics show us that for a variety of reasons, they are the group of people least likely to travel.

Growth of Business

Business travel has always been a major contributor to the tourism business. Business travelers are as much tourists as are vacation travelers, and many airlines and hotels could not survive without them.

Increasing Shorter Holidays

People tend now to split up their annual vacation allowance into several shorter holidays. In addition, many people in developed countries work only a four-day week, by working more hours each day. This means that those people can travel more frequently, but perhaps also for shorter distances each time, which may have a greater impact on domestic, rather than international, tourism.

TOURISM AND THE ELDERLY

Statistics indicate that generally about 20 percent of the people in a country do about 80 percent of the traveling. In the United States today there also are more people over sixty-five than in their teens. In fact, there are approximately 50 million elderly people over age sixty-five, and this number will increase as their health and life spans keep improving. U.S. Census Bureau estimates are that by the turn of the century 20 percent of the population will be over sixty-five years of age. Most of the developing countries have similar statistics. Nevertheless, studies show that the people most likely to travel are those between age twenty-five and fifty-five. This implies that retired and elderly people—those with both time and money on their hands—do not contribute greatly to tourism.

Indeed, the number of elderly people traveling, compared with the total number of people in that age bracket, is minuscule, and tourism industry marketing specialists would do well to cater to the special needs and wants of the elderly in order to attract more of them as customers. Two sectors of the travel industry that appear to be doing a good job of catering to the particular needs of this segment of the population are bus tour and cruise ship companies.

SOCIAL TOURISM

Social tourism is subsidized tourism to help the economically poor or otherwise disadvantaged potential tourists to travel. In other words, financial aid is necessary to provide these people with vacations. Social tourism has many forms and is more advanced in Europe than in North America, particularly in Eastern Europe. Social tourism can also be found in countries such as New Zealand and Japan and in North America where social agencies such as the YMCA, YWCA, Boy Scouts, Girl

Guides, and church groups support summer camps and offer subsidized vacations to the poor and the handicapped. In fact, even camping areas in government-operated parks are a form of subsidized vacation for those who can not afford, or do not wish, to travel and stay at expensive hotels.

Social tourism generally is offered to people of limited means whose vacations are subsidized by the government at various levels, by employers, by trade unions, or by associations. Paid holidays, by either government decree or union agreement, are a well-entrenched part of social life in today's developed nations. But even with paid holidays many people still do not take vacations. Sometimes they lack information about cheap or subsidized holidays, or vacation expenditures, on top of direct travel costs, for such things as accommodations and food are invariably higher than they would be if the person stayed at home.

The chartered airline tours that mushroomed in the 1960s were a form of social tourism. Associations would rent entire aircraft, or blocks of seats on an aircraft, from either a regular airline or an airline leasing company. These associations would then sell these seats, often at less than half the price of a regular economy-priced seat on a scheduled airline, to their members. Perhaps without realizing it, these associations were participating in social tourism by offering cheap travel to people who would otherwise probably not travel.

Types of Social Tourism

Some ways in which social tourism may be financed are

- Direct or indirect government subsidies.
- Organization of bulk travel with carriers and/or accomodation suppliers to reduce costs.
- Establishment by governments, employers, unions, or others of special travel-saving plans.
- Provision by employers of special vacation allowances or bonuses.
- Provision by government or employers of subsidized vacation sites for employees and their families.
- Payment by governments, employers, or unions of all vacation costs.
- Establishment of "vacation now, pay later" plans sponsored by employers, banks, or others.
- Reduced fares on railways for special groups such as the socially deprived or the elderly, or even for all workers during the holiday season.
- Price reductions in hotels during holiday seasons.

Social tourism should not be considered second-class tourism. For example, many of us take advantage of subsidized (that is, social) tourism without realizing it. A mother who uses a government-subsidized day-care center to look after her children so that she can earn an income may well put some of this income aside for a vacation.

Even free enterprise offers social tourism! For example, many airlines sell premium-priced tickets to business travelers, thereby allowing the airlines to offer seats at less than the normal economy fares to others who might otherwise not be able to travel. Many travelers seek out these low-cost air fares not only to save travel money but also to allow them to stay longer at their destination and spend more money there on accommodations, food, and entertainment, or to take another vacation later on. Hotels also practice a form of tourist subsidy. Many hotels in resort areas offer block sales of rooms to tour companies at relatively low prices. The tour companies then resell these rooms, along with travel arrangements, in a low-cost packaged tour. Finally, to promote and encourage international social tourism, the International Bureau of Social Tourism was created.

DISCUSSION QUESTIONS

1. Why do many people feel that they have to do something during their leisure/vacation time?

2. As recently as fifty years ago most people did not go away on their vacations. Why?

3. How have unions affected people's vacation periods?

4. Why do families now have more disposable income for vacation travel?

5. Discuss the reasons that people are traveling more today, with reference to the costs of travel.

6. Discuss how changing demographics are likely to affect tourism in the future.

7. Over the past fifty years, society has become more urban. How has this affected tourism?

8. People may take more frequent, but shorter, vacations in the future. Discuss how this might affect tourism.

9. Which two sectors of the travel industry best serve the elderly's travel needs?

10. Define social tourism, and give three examples of it.

PROBLEM

Assume that you are the manager of a restaurant in a town of about 25,000 inhabitants in the Rockies. This town is a popular summer and winter destination, and the restaurant is always full during the summer months and the peak ski-season winter months. During the shoulder-season months (April, May, June, September, and October) the restaurant has fairly little business, even though there is lots of tourist traffic. Most of these tourists are elderly travelers on bus tours through the Rockies who stay overnight in the town. Their breakfast and lunch meals are included in the price of their package tour, but in the evening they are free to eat in the restaurant of their choice. As the restaurant's manager, you notice that most of them go to other nearby restaurants and that few of them visit yours, even though your restaurant is a family operation offering standard fare (that is, nonethnic or specialty foods) at competitive prices. You do not seem to be getting your share of this elderly market.

1. List some of the things that you might do to find out why you are not receiving your share of this market.
2. List five recommendations for the restaurant owner to consider to help attract more of these elderly customers. To help you with these recommendations, talk to five or six elderly people (say, over seventy years of age). They do not have to be frequent travelers, but they should be people who dine out from time to time and are familiar with restaurants. Ask them why they choose particular restaurants and avoid others. Find out if they have any particular ideas about what they would like restaurants to do for them.

SUGGESTED READINGS

Clevedon, Robert. 1983. *The USA and the UK on Holiday*. London: Economist Intelligence Unit.

Conner, Karen A., and Gorden L. Breltena. 1979. "The Four-Day Workweek: An Assessment of Its Effects on Leisure Participation." *Leisure Sciences* 2(1): 55–69.

Cosgrove, I., and R. Jackson. 1972. *The Geography of Recreation and Leisure*. London: Hutchinson.

Devito, Richard. 1986. "The Senior Citizen Travel Market: Still in Its Growth Stage." In *The Practice of Hospitality Management II*, ed. Robert C. Lewis, Thomas J. Beggs, Margaret Shaw, and Steven A. Croffoot. Westport, Conn.: AVI, pp. 467–471.

Doxey, G. V. 1983. "Leisure, Tourism, and Canada's Aging Population." In *Tourism in Canada: Selected Issues and Options*, ed. P. E. Murphy. Victoria: University of Victoria, Western Geographical Series 21, pp. 57–72.

Dumazedier, Joffre. 1974. *Sociology of Leisure*. New York: Elsevier.

Haulot, A. 1981. "Social Tourism: Current Dimensions and Future Development." *Tourism Management* 2: 207–212.

Ibrahim, H., and R. Crandall. 1979. *Leisure: A Psychological Approach*. Los Alamitos, N.M.: Hwong.

MacCannell, D. 1976. *The Tourist: A New Theory of the Leisure Class*. London: Macmillan.

Mayo, Edward J., and Lance P. Jarvis. 1981. *The Psychology of Leisure Travel*. Boston: CBI.

McIntosh, Robert W., and Charles R. Goeldner. 1984. *Tourism: Principles, Practices, Philosophies*. New York: Wiley, pp. 146–150.

Mihovilovic, M. A. 1980. "Leisure and Tourism in Europe." *International Social Science Journal* 32: 99–113.

Neulinger, John. 1974. *The Psychology of Leisure*. Springfield, Ill.: Thomas.

Travel Motivators and Destination Life Cycles

Without people's motivation to travel, there would be no tourist industry. During the heady tourism expansion years after World War II the tourist industry paid little interest to tourists' motives for travel. Most sectors of the industry were too busy to be concerned with either why people traveled or why they were sometimes not satisfied with their travel experiences. But when business slowed down during the 1970s' oil crisis and subsequent recessions, the competition for a share of the traveler's discretionary income rose, and the tourist industry had to fight harder to obtain its share. This, in turn, created more interest in discovering the tourists' needs. For example, according to Taylor (1983), Tourism Canada changed its advertising to attract the different tastes of some of its tourist customers, such as the British, French, and Japanese. But before it could do this, Canada had to find out the travel motivators of each of these different markets.

Travel motivators are those factors that create a person's desire to travel. They can be divided into those that are not primarily related to the actual destination and those that are primarily related to the actual destination.

MOTIVATORS NOT RELATED TO DESTINATION

Non-destination-related motivators are easier to determine than are those that are destination related, and they include travel for business, education, health, and religion and visiting friends and relatives. In other words, motivators not related to a destination give people little or no choice about going to that destination instead of some other. The cause of travel, rather than the destination, is the determining factor.

Business

For many operators in the tourism industry, business travel is critical to success. On a year-round basis, about 85 percent of all air travel is business related. Many hotels are oriented toward business travelers. Convention centers are built to attract business travelers. Auto rental companies, particularly at airports, are almost entirely dependent on business persons. And many restaurants need their patronage to survive.

Political representatives and government employees can be included in the business category, as politics is a form of business, and politicians and government employees represent their various levels of government when they travel.

Participants in sporting events and entertainment are also business travelers, as they are in the business of sports or entertainment and travel because of their job.

An important aspect of business travel is that its demand changes relatively little in regard to variations in airfares, hotel room rates, restaurant meal prices, and other travel costs. An inelastic demand means that when prices increase, there is not a more-than-compensating decline in demand.

Education

Some people do not perceive students studying in another country as tourists. But they are, for they fit the definition of a tourist as long as their motivation to travel is to study and not to work at a job. Students' spending is important to the airlines but less important to hotels, restaurants, and some other branches of the tourism business, as students generally stay in dormitories or apartments and do not heavily patronize the hotels and restaurants at their destination.

Health

The earliest health travelers went to spas, because the water was thought to help cure such ailments as arthritis and rheumatism. Today, many of these spas are still operating and continue to attract tourists. Some have remained tourist destinations, but for another purpose. For example, one of the early spas was in Davos, Switzerland, which is now better known as a ski resort.

Today, diet resorts and similar places have taken the place of spas, motivating people to travel to them for health reasons. Perhaps in earlier years people did not have the same concern about losing weight!

Sea resorts became popular because of their fresh air and the assumed curative powers of saltwater. Sea resorts are more popular than ever today, but mainly because people want to acquire a tan or participate in water sports.

Finally, many people travel to distant destinations because surgery, or medication, is not available to them locally.

Religion

Religious travel can be differentiated into travel for reasons of spirituality and reasons of curiosity. If the travel is for reasons of spirituality, then it will fit into the non-destination-related travel category. This includes pilgrimages to places such as Lourdes or Fatima or trips to religious headquarters, such as Catholics traveling to Rome, Jews to Israel, and Muslims to Mecca.

Visiting Friends and Relatives (VFR)

Visiting friends and relatives (VFR) is probably the most important motivator of all travel. The mode of travel is usually the automobile, which benefits motels and campgrounds on the way, with little destination effect on hotels and restaurants. The route of travel for VFR is often more important than the destination location.

Also fitting into this category is the desire to visit the "homeland" that motivates many North Americans to visit countries in Europe, even if they no longer have any friends or relatives living there.

MOTIVATORS RELATED TO DESTINATION_____

Destination-related travel motivators are those that allow tourists to select where they go. In other words, tourists are not restricted to a specific destination. They can compare destinations and costs and then decide which destination is most appealing.

The causes of destination-related travel are often difficult to determine. They include such things as curiosity about other cultures, places, people, religions, and political systems, as well as the desire to see attractions such as art, drama, music, and folklore. This type of travel can also be motivated by the tourist's desire to be able to talk to others about a trip for reasons of ego enhancement or self-esteem, to follow a trend to a particular destination, or to be one of the first to visit a new destination. Also included in this type of motivation are the romance of travel, the use of leisure time to escape, the need for social contact, the desire for a change of routine, or merely the wish to have a new experience or to do nothing (such as lie on a beach and get a tan). Also included in this category are those who travel as spectators to view sporting events, to watch entertainment, to gamble, or to take part in recreational sporting events such as skiing, golf, tennis, fishing, and hunting.

MARKET RESEARCH

Although these categories have been created in order to tabulate people's motivations, it is important to realize that tourists sometimes travel for more than one reason, such as the business traveler who adds a few days of vacation to the end of a business trip. It therefore is important to those involved in tourism marketing to determine the reasons that people travel to certain destinations. This helps guide their advertising to induce repeat travelers to continue to go there and also to encourage those who have not yet been there.

To motivate those who have not been to a particular destination it is important for those in marketing to determine why they have not been there. For example, the Canadian government (Tourism Canada 1982) recently conducted a survey in Europe to determine what Europeans thought of Canada as a tourist destination. The results showed that Canada did not have a strong image in regard to having interesting people, places of historic and cultural interest, and an exotic and exciting atmosphere. Rather, Canada was seen more as a place for rugged tourists to fish and hunt, and not as a country of sophisticated cities with night life. This type of research information is useful for future advertising, to change Europeans' image of Canada.

Those involved in tourism marketing also must do market research on the demographic and socioeconomic makeup of potential tourists.

Demographic Data

Demographic research is obtaining statistical data about such things as tourists' age, sex, occupation, place of residence, education level, marital status, family size and composition, social class, race or ethnic group, family income, spending habits, number of cars owned, and second-home ownership. The objective is to classify tourists and potential tourists.

Some of these demographic data can be obtained from census figures. Other data can be gathered from questionnaires and personal interviews. Much of this research is carried out by the government at various levels. Past research shows that travel is generally closely correlated with income and education levels, as well as urban living. In other words, rural dwellers and those with lower incomes are less likely to travel.

Psychographic Data

Tourists are also often grouped behaviorally according to their psychographic characteristics. Psychographic data include such things as people's life-styles, self-images, attitudes toward marriage, attitudes toward travel, personality traits, interests, opinions, and motivations. That is, people are classified according to their values. Psychographic data are generally obtained from questionnaires and personal interviews. Note also that two groups of people can be demographically similar but psychographically different.

Psychocentrics and Allocentrics

Another way of looking at tourists psychographically was developed by Plog (1972), who views people on a continuum stretching out on either end of a center. Most people belong in the midcentric range. At one extreme from the center are the *allocentrics* who want an independent vacation experience, and at the other extreme are the *psychocentrics* who become part of the mass tourism market (for example, people in a tour group are psychocentrics). Plog suggested that different types of tourists are attracted to different tourist destinations depending on where they fit on the continuum between the allocentrics and psychocentrics.

New destinations generally appeal to the small number of allocentric adventurous tourists who make few demands, as they prefer to fit into the local culture. As the destination becomes more popular and changes its character, the allocentrics move elsewhere, seeking new "untouched" places. The midcentrics now become the destination's major source of tourists. In turn, as the destination gives way to larger and larger numbers of arrivals, it goes through another change and becomes a popular resort dependent on foreign investment and labor. Now the psychocentrics feel at home because the destination offers a range of facilities, attractions, and services "just like those back home" that divorce it from its previous natural geographic and social environment that initially attracted the allocentrics.

An allocentric is the type of person who travels to relatively "untouched" areas such as a remote place in Africa or an isolated island in the South Pacific. A midcentric aims for destinations such as Hawaii, the Caribbean, or Europe. The psychocentric is happy with a packaged vacation to Disneyland. Some of the characteristics of allocentrics and psychocentrics are as follows:

Allocentrics

- Are adventuresome and like to explore alone.
- Enjoy a sense of discovery and having new experiences.
- Seek out novel and different destinations before others have been there.
- Often have high activity levels.

- Prefer areas that are not "touristy."
- Will accept basic conveniences in accommodations and food.
- Enjoy meeting and dealing with people from another country or culture.

Psychocentrics

- Prefer the tour package vacation.
- Are not highly active.
- Enjoy commonplace activities such as sun, sand, and surf.
- Often prefer to drive to a destination rather than fly.
- Prefer a familiar tourist destination.
- Prefer accommodations, restaurants, attractions, and shops similar to those at home.
- Do not want a "foreign" atmosphere.
- Are comfortable being with other travelers like themselves.
- Prefer to have all travel arrangements made for them, such as on a packaged bus tour.

TOURIST DESTINATIONS

There are strong links between tourist destinations and motivations for travel, and so such destinations must be planned around these motivations or visitor expectations. It is therefore obvious that no destination will appeal to all types of people; each tourist destination must develop its own characteristics to satisfy its appropriate segment or segments of the market.

One should be careful not to link tourist destinations to a specific tourist type, because, as mentioned earlier, people sometimes have more than one motivation for making a trip or change their motivation from one trip to the next. For example, the allocentric may go on a mountain-climbing trip to Switzerland and act like an allocentric but on another occasion may take a psychocentric family weekend visit to Disneyland. Furthermore, owing to changes in age, income, and other factors over time, the allocentric can change into a psychocentric, and vice versa. Also, a particular destination can offer a range of travel experiences, even to the same person, depending on how the trip is packaged.

For these reasons it would therefore be risky for a tourist destination to depend solely on one type of tourist. Some destinations do this, but most are designed to accommodate more than one type of tourist, although it is rare to find one that tries to cater to all types of tourists. For example, Waikiki in Hawaii basically attracts the vacationing, recreational type of tourist. But it is also popular with the convention trade.

Defining a Destination

What is a tourist destination? It can be described as an area with different natural attributes, features, or attractions that appeal to nonlocal visitors, that is, tourists. These attributes, features, or attractions can vary as much as types of tourists vary. For example, whereas Disneyland attracts one type of tourist (generally, the family trade), the Munich beer festival attracts a completely different type of tourist, as the main attraction of a beer festival does not usually appeal to the family trade.

To determine whether an area is a true tourist destination, it is important to classify its visitors as local or nonlocal. If the area's appeal is primarily to local residents who have not had to travel far to get there, then it will not normally be classified as a tourist destination. But if it appeals to people who have to take a day trip to reach it, even if they are classified as excursionists (that is, not staying overnight), it will be considered a tourist destination. This means that any park, stately home, or beach that caters to people who have had to travel some distance to reach it can be considered a tourist destination. Some governments have established a distance break-even mark that differentiates a visitor from a local resident. For example, Statistics Canada uses a fifty-mile (eighty-kilometer) radius as the deciding distance.

This does not mean that residents visiting an attraction are not important if that attraction is not a tourist destination by definition. To the economy of that area, it can be just as important to keep local residents at home, encouraging them to visit and spend money at local attractions, as it can be to encourage tourists to travel farther to visit that destination. Even though concern for the economy as a whole is normally expressed on a national basis, that national basis is made up of all the areas within that nation.

DESTINATION LIFE CYCLES

Tourism destinations, just like any other product, have life cycles. These life cycles can be short term, medium term, or long term.

Short-Term Cycles

Short-term cycles are those that occur within a period of a year or less. These cycles are usually quite obvious, a good example being the seasonal cycle at a resort, such as the peak summer season at a seaside area or the peak winter season at a ski resort, with little to sustain business in the six-month-or-longer off-season. Sometimes tourist destinations have two cycles in a year, that is, both a summer and a winter season. For example, a mountain resort can have both a summer season, during which golf, lake swimming, horseback riding, and similar recreations attract tourists, as well as a winter season for skiing, skating, and other outdoor winter activities.

Although some destinations can provide year-round facilities, many of them still have a cyclical annual business. For example, a major tourist city may operate at capacity for vacationing tourists during the summer months and try to fill its accommodations during the balance of the year with convention business, but without reaching the peak summer demand for its facilities.

The amount of demand for most tourist destinations is based on the tourists' lifestyles, such as the children's school holidays. In France, for example, August is traditionally the vacation month when everyone wants to be away on holiday. The strains on the suprastructure (roads) and infrastructure (hotels, restaurants) of France and other surrounding European countries during this month, accordingly, are tremendous. This type of seasonal demand also causes considerable strain on the tourist industry and its labor force, thereby creating another problem. In highly seasonal areas, because such businesses must maximize their revenue in order to survive through the doldrum months, there may be price differentials (even price gouging) between the peak demand and the off-season periods, and these can affect even local residents who may wish to use a tourist facility. For example, a resident using a local restaurant may pay a higher price for the same menu item in the summer than in the winter.

Traffic congestion and the lack of parking during the peak season can cause similar frustrations and even hostility toward tourism and tourists. The extra community costs (for policing, for example) may also be a financial strain on some tourist communities. On the other hand, those employed in seasonal resort establishments that are open year-round often like the cyclical nature of the business because, as long as they have year-round employment, there will be a period each year when the demands on them decline considerably. In other situations—for example, a family-operated bed and breakfast establishment—the family may be quite happy to work hard for a few months during the peak season and then withdraw from the bed and breakfast business until the following year. In other situations many tourists take advantage of the lower rates for accommodations during a seasonal destination's off-season. Indeed, in order to minimize prices to their delegates, convention organizers often use facilities only during the off-season.

Medium-Term Cycles

Medium-term life cycles last for a period of a few years. The change is often slow and can be caused by such things as altered customer preferences, changes in demography, changes in the economy of the host area or the area of the majority of its tourist guests, currency-value fluctuations, and even changes in the local environment. For example, through the lack of proper care, an area can become so run-down and shabby that it is no longer attractive to tourists.

Once a destination is committed to a particular tourist market, it may have difficulty changing its orientation as it finds its market slowly disappearing. This happened, for example, when jet travel was introduced. Many British seaside resorts that catered primarily to domestic tourists found that their market disappeared when those tourists discovered that they could fly relatively quickly to more "glamorous" seaside areas in some foreign land. The domestic seaside resorts have not found their market easy to replace, but one way that some of them coped was to convert to a convention destination, as Brighton did.

Long-Term Cycles

Long-term life cycles are often described as having four stages: discovery, growth, maturity, and decline. Early in their life, destinations attract few visitors or tourists; they are in their discovery stage. As the destinations grow and become more popular, they attract more people. To do this they sometimes have to change, or become less "foreign," as they move through growth to maturity.

The type of tourist also changes from early in a destination's life cycle to its maturity. For example, the European visitor to Peru (early in its life cycle as a tourism destination) is likely to be far different from the European visitor to Hawaii. But the European visitor to Hawaii (a mature destination) will probably differ little from the Australian visitor to Hawaii. Note that Hawaii itself was in the discovery stage in the 1930s, being accessible only to the rich who had time to travel there by ship. It was only as a result of the post–World War II air travel boom that Hawaii was made accessible to the masses and able to grow to maturity.

As a destination matures it may become overcommercialized, relinquish the appeal that first made it unique, and then decline and die. Tourism destinations carry the seeds of their own destruction. To put it another way, tourism can kill tourism. In some cases the tourist facilities in the declining stage may be converted to some other use. For example, a hotel may be converted into condominiums for residential use or for a retirement home.

Not all destinations go through the four stages of discovery, growth, maturity, and decline—any more than any other product does. But in order to avoid decline, a tourist destination may have to change in some way or adapt to new markets. Some destinations never get past the discovery stage. For example, air flights to the Antarctic to view the penguins are popular with some tourists today. But it is unlikely that the Antarctic will ever become a mature tourist destination, owing to its relative inaccessibility and harsh climate. Other destinations may bypass discovery and growth. For example, a new resort built where nothing existed before may immediately become popular and be a mature resort. This was the case with Cancun in Mexico.

Social, Political, and Economic Changes

Life cycles can also be affected by social or political changes. This happened to Cuba, which was a favored destination of U.S. tourists before 1958. They went there primarily to gamble, but this changed overnight when Fidel Castro took power: The casinos were closed, and tourists stopped going there. Cuba has since emerged as another kind of tourist destination.

Political terrorism can also be a factor. The many acts of terrorism in the Middle East in the past several years have seriously diminished the popularity of many countries in that area as destinations for tourists.

Life cycles can also be affected by economic changes or even by changes in currency exchange rates. Finally, they can be affected by social tourism. Social tourism (discussed in Chapter 3) arises when a government provides subsidies to allow a destination to grow and survive.

A Classic Example

Many tourist destinations have gone through all four stages. For example, with the advent of rail travel, the early health spas gave way to the seaside resorts. A more recent example is Atlantic City in New Jersey. It went through all four stages, died, and has now been reborn. Initially, Atlantic City—with an excellent beach, relatively mild summers, and a splendid surf—was a family seaside destination in the latter half of the nineteenth century. The developers eventually moved in and added attractions and amenities that helped diversify its tourism. The local government added an amusement pier and Atlantic City's famous boardwalk. Luxury hotels were then added, and in the 1920s and 1930s the city was a prime tourist destination that was immensely helped in the 1930s with the introduction of the game Monopoly. A convention center was added, as were many more hotels and motels.

Unfortunately, the city did not have a large enough population to provide the work force to support the large influx of tourists, and so employees were brought in from outside. To house these employees, low-budget, dreary, and depressing rooming houses were built, which soon became dilapidated and caused urban blight. In addition, the convention center attracted mobsters who, in turn, discouraged family tourists. Decline set in, and Atlantic City fell out of favor for two or three decades. It was described by Mahon (1980, p. 15) as follows:

> But the hotels, once in the vanguard of oceanfront skyscraping luxury, no longer enticed tourists. Travelers, spoiled by the bland comforts of Hilton or the disinfected sameness of Holiday Inn, could not be lured to places where the bathroom was a commute down the hall. Many of the hotels shut, and there they stood, tired old white elephants, humiliated, a symbol of everything that had gone wrong.

Recently Atlantic City started a new life cycle and acquired a new appeal when legalized gambling was approved. New hotels have been built, along with casinos, nightclubs, and other entertainment establishments. Tourists are motivated to go to Atlantic City for different reasons than their predecessors were, but the tourist developers recognized that a new market existed and adapted to it. Unquestionably there is a link between tourist motivation and a successful tourist destination.

Airport Life Cycles

Airports also can have life cycles. For example, in the early days of flying before the jet age, and even during the early part of the jet age, airports in such places as Goose Bay (Labrador), Gander (Newfoundland), Reykjavik (Iceland), and Shannon (Ireland) were important stops for refueling and crew changes for flights from North America to Europe. The local economies of the areas around these airports benefited greatly from this traffic. But when longer-range jet planes were introduced, these airports were bypassed and thus came to the end of that particular phase of their life cycle. We see the potential for this to happen to many busy airports in existence today. For example, Anchorage in Alaska owes much of its prosperity to traffic generated by the oil business, but more of its wealth to the planes that connect it to the rest of the world. Sampson (1985, p. 14) described the Anchorage airport:

> In the concourse (travelers) are greeted by a huge stuffed polar bear standing up-right, a menacing arctic wolf and an exorbitant duty-free shop which gives few clues (apart from Alaskan salmon) as to its geography—displaying Korean tape recorders, Dutch cigars and Scotch whisky which have been flown up here to sell to people flying out. Few passengers ever leave the transit area, and many airlines have not been granted what is grandly called the "fifth freedom"—the freedom for passengers to stop over in a foreign country: the airlines can fly passengers through the place, but not *to* it. Looking at the rows of apprehensive faces of all colours and shapes, each with the same forsaken look, they seem all to have been denied the freedom to belong anywhere, like flying Dutchmen in search of an unattainable love.

Much of Anchorage's air traffic connects Europe and the eastern seaboard of North America to Asia. Because of their increased fuel capacity, today's bigger jets are capable of flying directly from Europe to the Far East and vice versa, thus bypassing Anchorage. Will airports such as Anchorage suffer the same life-cycle fate as that of Goose Bay, Gander, Reykjavik, Shannon, and others as technology leaves them behind?

DISCUSSION QUESTIONS

1. Define non-destination-related travel, and list three of the types of traveler who fit into that category.

2. Some types of travel are defined as inelastic. Explain what this means, and give an example of a type of traveler whose travel is generally inelastic.

3. Why is student-related travel important to some sectors of the travel industry and not to others? Give an example of a sector to which it is important, and another to which it is much less important.

4. In earlier times people traveled to spas for health reasons. Give an example of a health reason to travel today.

5. What are the two categories of religious travel? Which one is destination related, and which one is not?

6. Explain how destination-related travel differs from non-destination-related travel, and give four examples of destination-related travel.

7. What are five items that, in travel research, would be considered as demographic data regarding tourists, and how are demographic data usually obtained?

8. In travel research, what are psychographic data regarding tourists, and how are those data obtained?

9. Distinguish between a psychocentric and allocentric, and list three characteristics of each.

10. Discuss the problems of a seasonal short-term life cycle destination.

11. Tourism destinations are said to have four stages in their life cycles. What are they?

12. At what stage in its life cycle would you consider each of the following?
Hawaii
South Pacific
Western Europe
Africa
Asia

13. What factors, other than a change in tourists' desires, can cause a destination to move rapidly from one stage in its life cycle to another?

14. Based on your own knowledge of a specific tourist area, describe any steps that you think could be taken that might help prevent its eventual decline.

PROBLEM

Select a local tourist destination. Remember that a destination does not have to be an entire city, town, or area but can be a park, beach area, historic site, museum, or any similar location that attracts tourists. Remember also that these tourists do not have to be visitors who stay overnight at the destination. They can be automobile, bus, train, boat, or even airplane day trippers. Prepare a one-page report describing this destination and discussing from your perspective what life-cycle stage it is in. If possible, obtain statistics showing how this life cycle has been changing over the last several years and how, in your opinion, the destination's management may have adjusted to cope with different stages in this life cycle or with changes in customer demographics, life-styles, or other factors. If the destination is in its decline stage, can you determine the reasons? Has it been affected by social, political, or economic changes over the past several years? If appropriate, discuss the importance of the price differentials that it uses to cope with an annual seasonal life cycle.

REFERENCES

Mahon, Gigi. 1980. *The Company That Bought the Boardwalk*. New York: Random House.

Plog, Stanley C. 1972. "Why Destination Areas Rise and Fall in Popularity." Los Angeles: Travel Research Association.

Sampson, Anthony. 1985. *Empires of the Sky*. London: Coronet.

Taylor, G. D. 1983. "Canada's Tourism Trends for the 1980s." In *Tourism in Canada: Selected Issues and Options*, ed. P. E. Murphy. Victoria: University of Victoria, Western Geographical Series 21, pp. 29–55.

Tourism Canada. 1982. *In-Depth Studies of Attitudes to Canada*. Ottawa: Tourism Canada.

SUGGESTED READINGS

Gee, Chuck Y., Dexter J. L. Choy, and James C. Makens. 1984. *The Travel Industry*. Westport, Conn.: AVI, pp. 18–35, 38–50.

Jenkins, Roger L. 1978. "Family Vacation Decision Making." *Journal of Travel Research* 16(4): 2–7.

Mayo, Edward J., and Lance P. Jarvis. 1981. *The Psychology of Leisure Travel*. Boston: CBI.

McIntosh, Robert W., and Charles R. Goeldner. 1984. *Tourism: Principles, Practices, Philosophies*. New York: Wiley, pp. 137–146, 150–164, 171–174, 178–183.

Murphy, Peter E. 1985. *Tourism—A Community Approach*. New York: Methuen, pp. 79–89.

Neulinger, John, and Charles C. Thomas. 1974. *The Psychology of Leisure Travel.* Springfield, Ill.: Thomas.

Plog, Stanley. 1973. "Why Destination Areas Rise and Fall in Popularity." *Cornell Hotel and Restaurant Administration Quarterly* 12(1):13–16.

Reason, James. 1974. *Man in Motion: The Psychology of Travel.* New York: Walker.

Rubenstein, C. 1980. "Vacations, Expectations, Satisfactions, Frustrations, Fantasies." *Psychology Today*, May, pp. 62–76.

Attractions

CHAPTER OBJECTIVES

After studying this chapter the reader will be able to

- Differentiate between infrastructure and suprastructure.

- Discuss how climate affects certain types of tourism.

- Describe Butlin's Holiday Camps and Club Med.

- Give examples of how scenery can attract tourists.

- Explain how wildlife and sports can promote tourism.

- Discuss some of the specific problems of using the parks for tourism.

- Discuss amusement/theme parks and world's fairs and their role in tourism.

- Describe the role of shopping in tourism.

People do not travel vast distances and spend time and money to go somewhere that does not offer them something different. The uneven distribution of tourism around the world is evidence of this. There is a complex interrelationship between people's desire to travel and their attraction to a specific destination. It is the attractions of a tourist destination that encourage people to go there, and so no attractions means no tourism. But a destination must have more than just attractions; it must also have amenities, which can be categorized as either an infrastructure or a suprastructure.

The infrastructure comprises roads, airports, stations, utilities, communication, and similar items that make it easy for the tourist to reach and use a destination. For the typical tourist there must be few, if any, physical infrastructure barriers to a destination. The infrastructure is normally provided by the government, using tax revenues.

The suprastructure comprises amenities such as accommodations, food services, marinas, shopping, and entertainment. This suprastructure is normally provided by private enterprise, with few or no government subsidies. The infra- and suprastructures, combined with the attractions, differentiate the successful tourist destinations from the less successful ones.

NATURAL ENVIRONMENTAL ATTRACTIONS

Attractions can be categorized as either natural or manufactured. Natural environmental assets are usually the most successful in attracting tourists, but they must attract tourists in a way that allows the asset to be preserved. Tourism can be destroyed if those assets are exploited. Natural attractions can be subdivided into climate, scenery, and wildlife.

Climate

Sun and surf have always been natural attractions. Once rail travel became possible, railway lines were quickly built from major inland towns and cities to beach areas, and the people flocked to them.

Europe has many famous beaches, such as Brighton and Blackpool in England, Deauville in France, and Scheveningen in Holland, and the United States has the beach at Atlantic City in New Jersey, as well as many others. These beaches are relatively close to major population centers and are therefore easy and cheap to reach. As people become more affluent, they tend to move farther south where the sun is warmer and more pleasant in winter.

Nice and Cannes in France became popular with the more affluent classes in the early part of the twentieth century. Southern European beaches have always been popular with the Scandinavians, who have long, dark, and cold winters and whose beaches, even in the summer, are not as appealing. As the southern beaches became more popular with the less affluent, the richer people moved farther afield to the beaches of the Adriatic in Europe and Florida in the United States. Now, of course, even those sunny places have become popular with the less affluent, as have the beaches in Hawaii, Mexico, and the Caribbean, which draw people year-round for a vacation or a visit on a cruise ship.

Some organizations have capitalized on the public's desire for sun and beaches. In the 1930s Butlin Holiday Camps in England were organized, with the first one opening in Skegness in 1936, complete with entertainment, fun, and games. Butlin Holiday Camps are still operating today and appeal to a certain segment of the market. A greater force in the international sun and beach market is the Club Méditerranée, commonly abbreviated as Club Med. The first Club Med opened in Majorca in 1949, and there now are about eighty of them around the world. Club Med does not have overly organized entertainment, but each site does offer a wide variety of free sporting activities. According to one of its brochures, the philosophy of Club Med is to "give back to urban vacationers the village of old in all its freedoms but without its hypocrisy."

Many people visit beach areas not only for the sunshine but also for sporting reasons such as sailing or surfing. Today there are many world-famous recreational beaches such as Copacabana in Rio de Janeiro (Brazil), Montego Bay (Jamaica), Waikiki in Hawaii, and Surfers Paradise on Australia's Gold Coast. Unfortunately, because of overuse and effluent from sewage outlets and oil from ships, some beaches have become polluted. Others have become so crowded that people have to pay to use them. For example, the beaches on the Italian Riviera are crowded public areas. For some less crowded areas, one can pay for a day's access, and if one wants a reserved area of beach, it can be arranged through a membership in a club that owns a section of beach. A club membership entitles the member to access to a specific part of that beach for a summer season. One could call this a form of timesharing!

Of course, climate and beaches are not the only combination that attracts tourists. Skiers look for snow and mountains in the wintertime. Indeed, skiing has been the fastest-growing attraction of all in the past thirty years. For example, Austria's ski business has tripled in this period, and there are now some fifteen hundred ski lifts in that country. But the demand for skiing seems to have leveled off now, and many people feel that this is a good thing because, just as beaches can become polluted, so too can mountains, with lifts and ski runs.

Scenery

Tourists going to naturally scenic areas, such as mountains, are concerned about climate, but less so than are those who need sunshine to enjoy a beach or snow to enjoy skiing.

After trains made long-distance travel easier, Europeans were attracted to the Alps, and North Americans to the Rockies. Visitors to the mountains in those days wanted to hike and climb in them and admire them as they were, without the need for contrived sports such as skiing. Today, mountains still attract people for their natural beauty, as do other land phenomena such as canyons (for example, the Grand Canyon in Arizona), rock formations (Ayer's Rock in Australia), volcanos (Vesuvius in Italy), and coral reefs (the Great Barrier Reef in Australia).

Water, apart from the sea, can also be a scenic attraction, which is why tourists gravitate to places such as Niagara Falls (United States and Canada), Victoria Falls on the Zambesi River in Zimbabwe in Africa, England's Lake District, Iceland's glaciers and geysers, and Old Faithful geyser in Yellowstone National Park in the United States.

Tourists also flock to the multicolored displays of autumn leaves in New England or the Ardennes in Belgium, as well as to see the cherry blossoms in Japan or the tulips in Holland. England's moors attract other types of people. Tropical rain forests appeal to some, and others enjoy the desert.

Wildlife

Wildlife is another natural attraction. Some perceive wildlife as something to be observed during a visit to a park in Africa such as Serengeti in Tanzania, Murchison Falls in Uganda, or Kruger in South Africa, or during a trip to see the penguins of the Antarctic, the polar bears of the Arctic, or the many different forms of wildlife seen on a trip along the Amazon River in Brazil.

Other tourists view wildlife as something to be caught at the end of a fishing line or shot by a rifle. These tourists can be a major source of government revenue through fees paid for licenses to fish or hunt.

MANUFACTURED ATTRACTIONS

An alternative to natural attractions are the manufactured ones. Cities attract tourists simply because they are exciting places to visit, with their constant activity. This type of tourism is sometimes referred to as *urban tourism.* It is difficult to determine whether tourists visit cities because of their activity or because of their physical assets. Do tourists visit London because of its atmosphere or to visit such attractions as Buckingham Palace and the Tower of London?

Within cities there is an endless list of manufactured attractions such as the Leaning Tower of Pisa in Italy, the Roman ruins of Bath in England, or the Eiffel Tower in Paris. The preservation of many historic buildings is often supported by tourist visitors. Even churches or cathedrals can earn extra money by allowing tourists to make brass rubbings. But others have suffered from too many tourists. An example is Stonehenge in England which has now been placed behind a perimeter fence to protect it from people compacting the soil around the base of the stones and threatening to topple them.

Palaces such as Versailles in France and castles such as Windsor Castle in England attract others. Some tourists like to visit monuments such as the Arc de Triomphe in Paris. Others gravitate to restored villages such as Williamsburg, Virginia, or old battlefields such as that in Gettysburg, Pennsylvania, or Waterloo in Belgium.

Other tourists like museums. World-famous ones include the British Museum in London, the Deutschmuseum in Munich, the Louvre in Paris, the National Museum of Anthropology in Mexico City, and the Museum of Science and Industry in Chicago. Other tourists enjoy visiting historic universities or libraries. Government and political buildings also attract tourists. This category includes the Kremlin in Moscow, the Houses of Parliament in London, and the White House in Washington.

Many tourists are attracted to sites of past civilizations or archaeological sites such as the pyramids in Egypt, Stonehenge in England, the Mayan temples of Mexico, or Machu Picchu in Peru. Others prefer still-existing cultures such as that of the Basques in the French/Spanish Pyrenees, the Moroccans in Marrakesh, or the Dutch and Amish in Pennsylvania.

Many festivals around the world also draw tourists, such as the Mardi Gras in New Orleans, the Edinburgh Festival, Carnival in Rio de Janeiro, and Oktoberfest in Munich. Some festivals are religious. One of the more famous ones has been held for 350 years, usually once every 10 years: the Passion Play in Oberammergau in Germany.

FIGURE 5-1. The Tower of London: A popular attraction for visitors to England.

FIGURE 5-2. St. Paul's Cathedral, London, is famous for its history and architecture.

FIGURE 5-3. London's Tower Bridge: Another popular tourist attraction for England's visitors.

FIGURE 5-4. Neuschwanstein Castle in Bavaria, Germany, built by "mad" King Ludwig II, is visited by as many as ten thousand tourists a day.

FIGURE 5-5.   Linderhof Castle in Bavaria, Germany, attracts tourists year round.

Religious locations and buildings also attract large numbers of tourists to the Vatican in Rome, Westminster Abbey in London, and the Mormon Temple in Salt Lake City, Utah. In this category we could include religious shrines such as those at Fatima in Portugal and Lourdes in France.

Music, the arts, dance, and theater also bring in tourists. The Bolshoi Ballet in Moscow, the Vienna Boys Choir, folk dancing in many European countries, and the theaters of major cities including New York, London, and Paris could probably not survive without tourists.

Finally, handicrafts can be a major creator of tourism. Italy is famous for its leather goods, Czechoslovakia for its crystal, Ireland for its linen, the Cherokee and Navajo Indians of the United States for their ceramics, and the Canadian Eskimos for their soapstone carvings.

Sports

Sporting events also draw tourists, not only the participants who travel, stay in hotels, and eat in restaurants, but also many of the spectators who follow their baseball, basketball, football, ice hockey, or soccer teams to away matches. Participants and spectators of either amateur or professional sports are tourists when they travel.

Annual sporting events such as Wimbledon's tennis are big tourist revenue generators, and less frequent events such as the Olympics, held every four years, attract hundreds of thousands over a two-week period. And the major marathons now attract as many as twenty thousand participants and many more tens of thousands of visitors and spectators.

Entertainment

Other forms of entertainment, apart from sports, are also part of the appeal for some tourists. Included in this category are nightclubs and discos, restaurants, and gambling where it is legal (and sometimes where it is not). Major casino gambling areas are London, Monaco, the Caribbean, and U.S. cities such as Las Vegas and Atlantic City. Many cruise ships offer gambling as part of their entertainment.

The casino business, dating back to the early days of this century, has grown into a multibillion-dollar business today. Hotels, nightclubs, restaurants, convention and meeting centers, and gambling casinos are closely linked. Some casinos are privately owned, but in the United States many are owned by hotel chains such as Hilton and Hyatt. In some cases even governments run the gambling business. For example, the government-operated ferries of the British Columbia ferry fleet traveling between Seattle, Washington, and Victoria, British Columbia, installed slot machines on two of its cruise ferries for the 1987 summer tourist season. In that year there was a 21 percent increase in passengers over the previous year, and the profits from the machines more than covered what would otherwise have been an operating loss.

Gambling in a city like Las Vegas or Atlantic City is just one part of the total leisure concept that these resorts offer. Las Vegas in the 1930s was just a dusty railway town, but it is now a major resort with many types of entertainment in addition to gambling. Las Vegas attracts about thirteen million tourist visitors a year—more than the population of some individual European countries.

Parks

Natural or forest parks usually are owned by the government. These parks have great appeal to many people if they are not overcommercialized. Most governments recognize that parks provide unique recreational experiences as long as the attractions are compatible with the park's own natural ecological features.

Park operators have many difficult decisions to make. Should overnight accommodations be provided or only day visitors allowed? Should parks be created close to urban centers to avoid the problem of accommodation in the park? Should private cars be allowed in the parks and large parking lots built? Should there be only public transportation access to them? Should the parks offer campgrounds, and if so, how rustic should they be to avoid having to construct conveniences of all kinds? Finally, should an entrance fee be charged to help pay for the parks' maintenance?

National parks around the world have been preserved as a result of the demands of tourism. One of the first examples of this was Yellowstone National Park which was created in 1872 with the construction of access routes and tourist accommodations. Many of the national parks in Britain contain productive farmland and even urban areas. As the parks became more popular in Britain as tourist destinations, they thus required a more careful integration of tourism into an existing economic and social system. The government's philosophy was that landscape conservation took precedence over the demands of recreational tourists.

Despite additions to the parks in North America, the supply of national park space has not kept pace with the increasing demand, particularly in the eastern states and provinces. This puts pressure on the existing parks' landscape and habitat change, soil compaction and erosion, and wildlife. For example, trails have to be cleared; nuisance bears have to be removed; and when parks are used for skiing and campsites, trees have to be cleared. The dilemma is both making parks accessible to tourists and trying to preserve their natural environment. The competition for park usage can also be severe when different user groups stake a claim. For example, tourists in parks often conflict with mining or forestry. In other cases this conflict is between tourists and native Americans who want the parks preserved as their heritage.

Finally, the cost of preserving parks solely for tourism is expensive. When land for parks is removed from use by industries such as mining and logging, the operating costs are further compounded by the loss of revenue in the form of taxes that the government would otherwise receive.

Amusement and Theme Parks

Amusement and theme parks developed from the ancient carnivals, circuses, and tournaments of Asia and Europe. These early annual events provided gathering spots for people to trade goods, share news, and be entertained.

These events eventually developed into more permanent, and even year-round, amusement parks, with their carnival games, thrill rides, cheap food, and hucksters. Famous ones such as Coney Island in New York are destinations for both local residents and long-distance visitors. But owing to changing travel patterns and the lack of automobile parking space, many amusement parks find it difficult to remain popular. Those city amusement parks that have remained popular are the Tivoli Gardens in Copenhagen and the Prater in Vienna.

Theme parks have replaced amusement parks in North America. Disneyland in Anaheim (California) opened in 1955 and changed the local amusement park business by adding shops, shows, and restaurants integrated into a theme embracing adventure, fantasy, history, and science fiction. Cleanliness is of prime importance at the Disney parks. Disneyland and Disney World/Epcot in Orlando (Florida) are now major tourist areas. Similar parks are the various Six Flags, such as Six Flags

Over Georgia in Atlanta, and Wonderland near Toronto, Canada. These parks are so successful that similar types of theme parks are being built around the world. Disney has one near Tokyo and will open another near Paris in 1991. This will be the largest amusement/theme park in Europe.

Theme parks charge a basic entrance fee, but customers then pay no more for entrance to displays or rides or even for transportation throughout the park. The success of a theme park depends on how much its customers enjoy themselves, as it needs repeat business and word-of-mouth advertising. Such parks must continually update their attractions such as rides and live entertainment. In other words, they must offer perceived value, with no additional costs other than for food and merchandise.

Food and merchandise (souvenirs, for example) are not normally a major attraction to theme parks, but the food must be of high quality and affordable. There must also be a variety of food outlets to cater to different tastes and budgets. Generally, fast-food outlets predominate, as customers want to spend little time eating in order to increase their time for entertainment.

Theme parks operate on a customer-volume basis. The managers must know the customer capacity of their rides and entertainment outlets and must be able to increase this capacity in order to avoid long lines. They must know how long people are prepared to wait in queues before becoming frustrated. This scheduling is a major problem because, depending on weather and other factors, there can be large fluctuations in attendance from day to day.

Theme parks can educate and instruct as well as amuse and entertain. They act as a magnet to attract other educational and entertainment centers such as aquariums and marine displays, as well as hotels, motels, and restaurants.

World's fairs or expositions are short-term theme parks that may leave some of their displays and other offerings standing after the event. For example, the Space Needle tower and restaurant, a reminder of Seattle's 1962 World's Fair, is a landmark today for visitors to that city. World's fairs seldom make money during their six-month duration, but they do serve to put a city's name on the map and draw hundreds of thousands of tourists who may be repeat visitors in later years and may spread the word to other potential visitors.

Retail Shops

Many people visit cities because of the quality of their shops, such as those in New York, London, and Paris. Some famous stores, such as Harrod's in London or Bloomingdale's in New York, are known to tourists from around the world. Other shops, such as souvenir and local handicraft shops, are also economically important, for they are major employers and encourage local handicrafts that can benefit from tourist spending.

Most tourists probably do not visit a destination mainly to shop but often take advantage of it on arrival. For example, one of the biggest shopping centers in the world is the Ala Moana shopping center in Honolulu, which receives an estimated 20 percent of its revenue from tourists whose main reason for visiting Hawaii is probably not shopping.

Shopping Malls/Amusement Parks

One of the more recent innovations is a combined shopping mall and amusement park such as the West Edmonton Mall in Edmonton, Canada. This mall has five hundred retail shops, nineteen theaters, and one hundred restaurants. Also completely under cover are a miniature golf course, ice arena, ferris wheel, roller coaster, a water park with slides as high as 85 feet, and a 350-foot-long wave pool with waves as high as 6 feet. There are also submarine rides that cruise past coral reefs, live sharks, dolphins, exotic fish, and an ancient galleon. The mall's adjacent Fantasyland Hotel even has 120 of its 360 rooms designed as "theme" suites. Depending on his or her mood, a registering guest can choose a room with a Roman, Polynesian, Arabian, or one of several other themes.

Something Out of Nothing

Some attractions can be created where there was previously little or nothing to attract tourists. For example, an enterprising group had the idea of moving London Bridge—which was originally constructed across the Thames River in 1843 and was to be demolished to make way for a new one—to Lake Havasu in Arizona. The bridge was dismantled in London and transported, reassembled, and opened in 1971 in Arizona, complete with a model English village. It is now a tourist attraction.

The message is that for a location to become a tourist center, it must capitalize on its natural physical appeal and/or climate, its location, or its reputation, or even create something out of nothing!

DISCUSSION QUESTIONS

1. Differentiate between infrastructure and suprastructure.
2. Discuss how climate affects certain types of tourism.
3. Describe Butlin's Holiday Camps and Club Med.
4. Give some examples of how scenery can attract tourists.
5. What are the two ways of viewing wildlife as a tourist attraction?
6. How do sports add to tourism?
7. Discuss some of the problems of using the parks for tourism.

8. Briefly discuss theme parks and their role in tourism.

9. What long-term value can a world's fair or exposition have on tourism?

10. What role does shopping play in tourism?

PROBLEM

Select a local tourist attraction. It can be a historic site, museum, park, shopping center, or any of the many other possibilities mentioned in this chapter (or even one not mentioned!) that caters to tourists. Remember that a tourist to this attraction does not, by definition, have to stay in a nearby hotel overnight but can be a day visitor who has traveled there by auto, bus, train, boat, or even air. Write a one-page report describing those features of this attraction that actually draw the tourists. Are infrastructure and/or suprastructure important to it, or is it a natural attraction from which infrastructure and suprastructure would detract? Can you determine what type of visitor it draws? What does the attraction's management do to bring in visitors? For example, what highway signs, brochures, or other advertising media are used to catch people's attention and to direct them to this site? What features has management added to lengthen the visitor's stay (for example, historic displays, souvenir shops, or rides)?

SUGGESTED READINGS

Buck, Roy C. 1977. "Making Good Business Better: A Second Look at Staged Tourist Attractions." *Journal of Travel Research* 15(3): 30–32.

Cammeran, James M., and Ronald Bordess. 1981. *Wonderland Through the Looking Glass.* Maple, Canada: Belsten.

Dickson, Duncan R. 1984. "A General Overview to Theme Parks." In *Introduction to Hotel and Restaurant Management*, ed. Robert A. Brymer, Dubuque, Ia.: Kendall/Hunt, pp. 285–288.

Eadington, William R. 1976. *Gambling and Society.* Springfield, Ill.: Thomas.

Economic Consulting Services. 1983. "Developing Successful Theme Recreation Centers." *Real Estate Review*, Winter, pp. 1–4.

Franco, Victor. 1972. *The Club Mediterannée.* London: Shepheard Walwyn.

Gee, Chuck Y., Dexter J. L. Choy, and James C. Makens. 1984. *The Travel Industry.* Westport, Conn.: AVI, pp. 242–254, 258–268.

Mathieu, Susan M. 1981. "The S. S. Segwun: Marketing of a Successful Attraction." *Recreation Canada*, December, pp. 34–38.

Murphy, Peter E. 1985. *Tourism—A Community Approach.* New York: Methuen, pp. 41–51, 60–76.

Rosa, Duane J. 1984. "Casino Management: An Overview." In *Introduction to Hotel and Restaurant Management*, ed. Robert A. Brymer. Dubuque, Ia.: Kendall/Hunt, pp. 297–300.

Zehnder, Leonard E. 1975. *Florida's Disney World: Promises and Problems*. Tallahassee, Fla.: Peninsular.

Governments and Tourism

Tourism as we know it today could not exist if governments were not involved at the highest levels. For two countries to exchange tourists, they first have to recognize each other diplomatically and then draw up commercial agreements known as treaties of amity, commerce, and navigation. These treaties provide mutual protection and security for travelers in the two countries. In addition, the two countries may sign specific agreements regarding tourist matters such as

- Advertising and promotion.
- Exchanges of statistical tourist data.
- Requirements for passports and visas.
- The location of tourism offices in each other's country.
- Cultural exchanges.
- Air agreements (landing rights) in each other's country.

Governments are therefore interested not only in cooperation between each other in regard to international travel but also in such matters as tourism research, regulation, and promotion within their own country. Since the end of World War II many governments have become more and more involved in tourism policy and control, in the creation of tourism ministries and tourism departments not only at the national level but also at the state/province level and even at the city level. In many cases tourism departments are part of the country's ministry of trade and commerce because of the association of tourism with business. These various levels of government involvement with tourism have helped create a more competitive tourist situation and also have helped control its growth through tourism policy planning.

INTERNATIONAL AIR AGREEMENTS

One of the principal roles that the government plays in the international market-place—and which has a direct impact on the tourists' travel flexibility—is the negotiation of international air agreements. International tourism would be impossible without a system of agreements, which often require complex, lengthy negotiations between the two governments and the air carriers that wish to carry people between those two countries.

Even if an airline wishes only to fly over a country, negotiations are still required for what are known as "overflight privileges," and an airline allowed such a privilege often has to pay a fee to the nations over which it flies. In addition to landing rights in another country, fuel purchase and maintenance agreements also must be arranged, often at a high government level.

Many nations have government-owned, flag-carrying international airlines and want to ensure that these air agreements (with particular reference to airfares) remain in force. Many of these airlines are relatively small, marginally profitable, and frequently subsidized, and, without the requirement of agreements, would be subjected to market forces and the competition from much larger and more powerful privately owned airlines (such as those in the United States).

But it is also in the interest of these privately owned airlines to have international air agreements, as otherwise the national flag carriers could be heavily subsidized by their governments to keep them in business as a matter of national pride. A heavily subsidized airline could then undercut the private airlines by means of discounted fares. Furthermore, without agreements, the large airlines could concentrate on the more profitable international flights and leave the smaller airlines to struggle with the unprofitable routes. International agreements also ensure that where there is enough business for the airlines of two nations to offer service, a third one will not move in and cause problems for all three of them. Finally, international agreements usually impose a system of rates that prevents predatory pricing. They may also permit high prices to be maintained on very profitable routes, by keeping out the competition.

Freedoms

The agreements between nations for landing rights are called *freedoms,* which were drawn up at an international meeting known as the Bermuda Agreement of 1946. Technically, there are eight freedoms between two countries, but according to Gee, Choy, and Makens (1984, p. 193),

> only the first two technical freedoms have gained wide acceptance. The fundamental third and fourth freedoms and the contentious fifth and sixth freedoms remain the subjects of bilateral bargaining. Seventh and eighth freedoms usually are allowed only under special circumstances.

These eight freedoms are as follows:

1. An airline can fly over one country while on its way to another. For example, a U.S. airline can fly over Canada on its way to England.

2. An airline can land in one country for refueling while on its way to another country but cannot drop off or pick up passengers. For example, a U.S. airline can land in Canada for refueling while on its way to England.

3. An airline can drop off passengers in one country while on its way to another. For example, a U.S. airline can drop off U.S. passengers in London while on its way to Frankfurt, Germany.

4. An airline can pick up passengers from a foreign country and bring them back to its own country. For example, a U.S. airline can pick up German passengers in Frankfurt and bring them to the United States.

5. An airline may pick up passengers in a second country while flying to a third. For example, a U.S. airline on its way to Frankfurt may stop and pick up passengers in London before continuing on to Frankfurt.

6. An airline returning from a foreign country may stop at one of its gateway airports and drop off passengers before proceeding to a third country. For example, a U.S. airline picking up passengers in London may drop off some of those passengers in Anchorage (so that they can make connections to other airlines) before continuing on to Tokyo. In other words, most of the carried passengers do not originate in the United States, nor is it their destination.

7. An airline from one country may operate *only* between two other countries. For example, a U.S. airline may technically be able to fly passengers between Tokyo and Seoul, South Korea.

8. An airline from one country may operate only between two points in

another country. For example, a U.S. airline can technically carry passengers only between Tokyo and Osaka, both in Japan.

GOVERNMENT INVOLVEMENT IN DOMESTIC TOURISM

The government in most countries has both a direct and an indirect involvement in tourism. One direct involvement is in tourism research. The private sector of tourism generally has neither the capacity nor the immediate need to carry out macrotourism research. But if a country's tourism industry is to be internationally competitive, this research must be carried out, and that responsibility generally falls on its government.

Governments also own parks, airlines and airports, art galleries, museums, historic sites, streets and highways, railways, buses, harbors and ferries, subways, hotels, resorts, swimming pools, golf courses, and even liquor stores. Governments produce maps and charts, operate information centers, advertise, regulate fishing and hunting, require businesses to be licensed, employ inspectors, collect taxes, make loans or grants, and collect and analyze statistics. All of these direct and indirect government involvements apply to the tourism business just as they do to any other. Obviously, much of what government does is not directed exclusively at tourism but, rather, toward its broader objectives. However, apart from tourism, it is difficult to think of any other sector of a nation's economy that is affected more by governments, from the lowest to the highest levels.

Government Financing

Governments often have no choice but to help finance many tourism supply components, as the private sector of the industry has no desire, and no funds, to do this. Governments, for the most part, have no alternative but to be the provider of airports, roads, and utilities (water, sewer), although sometimes all or part of these may have private funding.

When the government does provide part of a tourism project's financing, it must weigh the costs of these items against the benefits of using the tax revenues in other projects such as education or health care. In developed countries that already have a good base of social investments, the government might have more money to fund tourism projects. In less developed countries a twofold problem exists. First, the government's tax revenues are not high because of the population's low per-capita income, and second, most of that government revenue is needed to provide basic social services.

Although competition for government funds for tourism is intense in developed countries, it is far more competitive in less developed ones. In addition, less developed countries often have little to attract private financing. In such situations the government has two choices: It can either borrow the needed funds from one of the several international banks that specialize in assisting countries to improve their economies or else provide incentives to entice private enterprises (such as international hotel chains) to do the development work.

Government Policies That Affect Tourism

Government policies that affect tourism can best be described by considering currency exchange rates and national monetary policy. Tourism expenditures by a country's citizens and by visitors to that country are affected by international exchange rates. But a government cannot establish exchange rates for the sake of the tourism industry alone.

The same is true for domestic taxation. Taxes on specific products such as gasoline, alcohol, and tobacco must be established within the general framework of a country's economy, even though these taxes indirectly affect tourists' expenditures. Finally, government expenditures on the infrastructure, such as roads, are paid for out of general tax revenues, even though the improved infrastructure benefits tourists, many of whom are from abroad.

INTERNATIONAL GOVERNMENT ORGANIZATIONS

There are a number of world and regional international organizations, sponsored by national governments and others, that are heavily involved in international tourism.

World Tourism Organization (WTO)

One of the most important international tourism organizations is the World Tourism Organization (WTO), with its headquarters in Madrid, Spain. The WTO represents all national and official tourist interests and is recognized as the official consultative body on tourism to the United Nations. The WTO's basic objective is the promotion and development of tourism with a view to contributing to economic development, international understanding, peace, prosperity, and universal respect for and observance of human rights and fundamental freedom for all without distinction as to race, sex, language, or religion. In achieving this goal the WTO pays particular attention to the interests of the developing countries in the field of tourism and collaborates with appropriate branches of the United Nations and its specialized agencies.

Some of the many ways in which the WTO is involved in tourism are

- Helping developing countries in tourist endeavors.
- Acting as an international clearinghouse for tourist information.

- Encouraging the application of new knowledge to tourism development and marketing.
- Promoting cooperation among all countries in technical matters affecting tourism.
- Harmonizing tourist policies among nations by formulating and applying international tourism principles.
- Standardizing equipment, terms, and signs to aid tourists.
- Recommending positive tourism measures, such as the creation of new tourist facilities.
- Promoting tourism and spreading an appreciation of its advantages.
- Conducting regular surveys of world tourism.
- Creating methods of forecasting, measuring, and marketing tourism that will be of use to national tourist organizations in their own endeavors.
- Encouraging research leading to improvement in the comparability of tourist statistics.
- Facilitating world travel by encouraging the elimination or reduction of government control on international travel and by such means as standardizing passports, visas, and frontier formalities.

International Civil Aviation Organization (ICAO) and International Air Transport Association (IATA)

Two other major world international organizations are the International Civil Aviation Organization (ICAO) and the International Air Transport Association (IATA). These two groups will be discussed in a later chapter.

Organization for Economic Cooperation and Development (OECD)

The Organization for Economic Cooperation and Development (OECD) was established in 1960 in Paris with the objective of promoting policies that would achieve the highest sustainable economic growth and development and raise the standard of living among its member countries, as well as to contribute to the expansion of the economy and to world trade. Because tourism plays an integral part in achieving these goals, the OECD has a tourism committee for coordinating tourism studies and arranging meetings among member countries to improve statistical methods of monetary exchange and accounting. The OECD also prepares an annual report entitled *Tourism Policy and International Tourism in OECD Member Countries*. Most of the more than twenty OECD member countries are from Europe; other members are Australia, Canada, Japan, New Zealand, and the United States.

Organization of American States (OAS)

The Organization of American States (OAS) has objectives similar to those of the OECD, but it limits its activities to North, Central, and Latin America.

Pacific Area Travel Association (PATA)

The Pacific Area Travel Association (PATA) was organized in 1951. Although many governments are members, there are more than one thousand other organizations that are nongovernment members. These include airlines, steamship lines, ground transportation companies, travel agents, wholesale tour operators, travel associations, hotels, tourism trade publishers, public relations firms, and advertisers. The major objective of the PATA is to develop, promote, and facilitate travel in the Pacific area, which includes North America. PATA achieves this objective by arranging conferences and seminars, producing publications and reports, and sponsoring training programs.

Other Organizations

Other regional international organizations also have objectives similar to those of the PATA. Some of these organizations are

ETC: European Travel Commission

CMTA: Common Market Travel Association

CTA: Caribbean Tourism Association

SATO: South American Tourist Organization

NATIONAL ORGANIZATIONS

Almost every country has a national organization responsible to a greater or lesser degree for tourism, and some countries have a separate ministry responsible for tourism policy and planning. In other countries the amount of government involvement may be much less.

The way that a government involves itself in tourism can dictate tourism's rate of development, as the government can help promote and advertise tourism both to and within its own country, can offer grants and/or low-interest loans for tourism development, can aid in tourism education and training, and can even (as is the case in some countries) control the currency exchange rate for tourists.

Eastern Bloc Countries

At one extreme are countries such as the Soviet Union where the government tourist agency Intourist and the government airline Aeroflot completely control tourism within that country. The government operates hotels, restaurants, travel agencies, resorts, transportation, and even festivals. In other words, there is virtually no aspect of tourism that is not government controlled. Similar situations prevail in other Eastern European countries such as Rumania, Bulgaria, Yugoslavia, and East Germany.

Other Countries

According to Kaiser and Helber (1978, p. 12) the "responsibility and accountability for tourism management lie with the government empowered to represent . . . people." However, according to Murphy (1985, p. 33) government involvement has been slow to emerge in the laissez-faire economies of the West and has come to the fore only with the development of mass tourism and its consequences for national trade accounts.

One of the more dramatic cases of a government's involvement in tourism is Spain, where tourism development and promotion have been used in that country's economic and social development plans to make tourism the country's largest export. Using the potential for mass tourism as the incentive during the 1960s, Spain invested large amounts of both public and private funds to create a tourism infrastructure. As a result, employment was created, and the standard of living was improved for the local people in the regions where tourism flourished. This happened not only in established tourist areas but also in other regions such as the offshore Canary Islands. Spain's example was paralleled by Yugoslavia, along its Adriatic coast.

Nations such as Spain and Austria have based most of their post–World War II development on growth in their tourism business. According to British Tourist Authority (1981, p. 13) figures, the average overall European tourism export earnings were 4.7 percent of total earnings, but in Austria it was 21.7 percent and in Spain 22.5 percent.

In France the Côte d'Azur region on the Mediterranean coast has traditionally formed the basis for France's tourism industry, and the government used its leverage to help develop the Languedoc-Roussillon coastal area to relieve pressure along the Côte d'Azur, again creating new recreation facilities for residents as well as tourists and job opportunities for the local people.

Other Western European governments are highly involved in tourism, but to a lesser degree than are the Eastern European governments. For example, in Spain and Portugal, tourism is centralized and controlled, with the government both financing and operating some hotels and other tourist facilities. Even in completely free-enterprise countries the government may still have an interest in tourism. For example, in New Zealand the government owns the Tourist Hotel Corporation which runs the major hotels, airlines, railroad and shipping lines, and travel agencies.

In other cases, notably in countries such as Jamaica and the Bahamas, the government has become involved by default, as it has had to take over bankrupt hotels and other tourist facilities.

Governments and Transportation

In many other cases the government's prime involvement in tourism is the part or full ownership of a major national airline. This is the case in most European and many other countries. In the United States, all the airlines are privately owned. In Canada, the major international carrier, Air Canada, is indirectly majority-owned (through a crown corporation) by the government, but all other carriers are privately owned.

Many governments also own and operate their railroad systems. This is the case with British Rail and the railways of most other European countries. In Canada the government indirectly owns Canadian National Railway, even though the other major railway, Canadian Pacific, is privately owned. In the United States, all the railways, just like the airlines, are private corporations. However, the U.S. government today does have an indirect involvement with passenger rail travel. In 1971, in order to reverse the declining level of passenger service offered by the privately owned railroads (which preferred to concentrate on more profitable movement of freight), the U.S. Congress created the national railroad passenger corporation known as Amtrak. Its purpose was to eliminate unprofitable rail routes and consolidate most of the remaining profitable ones into a single national system. Amtrak is neither a nationalized nor a private corporation, but the government subsidizes it in order for it to survive.

Other Concerns

When governments first become involved in the tourist industry, their concern is primarily with export earnings and economic growth. Later this concern tends to spread to the planning, social, and environmental aspects of tourism, as tourism, like any other economic activity, competes for resources such as land and even for employees with traditional industries such as agriculture, fishing, and forestry. Most governments today have become more aware of the limitations of tourism and recognize that it must be properly fitted in to other economic and social systems. The ramifications of economic, environmental, and cultural concerns will be explored more fully in later chapters.

Fragmentation of the Tourism Industry

Another problem that governments have come to recognize and wrestle with is the fragmentation of the tourism industry. The industry is made up of many small business operators who believe in the free-enterprise system and the minimization of government involvement in the way they run their businesses. This creates a major obstacle for governments at all levels in planning tourism development. It is not difficult for a government to decide on a tourism policy and establish a working plan to achieve this, but to communicate this plan to the many entrepreneurs involved and have them work within it is much more difficult. How can the activities of all these small business operators be coordinated so that they all will work toward a common objective? Conflicts can arise that lead to less happy tourists whom everyone wishes to please. Further strain is also placed on the area's natural and human resources. Because of the importance of planning in tourism development, this topic will be explored in more depth in a later chapter.

Governments and Tourism Policy

Some European governments have long been involved in tourism programs. Other European governments, which previously considered tourism as primarily a problem for the private sector, now view it as a vehicle for economic and social policy, particularly since oil prices rose in the early 1970s. The governments of Belgium, Britain, France, Germany, and to a lesser degree the Scandinavian countries, now give tourism a much larger economic role than previously, especially in the areas of increasing employment and exports. However, even with this increased involvement in tourism, the European governments (as is also the case in Canada and the United States) are principally involved in tourism marketing or promotional efforts to increase tourism demand. Nevertheless, two countries, France and Switzerland, have developed comprehensive tourism plans to serve both domestic and foreign markets.

BRITAIN

The British government views its role as establishing the right framework for tourism enterprise and initiative. In other words, it believes that the responsibility for developing and marketing the product rests with the private sector. Britain's 1969 Development of Tourism Act laid the foundation for that government's role in tourism planning. This formal involvement was precipitated by a growing travel deficit, and its objectives are to direct development to economically depressed areas, to encourage hotel construction, and to provide more effective promotion abroad (through the British Tourist Authority). The British Tourist Authority (BTA) is the external arm of the government and has offices in various foreign cities and has as its aim the encouragement of foreigners to visit Britain. According to the BTA (1986), "Research is the foundation of the Board's marketing strategy. The BTA carries out a continuous and extensive programme of research in overseas countries and amongst tourists visiting Britain."

Tourist Boards

When visitors arrive in Britain, they become the responsibility of the national and regional tourist boards. For example, the English Tourist Board (ETB) is a statutory body created in 1969 to develop and market England's tourism. Scotland, Wales, and Northern Ireland have similar boards.

The ETB's main objectives are to provide a welcome for people visiting England, to encourage people living in England to take their holidays there, and to encourage the provision and improvement of tourist amenities and facilities in England. The board has a statutory duty to advise the government on tourism matters relating to England and administers the government's grant and loan schemes for hotels and other tourist attractions. The ETB has twelve regional tourist boards and more than seven hundred officially recognized tourist information centers. Despite the government's generally laissez-faire attitude toward tourism in Britain, tourism there is highly organized and coordinated.

THE UNITED STATES

Until recently, the United States' official federal tourism agency was the United States Travel Service (USTS), a branch of the Department of Commerce. The USTS was created in 1961 to promote and develop tourism, but it did not have a tourism policy.

In 1982 the government passed the National Tourism Policy Act and created the U.S. Travel & Tourism Administration (USTTA). The USTTA's objective is to foster travel to the United States from abroad, as a stimulus to economic stability, and to stimulate the growth of the U.S. travel industry in order to reduce the nation's travel deficit and to promote U.S. inbound tourism as an export earner. The information office of USTTA is known as Travel USA. The act also allowed the creation of the Travel and Tourism Advisory Board, with representatives from the travel industry, organized labor, the academic community, and others. The act also created the Tourism Policy Council to coordinate federal tourism policies affecting tourism, recreation, and heritage.

Many people in the United States question the need for a government to be so directly involved in tourism when most of the beneficiaries are private enterprises. But the proponents of the government's involvement argue that the country's travel deficit is a national public problem and that it is the government's responsibility to try to resolve it.

Travel Industry Association of America (TIAA)

The Travel Industry Association of America (TIAA) was formerly known as the Discover America Travel Organization (DATO). The TIAA is a nonprofit association of companies and government organizations acting as a lobbying group for the travel industry. Its main objective is to develop and implement programs that benefit domestic travel suppliers and tourists on a national basis. It achieves this objective through its marketing efforts, research, and activities with the government.

State and City Organizations

Most states have a government-sanctioned tourist office responsible for the development and growth of tourism in that state. These offices often also participate in programs such as advertising, information, and publicity to draw attention to the state's tourist attractions.

Many major cities also have a stake in tourism and have established tourism and convention offices. Many of the largest cities also own convention centers to help attract business tourists.

CANADA

During the fifty years that the Canadian federal government has been involved in tourism, under a variety of different names, it has had no comprehensive strategy and little effective coordination between the federal government and other government levels and between governments and the private sector. In Canada, the federal government organization involved in tourism is known as Tourism Canada, a branch of the Department of Regional Industrial Expansion.

Tourism Canada is involved in three areas of tourism: development, marketing, and corporate affairs. However, about 80 percent of its budget is currently spent on marketing, through its Vacation Canada program to encourage Canadians to vacation at home. Canada currently has an extremely large travel deficit, with Canadians spending about $1.70 abroad for each $1.00 earned from international tourist arrivals in Canada.

Recently the Canadian government introduced what are known as Travel Industry Development Subsidiary Agreements (TIDSAs). These financial agreements were signed by the Canadian federal government and various provinces to help attract tourists and reduce the country's growing travel deficit.

Travel Industry Association of Canada (TIAC)

The Travel Industry Association of Canada (TIAC) is an umbrella association for the tourism industry, just as the TIAA is in the United States. It is recognized as the voice of the industry, even though it does not represent some of the main tourism participants. The TIAC is composed of both large and small tourist businesses as well as industry associations. It is primarily concerned with broad issues such as taxation, energy policy, and employee training when they affect more than one tourism sector or region.

Provincial and City Organizations

Each of the various provinces in Canada has a government branch responsible for the growth of tourism in that province, and it is heavily involved in advertising, information, and the promotion of provincial tourist attractions. Most large Canadian cities also have convention and visitor bureaus to help promote local tourism. Some of them, as well, own their own convention centers to attract business tourists to conventions and exhibitions.

SUMMARY

 According to Mings (1978), governments have three options regarding tourism. The first is to maintain their current involvement. The second is to withdraw completely from direct involvement in the tourism industry and not to give it financial support. The third is to rationalize the industry (when feasible) by assessing its problems and prospects and following through when this is economically, socially, and environmentally viable, with plans to remedy weaknesses and direct the industry toward long-term goals. In some cases a government may use any, or a combination of, these three alternatives, depending on the circumstances. Finally, all governments have one more important role to play, and that is to remind local residents of the economic value of tourism and to encourage those residents to be hospitable to tourists.

DISCUSSION QUESTIONS

1. List four of the matters that two countries must agree on before they can exchange tourists.

2. Discuss the importance of international air agreements to both the airlines and the countries involved.

3. Explain each of the first four international air "freedoms."

4. Why does the responsibility for tourism research generally fall on the government?

5. Explain the difference between a government's specific tourism policy and other government policies that affect tourism.

6. What is the WTO, and what is its objective?

7. What is the OECD, and what is its objective?

8. Explain what the PATA is, who its members are, and what its main objective is.

9. In many countries the government owns, or has an interest in, a national airline. Why do you think that all the airlines in the United States are privately owned and that the government has never been in the commercial airline business?

10. Explain what is meant by fragmentation of the tourism industry and the problems that this creates for government tourism policy and planning.

11. Explain the government's policy and how tourism is organized and coordinated in Britain.

12. Explain the government's role in tourism in the United States.

13. Explain the government's role in tourism in Canada.

PROBLEM

You are employed in a state's ministry of tourism. The ministry is responsible for grading visitor accommodations and publishing an annual catalog showing all auto routes in the state and listing along each route the available accommodations (hotels, motels, campsites, etc.). Each lodging is graded each year by state inspectors who visit each property and award it anywhere from one to five stars (with five the highest-quality category). The grading is based on physical appearance covering such matters as size and design of property, number of rooms or campsites, public areas, and similar items. There have been many complaints about this system, both from accommodation operators and visitors who feel that the grading is unclear, unfair, and even misleading. Why do you think these complaints are arising? What recommendations for changing the system would you make to your minister? Are there any difficulties that might arise in implementing your recommendations? What might be any added costs to the new system if it is implemented?

REFERENCES

British Tourist Authority. 1981. *The Economic Significance of Tourism Within the European Community.* London: British Tourist Authority.

British Tourist Authority. 1986. *National Facts of Tourism 1984/5.* London: British Tourist Authority.

Gee, Chuck Y., Dexter J. L. Choy, and James C. Makens. 1984. *The Travel Industry.* Westport, Conn.: AVI.

Kaiser, C., Jr., and L. E. Helber. 1978. *Tourism Planning and Development.* Boston: CBI.

Mings, R. C. 1978. "Tourist Industry Development at the Crossroads." *Tourist Review* 33(3): 2–3.

Murphy, Peter E. 1985. *Tourism—A Community Approach.* New York: Methuen.

SUGGESTED READINGS

Council of State Governments. 1979. *Tourism: State Structure, Organization, and Support.* Lexington, Ky.: Council of State Governments.

Gee, Chuck Y., Dexter J. L. Choy, and James C. Makens. 1984. *The Travel Industry.* Westport, Conn.: AVI, pp. 55–65, 68–83.

Government of Canada. No date. *Tourism Tomorrow: Towards a Canadian Tourism Strategy.* Ottawa: Tourism Canada.

Organization for Economic Cooperation and Development. 1979. *Tourism Policy and International Tourism in OECD Member Countries.* Paris: OECD.

U.S. Government. 1978. *National Tourism Policy Study—Final Report.* Washington, D.C.: U.S. Government Printing Office.

U.S. Travel Data Center. 1985. *Impact of Foreign Visitors on State Economies.* Washington, D.C.: U.S. Travel Data Center.

U.S. Travel Service. 1978. *Tourism: State Structure, Organization and Support—A Technical Study.* Washington, D.C.: U.S. Travel Service.

World Tourism Organization. 1978. *Role and Structure of National Tourism Administrations.* Madrid: WTO.

Tourist Statistics

Travel is the common thread in most definitions of tourism, and travel is also linked closely to time availability. Most vacationing travelers have blocks of free or discretionary time during annual vacations or on weekends, and it is during these periods that travel and tourism peak. Generally it is younger and older people who have the most discretionary time. Between those two ages most people are paying for a house and raising a family, and so the demands on their time and their pocketbooks take precedence over their ability to be tourists.

DEFINING TOURISM_____

When defining tourism, many people argue that it does not exist as a separate identifiable industry but represents a cross section of many industries. For example, many supplier groups cater to both tourists and nontourists, such as in transportation, entertainment, and food service, whose economic survival may depend not on the tourist but on local residents for year-round support. These tourism suppliers are only partly in the tourism business. One factor that differentiates the tourism industry from many other products that consumers purchase and use is that in tourism, the tourist, and not the product, does the traveling. The tourism product is a combination of all the various supplier entities that provide the tourist with the total travel experience and satisfaction.

McIntosh and Goeldner (1984, pp. 3–4) list four different perspectives of tourism that can be identified and must be considered before tourism and tourists can be defined. These four perspectives are the tourist, the businesses providing the tourist goods and services (hotels, restaurants, and others), the government of the host community or area, and the host community itself. McIntosh and Goeldner further define tourism as the sum of the phenomena and relationships arising from the interaction of tourists, businesses, host governments, and host communities in the process of attracting and hosting these tourists and other visitors.

Defining the Tourist

The word *tourist* derives from the word *tour*, or a circular trip that starts at a specific place and eventually returns there following a particular itinerary. When most of us think of a tourist we think of a person on vacation to visit a distant location, to see the sights, to visit friends and relatives, and to do little else but relax or possibly participate in leisure activities such as sunbathing or sports. Many people consider tourists as only those people who are traveling for vacation reasons. But there are many other types of tourists, such as business people, convention delegates, and other travelers.

The preceding chapter mentioned that one of the government's major roles is producing tourist statistics. But first a tourist must be precisely defined. There are many definitions of a tourist, and different governments, and different levels of government, use different definitions depending on the data they require. As Gee, Choy, and Makens (1984, p. 11) state:

> The criteria selected to distinguish one kind of traveler from another are often dependent on the particular situation and focus of interest of the researcher. The variations in definitions of tourism emphasize the difficulty in comparing data on tourism.

Definitions, therefore, are somewhat arbitrary and must be considered in their particular context when analyzing statistical data.

Visitors

For international purposes one of the most commonly used definitions of a tourist is that developed by the 1963 United Nations Conference of Travel and Tourism and also adopted in 1968 by the International Union of Official Travel Organizations (later the World Tourism Organization). This definition first defines a visitor as any person visiting a country, other than that in which he has his usual place of residence, for any reason other than following an occupation remunerated from within the country visited. This definition was created for international travelers, but it can easily be adapted for tourists traveling within their own country (domestic tourists) by substituting the word *region* or *area* for *country*. This definition of a visitor is further refined by defining a tourist as any visitor staying over twenty-four hours in a country and making an overnight stay for any of the following reasons:

Business	Meeting
Congress	Mission
Convention	Recreation
Family	Relatives
Friends	Religion
Health	Sport
Holiday	Study
Leisure	Vacation

In other words, virtually everybody visiting a country for more than a day and making an overnight stay is a tourist. However, a person who travels to another country for paid work does not meet this criterion.

Tourists Versus Excursionists

Visitors who stay for less than twenty-four hours are defined by the United Nations as *excursionists* or day visitors. A traveler visiting another country on a cruise ship is also considered an excursionist, as are the crew members who do not normally reside there. But foreign air or ship crews docked or on layover and who use the accommodation establishments of the country visited are tourists rather than excursionists. The main characteristic of an excursionist that differentiates him or her from a tourist is that no overnight stay is involved. Some authorities recommend that cruise ship passengers be included in a classification separate from visitors and excursionists. The reason is that these excursionists often sleep on the ship, rather than using local accommodations, but nevertheless often spend more than one day visiting the destination.

Visitor statistics are required in order that governments and private operators can know how many tourists and excursionists to expect. They also need to know the profiles of tourists and excursionists so that they can develop policies and plans to serve them and assess their impact on the culture, economy, and environment of the area or areas that are visitor destinations. And they also need to categorize visitors as either tourists or excursionists. Again, excursionists make no demands on hotel accommodations but demand more ground transportation and infrastructure and have a great interest in shopping and related facilities.

Accommodation Records

Many tourists use hotel or motel accommodations for their overnight stays, and so tourist information can be obtained from guest registration cards to form a basis for statistical information, along with information from border-crossing records if international tourists are involved. Accommodation records of overnight stays provide only one part of the total picture, however. Many tourists (for example, those defined as visiting relatives and friends), or those staying in bed and breakfast places, guest houses, or farms, provide no official record of overnight stays, and any statistics based only on accommodation records can provide only a conservative estimate of the total tourism picture.

Domestic Tourists

Domestic tourists are sometimes much more difficult to define than are international tourists and excursionists. Domestic tourists are those who travel only within the borders of their own country of residence. The definition of this type of tourist is much more varied than that of the WTO for international tourists. Some governments incorporate a mileage factor in their definition. The United States' National Tourism Resources Review Commission (1973, p. 5) defined a tourist as "one who travels away from home for a distance of at least 50 miles (one way) for business, pleasure, personal affairs, or any other purpose except to commute to work, whether he stays overnight or returns the same day."

The Canadian government defines a person as a tourist if he or she travels twenty-five miles beyond his or her community. Because definitions do differ from country to country, and even from area to area within a country for domestic tourists, and because domestic tourism statistics are often produced using a definition that suits the purposes of the group or organization for whom the statistics are being compiled, great care must be taken when interpreting statistics regarding domestic tourists.

USEFUL PLANNING STATISTICS

In order to plan tourism, tourist statistics are required. Some of the more important tourist profile statistics are the following.

Country of Origin

Probably the most important statistic in planning is the arriving tourists' country of origin, as this can indicate to some degree the tourists' requirements.

It is a strange fact that tourists, whose motive to travel may be to see how things differ in a foreign country, often want to have many things just as they are at home. This is particularly true of accommodations and restaurants. For example, Austria's economy is based almost entirely on tourism, and most of its tourists are Germans who speak the same language, come from the same cultural background, and eat much of the same kind of food as do Austrians. On the other hand, part of Austria is bordered by Italy, but it receives relatively few tourists from that country because of language and culture differences and a shortage of restaurants in Austria that specialize in pasta!

Similarly, many of the visitors to some of the southern coastal regions of Spain are British, and it is no coincidence that fish and chip shops are common in that area. Also, many of the hotels in the costa regions of Spain are known as "British," "Dutch," or "Scandinavian."

For the same reason, hotel chains such as the U.S.-based Holiday Inn are able to operate around the world, as they cater to the accommodation needs of North Americans who feel more comfortable with a familiar hotel name that they can count on to provide the same standards they would find at home.

Number of Visitors

The number of visitors who choose to travel to a particular tourist destination is a function of their desire to travel and competitive factors that tend to reduce that desire. The desire or motivation to go to a particular destination is influenced by that person's psychographic and socioeconomic profiles. The competitive factors that reduce this desire to travel are such matters as the time and cost to get there, the cultural differences between the tourist's country of residence and the destination country, and the seasonality of the destination. For example, the greater the distance to the destination is, the longer it will take to get there, and the greater the cost will be. This tends to diminish the demand to travel there. But both time and cost can be reduced by technological change, as we saw with the introduction of jet aircraft in 1959, after which both the time and the cost for a North American to reach Europe were reduced by about 50 percent. When travel time and cost are reduced, then demand generally increases, which can have a dramatic impact on tourist supply needs.

Counting the number of tourists who arrive at a destination is usually not difficult, particularly if they arrive by public transportation and/or cross at specific border points. Measuring tourist arrivals helps indicate changes in demand, not only annually, but also by season or month.

Length of Stay

Another important statistic is the length of visit to a country or area. If foreign visitors are primarily short-stay excursionists, then their demands on the infrastructure (roads, airports) and the suprastructure (hotels, restaurants, attractions) will be fewer than those of tourists staying for one or more days.

Excursionists travel primarily by auto or bus and, in Europe, also by train. They make heavy demands on this type of transportation. Tourists, on short-haul routes, may also make demands on transportation similar to those of the excursionists, but tourists traveling longer distances are more likely to travel by air, and so the need to plan adequate airports, and customs and immigration facilities at those airports, is much greater.

Longer-stay tourists also require adequate accommodation facilities, whereas excursionists have little or no demand for them. Shopping, however, is very important to excursionists and is often what attracts them in the first place. Shopping may also be important to longer-stay tourists, and also important to them are attractions (museums, historic sites, and so forth) and recreation facilities (sporting or entertainment).

In general, the longer the length of stay is, the greater will be the demand for hotels, restaurants, shops, and attractions. Indeed, one of the objectives of those involved in tourism is to try to lengthen the tourists' stay, for the longer they stay, the more money they will leave behind.

Visitor Days

Although visitor arrivals are a useful broad measuring tool, more valuable is the number of visitor days (or nights). To calculate this, multiply the number of arrivals by the average length of stay. These data are useful to tourism planners because they indicate the need for more or fewer utilities, parking spaces, and park, beach, or other recreation areas. Similarly, developers of accommodation facilities need this information to plan the size of new hotels or to expand existing ones.

Per-Capita Spending

Closely related to length of stay is the visitors' average per-capita spending. To provide a meaningful statistic for comparison, this figure is usually calculated on a daily basis: total per-capita spending divided by the number of days of stay. This figure is not always easy to obtain, although tourist surveys can be of some help. Alternatively, if a jurisdiction has a sales tax on hotel rooms, merchandise sales, or restaurant meal sales, tax revenues can be used to provide these data. For example, consider the following data concerning a destination's use of hotel rooms for a typical month: This destination has a 5 percent rooms tax, and the rooms tax collected this particular month is $50,000. Studies have shown that 25 percent of total tourist spending is for hotel accommodations. In addition, at this destination, the money spent by tourists staying in hotels is estimated to be 80 percent of the total overall spending at this destination, the remaining 20 percent coming from VFR arrivals. Also during this month, there were five thousand visitor arrivals, whose average length of stay was five days.

Per-capita spending is calculated as follows:

$$5\% \text{ rooms tax collected} = \$50,000$$

Total amount spent on hotel rooms is therefore

$$\$50,000 \,/\, 5\%, \text{ or } \$50,000 \,/\, 0.05 = \$1,000,000$$

Because the amount spent on hotel rooms represents 25% of total hotel guest spending, total expenditures are

$$\$1,000,000 \; / \; 25\%, \text{ or } \$1,000,000 \; / \; 0.25 \; = \; \$4,000,000$$

Furthermore, this $4,000,000 represents the total expenditure of those staying in hotels, whose expenditures are 80% of all visitor expenditures. Therefore total overall expenditures are

$$\$4,000,000 \; / \; 80\%, \text{ or } \$4,000,000 \; / \; 0.8 \; = \; \$5,000,000$$

If there are 5,000 arrivals with an average 5-day stay, then the total number of visitor days will be

$$5,000 \; \times \; 5 \; = \; 25,000$$

Per-capita spending is thus

$$\$5,000,000 \; / \; 25,000 \; = \; \$200 \text{ a day.}$$

Even on a per-capita spending per day basis, however, this figure must be used with caution. For example, a Canadian tourist to the United States might spend an average of $200 per day, whereas a visitor from Germany might spend only $180 per day. This might indicate that the United States should spend more of its advertising budget in Canada to encourage more visitors from that country. But if the tourist from Canada stays on average only ten days (total spending $2,000), whereas the visitor from Germany stays fourteen days (total spending $2,520), then advertising more heavily in Germany might realize a higher total.

Remember that Latin Americans visiting Europe spend more per capita per day than do North Americans. This seems to indicate that European countries should do more to attract Latin American tourists. But perhaps the travel distances are too great for this to be feasible, or Latin Americans may not be inclined to visit Europe in great numbers, anyway. For these reasons it may still be more profitable for European countries to concentrate on the large numbers of North Americans who do come. In sum, average daily per-capita spending and length of stay are closely linked to market size and demand in regard to total tourist spending.

Reason for Visit

There is a close relationship between the purpose of a visit and the demand for tourist services. We have already seen this in distinguishing excursionists from tourists. But even tourists can have different demands. Consider, for example, business travelers. Business travelers going to a foreign country generally travel by air because it saves them time. Business travelers therefore make heavy demands on airlines and airports. VFR travelers are more likely to travel by auto, bus, or train and often find more important the facilities and attractions en route. Also, if the

VFR travelers are staying with friends and relatives at their destination they will make no demands on destination accommodations and few demands on restaurants, compared with those of the business travelers. In addition, the business travelers' per-capita daily spending is invariably far higher than that of the VFR tourists, although the latter's length of stay is usually longer than the business travelers'.

Type of Accommodation Required

There is a similar relationship between the type of traveler and the kind of accommodation required. For example, VFR travelers may require some accommodation en route. It usually is low-priced and offers few frills, such as a camping site or a pad for a recreational vehicle (RV). Campers and RV travelers may also require only grocery stores en route rather than restaurants. On the other hand, business travelers often require more expensive and luxurious accommodations (because of their need to entertain) than does the typical package tour tourist. For example, the bus tour travelers' demands for accommodations are generally much more modest than the business travelers'.

Generally, the type of tourist is also closely correlated with his or her average daily per-capita spending: The camper's average daily spending might be very low compared with that of the bus tour package traveler, whereas the business traveler's spending will be at the top of the list.

Type of Transportation Used

A tourist's method of travel can indicate the type of infrastructure and suprastructure required. Another aspect of this is that the travel method used on arrival may differ from that used on departure. For example, many people fly from their home country to a foreign country. From there they leave on a cruise ship that takes them to another foreign destination, from which they fly back directly to their country of residence.

Time Period of Tourist Arrivals

Determining the peaks and valleys during the year for tourist arrivals and departures is helpful in many ways. One of these is staffing, so that adequate personnel are available at border points and in hotels, restaurants, and tourist attractions.

Some destinations have more than one peak period. For example, many winter ski resorts are also popular summer tourist destinations. In such cases, tourism planners are often interested in pinpointing when the shoulder tourist seasons are, so that attractions and appropriate advertising can be planned that might bring in tourists at that time and so lengthen the tourist season.

Socioeconomic Profiles

Also useful are socioeconomic data about tourists, such as their ages, marital status, family size, occupation, and income levels. This information is particularly useful in planning advertising so that the message can be oriented to potential tourists who have profiles similar to those who have already been tourists. Also useful are the socioeconomic profiles of residents of a foreign country who are not currently potential tourists to a host country, so that the host country can adapt its advertising accordingly.

OBTAINING TOURIST DATA

A number of different methods, or a combination of methods, may be used to obtain statistical data about a country's tourists. For example, border-crossing points or ship or plane arrival locations can yield detailed information if arriving tourists fill in forms providing certain basic data. These forms are then collected by customs or passport officers.

The basic information obtained is the number of travelers, their origins, their destinations, their lengths of stay, and their mode of travel. Carriers (such as airlines and ships) can also provide similar information. Hotels and other accommodations of the industry can provide information concerning lengths of stay and even how much the visitors spent on accommodations and meals. They can also provide information that might be helpful in analyzing the distribution of demand for various types of accommodations.

Banks can offer information concerning exchanges of foreign currencies which can be helpful in calculating total incoming tourist spending (as well as providing information about how much money is spent abroad by a country's own residents!).

Nonetheless, these sources may not provide complete data, particularly about visitors traveling by automobile and staying with friends or relatives rather than in hotels or motels.

Sampling

One useful source of information about visiting tourists is questionnaires that are completed at a country's entry or exit points. It is not necessary to have every arriving or departing tourist questioned but to sample enough of them so that their answers will be representative of all tourists.

What About Domestic Tourists?

Most of the comments so far in this chapter have related to international tourists. But of more importance to a city, area, or region are data from all tourists, both domestic and international. Indeed, the tourism of some areas may not depend on international tourists but, rather, on domestic tourists. However, the type of data needed are generally the same as that for international tourists, that is, tourist profile information that will be useful for tourism policy formation, planning, and promotion.

Gathering domestic tourist data is a bit more difficult, as there often are no "border" crossing points as there are with international tourists. In some cases there may be highway border-crossing points between states, provinces, or counties. In such cases sampling questionnaires can provide the necessary information. And if tourist information centers are used, those stopping at the center can be asked to fill out a questionnaire about their trip, and overall visitor statistics can be estimated based on this sample.

There is another difficulty for a new tourism destination that is being planned; that is, there are no data on past tourists to use, and for that reason any market research on potential tourist profiles may be more costly to obtain and much less reliable.

Countries also need information about their own residents returning from a trip abroad. A typical sampling form used by the Canadian government is illustrated in Figure 7-1.

Statistical Trends

The greatest value of statistical information is not the data for any particular period or year, but any changes over time. A changing trend may indicate a need to reorient advertising or to adapt policies and plans to incorporate the new tourist profile.

One simple method of forecasting future tourist demand is trend analysis, which uses tourist information, such as tourist arrivals, for the previous, say, five years to project their trend of growth into the future. For example, if the growth rate has been an average of 5 percent over the past five years, it may be reasonable to predict that it will continue to grow at this rate over the next several years.

The advantage of using trend analysis is its simplicity. But such forecasts must be carefully interpreted, as they are based on the assumption that past growth trends will continue. Also, even though in our example the *average* growth rate was 5 percent a year, there could have been some severe fluctuations from year to year, and trend analysis will not show the cause of such fluctuations or whether there will be fluctuations in the future.

There are more sophisticated ways of forecasting from past trend data, but these methods are beyond the scope of this textbook. But reliable forecasts are necessary, as tourist suppliers frequently depend on outside financing to help them complete their projects, and those supplying financing often require forecasts in order to decide whether the project will be financially feasible.

Statistics Canada Statistique Canada

D-

International Travel Section

QUESTIONNAIRE FOR CANADIAN RESIDENTS TRAVELLING OUTSIDE CANADA

Statistics Canada on behalf of the Government and the tourism industry requests your co-operation in completing this questionnaire. The information you report will be used to estimate total expenditures by Canadians abroad for the travel account of the Balance of Payments and for development and marketing purposes to improve Canada's tourism product at home. Please report on the trip for which you received this questionnaire, from the time you left Canada until you returned. This survey requires no signature or identification but your reply is important in maintaining a low cost approach to collecting this information. Thank You.

Authority-Statistics Act, Chapter 15, Statutes of Canada 1970-71-72

1. Please give your place of residence.

(nearest city or town) (province or territory)

OFFICE USE ONLY

L# Q#

2. (a) Please enter where and when you left Canada.

(border crossing or airport) Day Month Year

(b) Please enter where and when you re-entered Canada.

(border crossing or airport) Day Month Year

3. Was this your first trip outside Canada this year?

1 ☐ Yes or 2 ☐ No

If Yes, was this your first trip ever outside Canada?

1 ☐ Yes or 2 ☐ No

4. Please show the number of persons in the travelling party in the following **age** and **sex** groups. The travelling party includes **yourself** and those persons you are reporting for on this questionnaire.

	Under 2 yrs.	2 to 11	12 to 19	20 to 24	25 to 34	35 to 44	45 to 54	55 to 64	65 and over	Total
Male										
Female										

5. Check the **main** reason for this trip.

1 ☐ Employed in other country
2 ☐ Attending convention, conference or seminar
3 ☐ Other business reason
4 ☐ Educational study
5 ☐ Visiting friends or relatives
6 ☐ Other pleasure trip
7 ☐ In transit to/from other parts of Canada
8 ☐ Other (specify)

6. What means of transportation did you use . . .

	To leave Canada?	To return to Canada?
Automobile	1 ☐	1 ☐
Commercial plane	2 ☐	2 ☐
Private plane	3 ☐	3 ☐
Bus	4 ☐	4 ☐
Train	5 ☐	5 ☐
Commercial boat/ship	6 ☐	6 ☐
Private boat	7 ☐	7 ☐
Other (specify)	8 ☐	8 ☐

7. (a) On leaving Canada, did you travel . . .

1. ☐ To USA only? or 2. ☐ Directly to other countries? or 3. ☐ To other countries via the USA?

(b) On returning to Canada, did you travel . . .

1. ☐ From USA, only? or 2. ☐ Directly from other countries? or 3. ☐ From other countries via the USA?

8. If commercial transportation was used during your trip, please answer this question for persons covered in question 4 (exclude local transportation).

(a) Name of carrier(s) (plane, boat, bus and/or train) LEAVING — Fares paid Canadian $

Name of carrier(s) (plane boat, bus and/or train) RETURNING — Fares paid Canadian $

(b) If you paid a round trip fare identify the carrier(s) in (a) and give amount paid here

Canadian $

or If you purchased a "Package Tour" (fare includes meals and/or accommodation), identify the carrier(s) in (a) and indicate the amount paid here.

Canadian $

(c) Transportation used.

1 ☐ Scheduled service 2 ☐ Charter service 3 ☐ Other (please specify)

9. Please estimate as nearly as possible nights and spending outside Canada by the persons covered in question 4. Include cash or credit card transactions for food lodging, entertainment, merchandise, gifts, automobile operation, local transportation, etc. **but exclude international transportation fares reported in question 8.**

(a) Total nights outside Canada

(b) Total spending (CDN$) (less fares) or √ ☐ if nil

(c) Please name the state(s) or country(ies) visited and enter the amount spent in each even if you did not stay overnight.

Name state(s) visited in U.S.A. Name other country(ies) visited	Amount spent in each	Night(s) stay in each	Type of lodging used in each	Name state(s) visited in U.S.A. Name other country(ies) visited	Amount spent in each	Night(s) stay in each	Type of lodging used in each

10. If this trip was to or from other parts of Canada via the U.S.A., name provinces/territories visited.

Country	Nights	$	Acc.

11. Which of the following activities did you participate in during this trip? (mark as many as applicable).

1 ☐ Attend business or convention meetings
2 ☐ Participate in outdoor recreation and sports
3 ☐ Attend events and attractions
4 ☐ City recreation and entertainment
5 ☐ Visit friends or relatives
6 ☐ Shopping
7 ☐ Sightseeing
8 ☐ Other (specify)

12. Comments.

4-2500-43: 8-5-85 TB/CT-REG. 8101301 THANK YOU FOR YOUR CO-OPERATION (Français au verso)

FIGURE 7-1. Canadian government visitor survey form.

DISCUSSION QUESTIONS

1. What is the WTO's definition of a visitor?
2. Explain the difference between a tourist and an excursionist.
3. Explain why the country of origin of foreign tourists is an important statistic for a host nation.
4. Discuss the importance of knowing the number of visitors to a destination.
5. Discuss the value of "length of stay" information about tourists.
6. Explain how visitor days are calculated, and discuss their importance.
7. Why is a tourist's per-capita spending information important, and how is it related to length of stay?
8. Discuss the need for a host country to know the reason that tourists are traveling there.
9. Explain why different types of tourists make different demands on the type of accommodation they need.
10. Why is it important for a country to have information about how tourists arrive there?
11. How can a country use information about tourism's shoulder periods and what kinds of tourists come during those periods?
12. What is a tourist's socioeconomic profile?
13. Discuss some of the ways in which international tourist statistics can be obtained.
14. How can a country obtain information about its domestic tourism?
15. Why is the trend of tourist statistics important, and how can it be used in forecasting?

PROBLEM

A destination area imposes a 4 percent tax on hotel rooms. During a particular month the total tax collected was $40,000. The amount of money that visitors spend on hotel rooms represents 20 percent of their overall total spending. Furthermore, the hotel guests' total spending represents 75 percent of all visitor spending, the remaining 25 percent being from visitors staying with friends and relatives. During this particular month there were four thousand visitor arrivals. The average length of stay is six days. Calculate a visitor's daily spending.

REFERENCES

Gee, Chuck Y., Dexter J. L. Choy, and James C. Makens. 1984. *The Travel Industry.* Westport, Conn.: AVI.

McIntosh, Robert W., and Charles R. Goeldner. 1984. *Tourism: Principles, Practices, Philosophies.* New York: Wiley.

National Tourism Resources Review Commission. 1973. *Destination U.S.A.* Vol. 2: *Domestic Tourism.* Washington, D.C.: U.S. Government Printing Office.

SUGGESTED READINGS

Gee, Chuck Y., Dexter J. L. Choy, and James C. Makens. 1984. *The Travel Industry.* Westport, Conn.: AVI, pp. 5–11.

Gough, J. H., and P. D. Ghangurde. 1976. *An Alternative Method of Surveying International Travellers at Frontier Points, Methodology Report.* Ottawa: Statistics Canada.

Leiper, Neil. 1979. "The Framework of Tourism: Towards a Definition of Tourism, Tourist and the Tourism Industry." *Annals of Tourism Research* 6(4): 390–407.

McIntosh, Robert W., and Charles R. Goeldner. 1984. *Tourism: Principles, Practices, Philosophies.* New York: Wiley, pp. 189–201, 395–435.

U.S. Travel Data Center. 1983. *Impact of Foreign Visitors on State Economies.* Washington, D.C.: U.S. Travel Data Center.

World Tourism Organization. 1986. *Yearbook of Tourism Statistics.* Madrid: WTO.

World Tourism Organization. No date. *Guidelines for the Collection and Presentation of International Travel Statistics.* Madrid: WTO.

Transportation Methods

The amount of travel that people do (and thus the amount of tourism that is generated) parallels improvements in the methods of transportation. Most of these improvements have been with us for only a relatively short period of time. Consider, for the sake of convenience, that humans have been on earth for 240,000 years and that we will condense the time from that period to the present into a twelve-hour clock starting at midnight and running to now, midday. In other words, each hour on our clock represents 20,000 years. Therefore, at only thirty seconds before midday was the steam engine invented, and the basis of mass tourism with the use of the steam engine for train travel has been around for only the last half-minute of our twelve-hour clock.

IMPROVEMENTS IN TRANSPORTATION_____

The first road vehicles were two-wheeled carts, with rough stone disks serving as wheels. These carts were used on the roads radiating from Babylon during about 2000 B.C. From these crude beginnings the Egyptians and Greeks developed the chariot. Donkeys and oxen were also used for transportation, as were camels in Asia where camel caravans opened up trade routes that eventually connected to the sea systems developed by the Phoenicians around the Mediterranean seaports. As donkeys were replaced by horses and horses provided the locomotion for carriages, more people were able to travel, although few of them did, as they had neither the reason nor the money to do so, except in Roman times.

Durant (1944, p. 324), in his history of civilization, described the transportation and communication system that formed the basis of the Roman Empire as "a commercial revolution comparable in kind with that which the railroads effected in the nineteenth century." He states that the roads of Europe from the Middle Ages until the nineteenth century were inferior to those of the Roman Empire. Indeed, the Romans had more than fifty thousand miles of paved highways, which is more miles of road than the U.S. Interstate Highway System embraces today.

Coach Travel

Throughout the Middle Ages and until about the end of the eighteenth century, road conditions in Europe did not encourage the use of wheeled transportation, and most people therefore traveled by horseback. In North America they followed the trails created by the native Americans.

However, road travel improved considerably with the invention of the more comfortable stagecoach, whose carriage was suspended rather than rigidly fixed. The word *coach* comes from the Hungarian town of Kocs where it was invented in the fifteenth century. By the mid-1600s there was a daily coach service in the summer from London to Oxford in England, but the roads at that time were still very rough, dirty, and dusty, as tarmac (macadam) was not used for road paving until about 1815. Also, there was little need for roads beyond the large coastal towns, as most people still traveled to and from those towns by ship, both in North America and Europe.

Conestoga Wagons

The first Conestoga wagon was built in the United States in the mid-seventeenth century. It was pulled by up to six oxen, mules, or horses. A descendant of the Conestoga wagon was the prairie schooner, made famous by its almost universal use in the migration across the western plains and prairies of North America. It had an upward slope at either end, with the wagon covered by canvas. It was named in memory of the white-topped schooners of the sea and was used by the tourists of its day who opened up the U.S. Midwest to trade and commerce.

Stagecoaches

Slow and clumsy stagecoaches were operated irregularly in England and North America from the early part of the eighteenth century. Stagecoaches first made the four-hundred-mile trip from London to Edinburgh in 1785, taking ten days in summer and twelve days in winter. Also in 1785 the first stagecoach connection was established between New York and Albany. Improved roads encouraged the use of the stagecoach, and it in turn encouraged the improvement of roads. Typically, coaches traveled about forty miles a day in summer and twenty-five miles in winter, over a fifteen-hour day. They carried anywhere from eight to fourteen passengers.

In Europe and later in America, the first horse-drawn urban omnibuses were introduced early in the 1800s. They carried passengers both inside and on the roof. The great period of the coaches ended in the early nineteenth century when the railroads were built.

Before the Industrial Revolution, wayside inns were located along the roads for the stagecoach travelers, but there were no common carriers (organizations licensed to provide public transportation), and people had to make their own travel arrangements.

Canal Travel

Canals also were used for travel in both the United States and Europe, from the late seventeenth to the late nineteenth centuries. Extensive canal systems connected rivers in England, Belgium, France, Germany, and Holland and were important to the movement of both people and goods. Today they are no longer as important to moving goods, except perhaps in countries such as Holland where the dikes, built for flood control, created canals that are still heavily used for commerce today as well as for leisure boat travel.

Steam Engine

The incredible improvements that the invention of the steam engine provided in the early 1800s for ship and rail transportation ushered in the beginning of organized mass transportation. These improved transportation methods then heightened people's desire to travel. The railways offered fast, convenient, safe, and relatively comfortable travel at comparatively low prices.

But the arrival of the automobile offered even more convenience and flexibility, and the airplane offered the greatest speed. Accordingly, in North America—states the Transportation Policy Associates (1985)—the railroads have suffered more in terms of changing travel modes than have other forms of transportation. The average annual growth rate from 1939 to 1984 of passenger miles increased 3.7 percent for private automobiles, 13.4 percent for airlines, and 2.4 percent for buses. But for the railways there was a decline of 1.6 percent.

Transportation and Hotels

In earlier years when travel was by horse or even by foot, most long-distance inland travel was by river or canal, and so hotels were built at the river or canal landings or, in the case of sea travel, at the docks. It was here that travelers gathered and the local community life was centered. As inland travel modes were taken over by the railroads, the city center became the railway station with its nearby hotels.

When the railroads became popular in Europe in the early 1800s, they encouraged the building of new hotels close to their stations. This, of course, spelled the end of the hostelries that were strategically located along the canal, river, or stagecoach routes, although some still survive today as historic inns used by today's motorists. Oddly enough, in the United States, major railway hotels were often built before the arrival of the railroad. They were built in strategic communities, mainly west of the Mississippi, in order to help ensure that the railroads would come through those communities.

Many of the railroads, both in North America and Europe, built and operated their own hotels adjacent to their stations for the convenience of their rail customers. Indeed, the railroads became the first operators of chain hotels. They were not alone, however, in adopting this vertical integration concept. The steamship companies, whose development and growth paralleled that of the railways in the 1800s, also were often in the hotel business. For example, Matson Navigation at one time owned a number of hotels in Honolulu and was instrumental in helping develop the tourist industry in that area. The link between its ship passengers and their accommodation needs was an obvious one.

When the automobile began to make inroads in the 1920s and 1930s, the railways began to lose their predominance as a passenger transportation medium. Roadside accommodations and services became far more important than city centers to the automobile traveler. Eventually, as the automobile became the main mode of intercity movement, many of the highways built to accommodate the auto traveler by-passed the cities and towns. Traditional city hotels became obsolete and were replaced by various kinds of motor hotels situated along the highways and supported by peripheral services such as gas stations, restaurants, and attractions.

More recently, bus companies (such as Greyhound and Trailways in North America) have been associated with hotels, as have the airlines, although in the latter case the "marriages" have not always been successful, and some of the airlines have been divorcing themselves from their accommodation enterprises. Gomes (1985, p. 39) commented:

> Despite the fact that, in some years, the profits made by Inter-Continental Hotels and Hilton International have been one of the few bright spots in the otherwise dismal operating results of their airline parents (Pan Am and TWA, respectively), the integration of lodging with the transportation business was, at best, only marginally successful in generating additional traffic for the integrated businesses as a whole.

Nevertheless, the transportation method used and the accommodation sector of the tourism industry have always been closely connected, as the *raison d'être* of the accommodation sector has always been to provide temporary housing for travelers.

Indeed, the evolution of travel has affected the types of communities, whether cities or recreation resort areas, in which travelers congregate.

OTHER IMPROVEMENTS

Along with all of these improvements in travel modes were parallel improvements in education, reduction of the workweek providing more leisure time, increased pay rates providing more disposable income, and increased security of travel. In addition, communication has improved. For example, we can readily find out what is available in the way of tourism experiences through advertising and can make reservations with ease. All of these various factors have affected travel. And all these improvements allow us today to visit places that were once accessible to only a few. For example, before World War II, Hawaii was visited only by those who had the money and the time to travel there by luxury liner. But today as many as fifteen thousand tourists a day arrive in Hawaii by jet from many parts of the world, at relatively low cost.

Accessibility

For ordinary tourists to go to a destination it must be easily accessible at relatively low cost. Europe offers a case in point. There is plenty of air service at relatively low cost from North America to Europe, and so Europe is an attractive destination for North Americans.

For North Americans it takes about the same amount of time to fly to cities such as Rio de Janeiro, Buenos Aires, or Santiago in Latin America. But compared with Europe, few North Americans go to Latin America because the cost of flying there is about twice as high as it is to go to Europe. Thus destinations must be accessible in both convenience and cost.

An interesting question is why the cost to fly to Europe is so much lower. Did the price go down because so many North Americans wanted to go there, or did North Americans go there because the prices were low? For the airline carriers it is a question of economies of scale: The more people who fly, the more flights that can be offered, and the lower will be the airlines' per-passenger operating costs. Furthermore, the more competition there is among the airlines, the lower the prices will be for their customers.

Choice of Transportation Mode

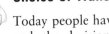

Today people have a choice of transportation to get to many destinations. In general, the decision of which to use probably depends on a combination of three factors: length of trip, number of people in the group (for this affects total overall cost), and disposable income available for travel. Other considerations affecting this decision may be found among the following:

- Availability, frequency, and flexibility of each mode (that is, its convenience).
- Time it takes to travel to a destination using various travel modes.
- Relative comfort or luxury of one travel mode over another.
- Ground services or terminal facilities available for each travel mode.
- Status or prestige involved.

TRAVEL MODES AND TYPES OF TOURISM

A major concern of tourist industry suppliers is motivating tourists to travel, and their mode of transport can have a significant effect on the tourism facilities actually offered, as well as on the type of tourism chosen. Generally, tourism can be categorized as either destination or transit.

Destination Tourism

Destination tourism refers to travelers who plan to arrive at a destination directly from home, stay for several days or weeks, and then return directly home. Destination tourism locations are sometimes referred to as *tourist resorts*, especially in regard to vacation travel. For example, we think of a place like Hawaii as a destination resort. Such resorts must be able to attract and retain tourists for more than a day or so. But a location can be a destination without being a resort. For example, most large cities are also business centers, and business travelers are frequently destination travelers, even though they do not think of their destination as a vacation resort.

Many convention travelers often combine work with a vacation at a destination resort. Many destinations accordingly also cater to both business conventions and vacation travelers, as the destination often needs the convention traffic to survive in the shoulder and off-season periods.

People who travel to destination areas make the greatest demands on local resources such as hotels, restaurants, and attractions. Frequently these tourists use the airlines as their mode of travel, as vacationers, in particular, tend to go to destinations that are quite far from home. Resorts such as Hawaii could not survive without adequate air-scheduling support. Business travelers also depend on the airlines to go to their destinations, as a reduction in travel time is important to them. However, budget travelers often travel to their destinations by train, bus, or automobile, but there are relatively few of these types of arrivals, compared with air travelers, particularly if their destination is far away.

Transit Tourism

Transit tourism is the principal type of tourism used by auto, bus, and some train travelers, particularly those on VFR trips. The greatest demand by transit tourists is for hotels, restaurants, campgrounds or trailer parks, and even attractions, en route. These travelers, as they have the flexibility to do sightseeing if traveling in their own vehicles, will even leave the main route to visit historical, cultural, architectural, natural, and even commercial attractions. Indeed, many commercial tourist attractions have been purposely built near convenient stopping points on major transit routes.

Travel time for transit travelers is not as important as it is to destination vacationers anxious to be there as soon as possible or to business travelers who often must be there as soon as possible. Even though transit travelers may stay at a specific destination for days or weeks, they make fewer demands on hotels and restaurants there than do destination travelers. Transit travelers also have little need for local public transportation if they have their own vehicles with them.

Combined Destination/Transit Locations

Some locations are both good destination and good transit spots. For example, Hawaii is often considered to be solely a destination area, and for most visitors to Hawaii, it is. But for travelers from North America who are going on to Australia, New Zealand, or other areas in the South Pacific, Hawaii is a convenient place to stop for a day or two before moving on.

Similarly, big cities like London, Amsterdam, and Paris serve as both destination and transit cities. They are convenient transit stopping-off points for North American visitors to Europe before they move on to other areas. These cities also serve as destinations for vacationers who wish to use the shops and visit the attractions. And they also serve as commercial destinations for business travelers.

Transportation Facilities

For many people, part of the experience of tourism is the excitement of planning a vacation trip and enjoying the actual travel experience. That is, it is not the destination of the trip alone that provides satisfaction. For example, there always seems to be an air of excitement at railway stations and airports as family and friends gather to see off someone who is traveling. F. Scott Fitzgerald (1941, p. 7) described a 1930s airport as follows:

> I suppose there has been nothing like airports since the days of the stage-stops—
> nothing quite as lonely or sombre-silent. The old red-brick depots were built right
> into the towns they marked—people didn't get off at those isolated stations unless
> they lived there. But airports lead you way back in history like oases, like the stops

on the great trade routes. The sight of air travelers strolling in ones or twos into midnight airports will draw a small crowd any night up to two. The young people look at the planes, the older ones look at the passengers with a watchful incredulity.

Compare this with Sampson's (1985, pp. 285–286) description of an airport today:

> The planes land at airports which all appear to be insulated from any known city or land. While the great railway termini took their architecture from temples or cathedrals which soared above the tracks, the airports took their origins from the hut and the hangar, and grew into cavernous metal barns, looking not on to a track but on to the great nowhere in the sky. The vast echoing airports like Honolulu, Anchorage or Pago Pago, where the jumbos stop to refuel and disgorge their transit passengers in the middle of the night, have all established the same kind of non-identity, as the flutterboards announce the names of every city but their own, and the duty-free shops sell imports from other airports. The transit lounges, cut off from both time and space, can generate a unique sense of numbness and not belonging—the feel of not to feel it. It is not surprising that many passengers, when they return to their same narrow seat, the same music inside the same cylindrical space, feel that, however cramped and eccentric, it is yet a kind of home.

This description would probably fit many airports, including London Heathrow's Terminal 3, from which many long-distance international flights depart. Crowds at peak periods are so dense that passengers waiting to be called for their flight departures can find a seat only with difficulty, and food and drink can be purchased only after interminable waits in line. This is tedious rather than exciting.

But many air terminals like Heathrow were built long before those responsible realized their need to cater to the mass movements of tourists today. Newer airports are being constructed to take better care of the travelers' needs and to return that air of excitement. For example, London Heathrow's recently opened Terminal 4, used primarily by British Airways' overseas flights, is vastly different from Terminal 3. It is open, spacious, and attractive. A similar example is United Airlines' recently opened terminal at Chicago's O'Hare airport. It is bright and brightly decorated and contrasts vividly with its older adjacent terminals at that same airport.

Transportation Modes and History

It is interesting, in summary, to consider how transportation and communication may have affected history. In regard to North America, Wells (1961, pp. 791–792) described the effect:

> Had the people of the United States spread over the American continent with only horse traction, rough roads, and letter writing to keep them together it seems inevitable that differences in local economic conditions would have developed dif-

ferent social types, that wide separation would have fostered differences of dialect and effaced sympathy, that the inconvenience of attending Congress at Washington would have increased with every advance of the frontier westward, until at last the States would have fallen apart into a loose league of practically independent and divergent nations. Wars, for mineral wealth, for access to the seas, and so forth would have followed and America would have become another Europe.

But the river steamboat, the railway, and the telegraph arrived in time to prevent this separation, and the United States became the first of a new type of modern transport state, larger, more powerful, and more conscious of its unity than any state the world had ever seen.

It is interesting to speculate how tourism, both domestic and international, would have been different if history had not unfolded as Wells described it.

DISCUSSION QUESTIONS

 1. When people traveled by coach or carriage, why was an inland network of roads not important?

2. What impact did the invention of the steam engine have on travel?

3. Discuss how changes in transportation over time have affected the accommodation sector of the tourism industry.

4. With improvements in travel modes in the nineteenth century, people were able to travel more easily. What other factors increased their ability to travel?

5. How would you explain the importance of accessibility in adding to tourism growth?

6. What are the three major factors that influence the choice of travel mode?

7. Apart from the three major factors that influence the choice of travel mode, what other factors might a tourist consider?

8. What is a destination tourism area?

9. Why do convention organizers frequently choose a destination tourism area as a site for their conventions?

10. Discuss transit tourism.

11. Which sectors of the tourism industry can benefit most from transit tourism?

12. How can an area be both a destination and a transit tourism location?

PROBLEM

Select one method of transportation, and study how it has affected tourism in your area or, if you live in a large metropolitan center, how it has affected a specific part of that area. For example, if you live in a large seaport city used as a departure and arrival point for cruise ships, you might decide to find out what impact that business has had over the last several years on the hotels and other businesses in the area that cater to the arriving and departing cruise passengers. On the other hand, you may live in a small town that is now bypassed by a highway. Automobile travelers who used to use this town as a natural stopping point for meals and shopping or even for an overnight stay now no longer stop. Once you have made your selection and done your research, prepare a one-page report of your findings, addressing such questions as, How were the businesses affected? What did they do to cope with this change in transportation methods? What is the projection for future changes?

REFERENCES

Durant, Will. 1944. *Caesar and Christ*. New York: Simon & Schuster.

Fitzgerald, F. Scott, 1941. *The Last Tycoon*. New York: Scribner.

Gomes, Albert J. 1985. *Hospitality in Transition*. Houston: Pannell Kerr Forster.

Sampson, Anthony. 1985. *Empires of the Sky*. London: Coronet.

Transportation Policy Associates. 1985. *Transportation in America*. Washington, D.C.: Transportation Policy Associates.

Wells, H. G. 1961. *The Outline of History*. New York: Doubleday.

SUGGESTED READINGS

Transportation Policy Associates. 1985. *Transportation in America*. Washington, D.C.: Transportation Policy Associates.

Automotive Travel

In most developed countries as much as 80 to 90 percent of all travel is by automobile. The first automobile was invented in Germany in 1885 by the firm of Daimler-Benz, which is still in business producing such cars as the Mercedes Benz. France also pioneered in automobile development, and even today we use many French automotive words such as *garage*, *chassis*, and *chauffeur*. Cars were commercially available in the United States as early as 1898. The auto quickly became popular, and in its early years some areas had more automobiles than miles of paved road. Steam-driven cars were initially more common than gasoline-driven ones. But they required considerable engineering skills to drive them, and they gradually gave way to the water-cooled, piston type of internal combustion engine still used in autos today.

PRIVATE AUTOMOBILES

In 1908 Ford Motors in the United States developed the Model-T and mass-produced it on assembly lines. Between 1915 and 1925 the cost of the Model-T dropped from just over $800 to about $250. By the early 1930s there were well over twenty million cars in use in the United States.

Autocourts and Motorcourts

In the Depression years of the 1930s, most ordinary families and business travelers used the automobile as a common form of transportation, and in the United States, low-priced overnight accommodation buildings were constructed along the highways. These buildings were known as autocourts or motorcourts. Today we know their successors as motels or motor hotels.

Public acceptance of the automobile in North America was so great that it was a major cause of the decline of passenger train travel. After World War II, with the massive acceptance of the automobile, the drop in passenger train travel was so great that there now is little passenger rail travel anymore in North America.

Highway Systems

Today, the U.S. Interstate Highway System, started in 1954, links 90 percent of U.S. cities with populations over fifty thousand. In Canada, the Trans-Canada Highway links St. Johns, Newfoundland, in the east with Victoria, British Columbia, in the west—a distance of about five thousand miles.

In Europe, the German *autobahns* built in the 1930s prompted other countries in Europe to build similar highways, and so long-distance auto travel across the many countries in Europe is as easy today as auto travel is in North America. The public's love affair with the automobile was only slightly dampened when oil, and therefore gasoline, prices shot up in the early 1970s.

Advantages of Auto Travel

Automobiles offer travelers many advantages over other forms of transportation. Buses, rail, and ships (and, more recently, airplanes) have fixed starting and ending points and inflexible schedules. The introduction of the automobile thus offered an alternative way to travel and allowed many new destinations to be opened. Nevertheless, many other destinations created initially by ships and trains are still popular today as automobile destinations.

The automobile driver can control the route taken, the departure and arrival times, and any stops made on the way. Baggage can be easily transported. And for budget-conscious families, more people than the driver can be transported with little additional cost. In addition, the automobile is available on arrival at a destination and allows people to plan distant travel trips on their vacations. It is no wonder that the automobile, with all its flexibility, has become so popular and dominant in travel.

As for cost, there is little doubt that the per-person cost of travel is less when two or more persons travel by automobile. This is particularly important to families and for trips of up to about a thousand miles. Beyond that distance, air travel can seem quite attractive even for families, as the extra cost of meals on the road and highway accommodations tend to make the airfares quite competitive.

The U.S. Bureau of Census's 1977 National Travel Survey showed that about 82 percent of all trips taken in the United States are by auto, and a study by Pizam and Pokela in 1983 showed that automobiles accounted for 75 percent of all "tourism-related" travel in the United States. There is little doubt that most intercity transportation is by automobile; this has been so for decades and is likely to continue in the future. Finally, the automobile has diffused tourism more than any other form of tourism has, as any community can become a tourist destination if it is accessible by car or other automotive vehicle.

Impact of New Highways

The better highways of today have also had an impact on many towns and villages that at one time might have benefited greatly from automobile travelers. For example, towns on busy travel routes might have been popular stopping spots for automobile travelers when roads were not as good as they are today. A good road system saves money, for a poor road system costs the automobile driver (as well as other users) more money for fuel as well as extra vehicle maintenance. But it is not only the direct user of highways that wants to have good, well-maintained roads. Tourist establishments also have an interest in this, as poor highways only encourage potential users to seek out alternative routes or even alternative methods of travel.

The new highways intentionally bypass towns to speed traffic. This time saving is advantageous to the long-distance automobile travelers, and the new highways also reduce traffic congestion in towns that travelers previously had no choice but to travel through. On the other hand, businesses that previously benefited from these tourists find their livelihood severely damaged. But these new and better highways create their own favored stopping points that draw new businesses such as motels, restaurants, and attractions. A case in point is the soon-to-be-built channel tunnel (affectionately known as the chunnel, but officially known as the Eurotunnel) to link France and England by 1993. The chunnel's entry and exit locations are critical to tourist businesses that have a vested interest in them. It is interesting to note that for cost reasons, this tunnel will be primarily a rail one; automobile traffic will be transported on drive-on trains.

Recreational Vehicles

Recreational vehicles (RVs) have become a popular form of travel in recent years. One of the major reasons for this is that they have allowed the costs for family travel to be minimized as a result of self-catering. That is, the travelers provide many of their own services such as meal preparation and accommodation. Families who use this form of transportation, food, and lodging still think of it as a form of vacation (despite all the work they have to do themselves) because it gives them a break from their normal life-style and permits them to get away from their urban roots for a while, even if they have to make their own beds and do their own dishes. At least the money saved can be spent on shopping and visiting attractions en route.

The growth in the RV vacation has also fostered a parallel growth in the need for RV campgrounds. Over the past twenty years there has been a dramatic growth in private and government camping areas providing easy access from major highways and tourist attractions. The better campgrounds offer water and electricity hookups and sewage disposal for RV travelers, as well as hotel-type reservation systems. Many of these campgrounds, such as Kampgrounds of America (KOA), are franchised.

Automobile Clubs

Many automobile owners belong to state or provincial automobile clubs in North America, and to the national automobile club of their country of residence in Europe, such as the Royal Automobile Association in Britain. In North America the various state and provincial associations are generally affiliated with a national association, such as the American Automobile Association (AAA) in the United States and the Canadian Automobile Association (CAA) in Canada. Most of these associations offer insurance protection to their members and also publish travel maps and tour books. In addition, many of them have their own travel agencies to serve both their own members and the public at large.

There are also some international auto associations such as the World Touring and Automobile Organization (located in London), the Inter-American Federation of Automobile Clubs (in Buenos Aires), and the International Automobile Federation (in Paris).

Oil Companies

One group that has a vested interest in automobile travel is the oil companies. Oil companies aid the traveler with both their fuel services and their road maps.

TAXIS, BUSES, AND AUTO RENTALS

People traveling by train, ship, and airplane frequently can reach their final destination only with the ready availability of public automobiles in the form of taxis. A less expensive form of transportation is often available for airline passenger arrivals: the airport limousines or buses that take them to a central downtown location. In North America these limousine and bus operators are generally private companies that have a contract to provide the service. In Europe they are often operated by the national airline of that country or by a subsidiary of that airline and are therefore not as vulnerable to any possible competition.

Note that the terms *bus*, *coach*, and *motorcoach* are often used interchangeably to describe commercial bus companies. For the sake of simplicity we shall use the word *bus* to refer to all of these terms.

Scheduled Buses

The horse-drawn omnibus first appeared in Paris in 1827, in London in 1829, and in New York in 1830. It carried passengers on the inside and on the roof. Buses were motorized early after the invention of the automobile. Buses with sleeping berths for intercity runs first appeared in North America in the 1930s but were soon discontinued.

Today, buses are a major form of long-distance automotive ground transportation. Buses are a cheaper form of transportation than the auto or train for long-distance travel because their fuel costs are lower per passenger carried. Statistically buses are also the safest form of transportation.

Although at one time intercity bus travel was as popular as train travel, the automobile eventually hurt the bus business, just as it did train travel. However, bus travel is still thriving both in North America and Europe between the many towns and cities it still does serve. Indeed, some bus companies in Europe are tied in with the railways and offer arriving and departing train passengers timetabled connections from the railway station to the smaller towns and villages not serviced by rail.

To attract travelers, bus companies have made many technological improvements to their coaches in recent years. These improvements include quieter engines, contoured seats, larger windows, air-conditioning, toilet facilities, and even hostess service.

Some bus companies have grown into conglomerates by branching out into other tourism fields. For example, the well-known U.S. Greyhound Company, formed in 1928, now owns restaurants, institutional foodservice operations, car rental companies, and it also deals in aircraft leasing, money orders, and insurance. Another large bus company in North America is Trailways.

Besides these two industry giants, there are many small family operations. The bus industry in the United States provides more services and accessibility to more communities than does any other form of public transportation. For example, it provides service to about fifteen thousand communities. In contrast, Amtrak rail services only five hundred, and the various airlines about seven hundred. The major advantage that buses have over rail and air is this accessibility. Bus companies can start a new service between cities very quickly if the demand is there. No large investment is required, as the roads already exist. The airlines and rail companies do not have this flexibility. The bus companies' labor costs also are low, as a traveling bus needs only a driver, whereas a train needs a larger crew, and a plane a very large crew in relation to the number of passengers carried.

Until 1982 the fares and routes of the U.S. intercity bus industry were regulated by the Interstate Commerce Commission. However, deregulation of the industry in that year removed many of the restrictive regulations for new entrants into the industry. In North America the American Bus Association (ABA) is the national organization that is the main source of industry statistics. Its members are carriers from both the United States and Canada.

Bus Tour Companies

In addition to the regularly scheduled bus routes, there are also tour bus operators who offer group package prices that include all transportation, hotels, baggage handling, and most meals and that take care of all of the small details for travelers who wish this form of travel experience. Some tour buses are equipped with tape recordings (in many languages in some cases) describing tourist attractions on their routes or city tours.

The tour and charter bus business is the fastest-growing segment of the bus industry in North America. A 1982 ABA study on bus travel showed that almost 55 percent of all bus passengers were on charters and tours. These tourists provide income not only to the bus companies but also to the accommodations, foodservice, and attractions sectors along the way. Because the bus industry is now deregulated in the United States, it is easy for new bus tour operators to enter the market, and

FIGURE 9-1. European bus tours are an easy way for elderly, and some not so elderly, tourists to see the sights.

many small new companies have done so, many by becoming franchisees of larger companies.

Much of the bus tours' growth can be traced to the many more Europeans who visit North America now. Many of these tourists are used to bus travel, as it is a common form of travel for most European residents. It is harder to "sell" North Americans on bus travel, as bus tours are often perceived as being only for the elderly, and many do not go to the most popular destinations. Buses are also seen as slow and uncomfortable, even though today they are not. The European bus tour operators have also perfected their art and have developed buses with seats that recline like airline seats, and slide sideways toward the aisle to create more room for passengers during a trip. Most buses also have built-in bars that dispense cold soft drinks and beer. Some of the larger European jumbo buses have both upper and lower decks and seat as many as eighty passengers. The tour guides that accompany these buses are also multilingual, as the bus tours often take in several different countries on each trip. Passengers need have no fear of foreign-language problems.

Bus Sightseeing

Buses are also operated in most cities of any size in both Europe and North America for local sightseeing tours that might run for an hour or two or for as long as twelve hours. These sightseeing bus tour operators are usually independent entrepreneurs that often compete with one another locally in Europe. However, in North America they tend to be franchisees of major companies like Gray Line (not the same as Greyhound) or American Sightseeing International, against which independent operators cannot easily compete financially. Bus tour operators in North America are represented by the National Tour Association (NTA).

Car Rentals

There are an estimated thirty thousand car rental outlets in North America. Mostly they are big-name companies such as Hertz, National, and Budget (among others) that operate on a franchised basis and tend to dominate at airport locations throughout the world.

The larger companies are able to prevail largely because of their national and international advertising. However, it is not a difficult or costly business for any entrepreneur to enter: All that is needed is an office and a parking lot, both of which can be leased. Automobiles can also be leased or else heavily financed, and the inventory of cars needed can be easily increased or decreased depending on the season. As a result of this ease of entry, the auto rental business is extremely competitive.

The car rental business orients its advertising primarily to business travelers, but they also offer fly–drive and train/auto packages that appeal more to vacation travelers.

DISCUSSION QUESTIONS

1. Explain how motels originated.
2. In North America what was the impact of the automobile on passenger trains?
3. What advantages to travelers does the automobile have over other forms of transportation?
4. What is the impact on the tourism business of a new highway that bypasses a town?
5. Why is the specific location of the channel between England and France critical to some segments of the tourism industry, and what are they?
6. Discuss the effect of recreational vehicles on tourism in recent years.
7. To some travelers, what are the advantages of scheduled bus travel?
8. Buses and trains are frequently competitive methods of travel. In what way do they sometimes work together in Europe?
9. Discuss scheduled bus travel in North America, including some of its advantages.
10. What advantages does a package bus tour offer to some tourists?
11. Discuss the growth of the bus tour business in North America in recent years.
12. How do local sightseeing bus tour operators differ in Europe and North America?
13. Explain what is meant by the statement that the auto rental business is easy to enter.

PROBLEM

Select one method of automotive travel (passenger automobile, scheduled bus, tour bus, sightseeing bus, auto rental, RV) and investigate how it has been affected in your area, either positively or negatively, by changes in tourism in the last ten years. If you live in a large metropolitan center, you may want to concentrate on that type of travel's effect on one specific section of your city. Once you have made your selection and done your research, prepare a one-page report of your findings, addressing such questions as, Has the segment of automotive travel you selected for your research been affected by other forms of automotive travel or by other different forms of travel? Has this effect been positive or negative? What are the projections for future changes, and how will they be handled?

REFERENCES

Pizam, A., and J. Pokela. 1983. "The 1979 U.S. Gasoline Shortage and Its Impact on the Tourism Industry." *Tourism Management* 4: 94–101.

SUGGESTED READINGS

Altshuler, Alan et al. 1984. *The Future of the Automobile: The Report of MIT's International Automobile Program.* Cambridge, Mass.: MIT Press.

Congressional Budget Office. 1982. *The Interstate Highway System: Issues and Options.* Washington, D.C.: Congressional Budget Office.

Curtin, Richard T. 1980. *The RV Consumer: Current Trends and Future Prospects.* Chantilly, Va: Recreation Vehicle Industry Association, pp. 1–46.

Gee, Chuck Y., Dexter J. L. Choy, and James C. Makens. 1984. *The Travel Industry.* Westport, Conn.: AVI. pp. 170–171, 175–181.

Green, F. B. 1978. "Recreation Vehicles: A Perspective." *Annals of Tourism Research*, October–December, pp. 429–439.

Rail Travel

The earliest trains were simply horse-drawn carriages on steel rails used primarily in mining. The first steam-operated train running on steel rails was introduced into England in 1825. The train at that time was perceived mainly as a mover of goods rather than people. It was not until 1830 that the first passenger train operated from Stockton to Darlington in northern England.

In 1829 two British train locomotives were imported into the United States, but they were found to be too heavy for the existing tracks, and so the U.S. railways had to design their own trains. The Baltimore & Ohio railroad was the first U.S. railway to begin steam engine operations, in 1830.

The early passenger coaches were simply stagecoach bodies mounted on train wheels, with the passengers inside and the luggage on top. Other coaches were new coal wagons, with wooden benches for seats, open to the elements and the train engine chimney's soot. When the train was first introduced the stagecoach lobby could see the demise of their own business. The lobby worked hard to have a law passed that required trains to be preceded by a man on a horse, waving a red flag, and spread the idea that it could be scientifically proved that the human body would disintegrate and disappear if it reached a speed of 40 mph!

Feifer (1985, p. 166) describes what some people thought about the advent of rail travel:

> The railway burst upon the nineteenth century much as space travel hit the twentieth century: it revolutionized ideas about where and how humanity could

travel. It opened up great vistas on one hand, and assaulted cherished ways on the other. Thundering, massive, belching smoke and hurtling along at unprecedented speeds, the train was a monstrous apparition across the gentle green hills of England. It drowned out the church bells, terrified the livestock, polluted the air. Surely it was committing even worse outrages on the fools who were actually inside—their lungs were getting too much air; the vibrations were interfering with their brain functions; . . . and what if they fell out?

And even John Ruskin declared that travel by train was like being sent somewhere in a parcel or concentrating one's dinner into a pill. Some people today describe air travel that way.

GROWTH OF RAIL TRAVEL

After 1830 the railways grew so fast in Britain that their track mileage soon surpassed that of the canals. Within a few years, in 1835, the first express route was developed. The Great Western Railway (GWR) was built to link London with the seaport of Bristol (a distance of about 120 miles). The GWR (affectionately known in those days as God's Wonderful Railway) was used by emigrants traveling to Bristol and then going on by ship to the colonies and the United States.

Six years later, in 1841, the first rail tour was introduced by Thomas Cook (the founder of what is now a well-known worldwide travel agency) who chartered a train that ran from Loughborough to Leicester in England. It was not long after that passenger trains began linking major population centers with the spas and seaside resorts in Europe and in North America. This started the final decline of stagecoach and canal passenger travel.

The United States' Atlantic coast was connected by rail with the Great Lakes in 1850, with Chicago in 1853, and with the western side of the Mississippi three years later. The first transcontinental railroad was built in the 1860s, with the Union Pacific Railroad going westward from Nebraska and the Central Pacific Railroad going eastward from California. The two were joined at Promontory Point, Utah, in May 1869. One of the problems with the early U.S. railroads was that the tracks of different companies varied in width, and so the carriages of one company could not travel on the lines of another. It was not until the mid-1880s that a standard gauge was adopted by all railroads.

Pullman Coaches

Because of the long distances involved, the United States and Russia used train sleeping cars much earlier than did the railways of most other countries. The Pullman coach—a luxury sleeping car—was introduced in 1859, and the first dining car, The Delmonico, was first used in 1868 in the United States. At about the same time Wagons-Lits in Europe began operating sleeping and dining cars. Dining cars were noted then for their quality of food and service.

The first U.S. transcontinental train ran in 1869, a trip that took seven days from coast to coast. These transcontinental trains often carried barbers and manicurists and provided paintings as part of the decor, as well as libraries for entertainment. Electric light was first used on trains in England in 1881, on the London, Brighton and South Coast Railway.

Orient Express

In 1883 the Orient Express was introduced in Europe and ran from Paris to Istanbul. The London-to-Istanbul Orient Express run was not introduced until much later, in 1913. The Orient Express was a sumptuous train with silk-walled carriages, Turkish-carpeted drawing rooms, mosaic-tiled bathrooms complete with hot showers, and tapestried dining cars with waiters dressed in eighteenth-century-style silk breeches and powdered wigs.

Famous as it was, the Orient Express stopped running in 1977 for financial reasons but was revived in 1982 with two luxury (and high-priced) routes: one from London to Venice (known as the Venice Simplon Orient Express) and the other from Paris to Istanbul. The coaches used are beautifully restored carriages from earlier days that are authentic to their last detail. For those unable to take the time for a trip on this romantic and exotic train, it can be vicariously experienced in the comfort of home on videocassette!

New Destinations

By the end of the nineteenth century, many northeastern U.S. resorts, such as Atlantic City in New Jersey, were well serviced by trains, and Florida was also being opened up by the railways as a tourist destination for those northerners who wanted a warm winter.

By the turn of the century the railway station had become the focal point of most communities. Towns often radiated out around the station, and virtually all travel was dominated by trains. By the 1920s there were twenty thousand intercity trains in the United States, with such grand names as the Broadway Limited, the Twentieth Century Limited, and the Golden State Limited.

The French Riviera also developed quickly after World War I because of its popularity with North Americans, who, after crossing the Atlantic by ocean liner, would arrive at London's Victoria Station. From there they would take the morning Golden Arrow train to the southeast English coast, cross the channel by ferry, and link up with the Flèche d'Or (the Golden Arrow) for the trip to Paris where they would then connect with the Train Bleu (the Blue Train) for the trip to the Riviera.

Start of Decline

By the 1930s the railways in North America began to carry smaller and smaller passenger loads as more and more people bought cars, found them cheap to operate, even on long trips, and found they were far more flexible in routing and scheduling than were the railways. But the railway companies were still building bigger and better locomotives, such as the diesel, as well as lighter and more streamlined coaches, and by 1939 the cross-continental travel time in the United States had been cut to four days. In North America and Europe, World War II made severe demands on the railways as they were heavily used by military personnel and their families.

Railways and Hotels

Many of the hotels built near stations or at resorts in that time were owned by railway companies. Some of them are still famous hotels today, such as the Greenbrier Hotel at White Sulphur Springs, West Virginia, and the Banff Springs Hotel at Banff Springs, Alberta. These hotels are still operating successfully today, even though their guests no longer arrive by rail in significant numbers.

Many of the resorts and cities exist today because of the railways. For example, the first casinos built in Las Vegas were established near the railway station for the amusement of people traveling by train. Today Las Vegas is a major tourist destination no longer principally serviced by rail passengers.

RAIL TRAVEL TODAY

After 1945, what the automobile had not done to kill off passenger train travel in North America, the airplane did. Some pockets of high-density train travel in North America still survive (for example, the northeast corridor of the United States and routes such as Toronto to Montreal in Canada), but the glory days of the train were gone. The rail companies in the United States were also privately, rather than government, owned, as is the case in Europe, and these private companies seemed to be more interested in transporting goods rather than people.

Goods Versus People

One of the problems of the rail passenger trains is that they are hard on tracks because of differences in their design from that of freight trains. Passenger trains need to travel at higher speeds than do freight trains and thus, particularly on curves, create greater stresses. Concrete ties have proved superior to wooden ones, but nevertheless the friction of steel wheels on steel rails, with the added pressures of high-speed curves, creates extra demands that freight trains do not make. Canted curves must also be built to contain the centrifugal force created by passenger trains' speeds. Thus there is a conflict between freight and passenger trains' using the same tracks.

Also, because there were so many different U.S. railways, each one could provide only part of the total services of moving people long distances, and none of them could plan the entire service. As Galbraith (1967, p. 364) described it:

> Most American railroads have had a pattern of development different from that of the firms of similar size; . . . there has been no similar capacity for taking control of prices, demand for the services, labor and capital supply and the other requisites of successful planning. . . . In Japan, France, Canada and other countries where there has been one national system or one or two dominant systems, the industry has had greater control over the requisites of its planning and its comparative performance and survival value have been much better.

Gee, Choy, and Makens (1984, p. 172) list four reasons for the demise of North American railroads since the end of World War II:

1. The construction of a national highway system, which permits easy travel virtually anywhere in the nation by private automobile.
2. The growth of the airline industry, which permitted fast, inexpensive, and safe mass transportation.
3. The heavy fixed-cost nature of railroads in which large capital expenditures are needed for equipment and to upgrade roadbeds and rails.
4. A philosophical and political conflict concerning the proper roles of government and private enterprise in the railroad industry.

Amtrak and Via Rail in North America

In the early 1970s the U.S. government established a private corporation known as Amtrak, and the Canadian government a similar one known as Via Rail, to rent the tracks from the railway owners and run passenger trains on them. These corporations have cut routes and introduced better equipment, but neither Amtrak nor Via Rail have proved very successful at generating a profit and survive only because of government subsidies.

According to McIntosh and Goeldner (1984, p. 52) Amtrak's three purposes are (1) to provide modern efficient intercity rail passenger service within the nation's basic rail system, (2) to employ innovative operating and marketing concepts to develop the potential of modern rail service in meeting intercity needs, and (3) to strive for operation on a "for profit" basis.

Both Amtrak and Via Rail have improved their service over the years, by adding new physical plant rather than using secondhand equipment from the previous owners. However, these North American rail lines have only limited capacity that compares badly with that of the European and other systems. For example, Amtrak currently has about 2,000 coaches operating over a twenty-thousand-mile network, whereas France has more than 8,000 cars operating over about the same trackage, and Japan has 26,000 cars for about thirteen thousand route miles.

One more recent development is that Amtrak is now working with travel agents to build rail tour packages, much as the cruise ship industry has done with its fly–cruise concept (to be discussed in the next chapter). The charter train business also appeals to individuals who wish to travel in group tours on trains. These trips include meals, bus excursions, hotels, guides, and even sleeping accommodations on some trains.

Trains in Europe

The decline in rail travel was not as great in Europe, mainly because the car did not make as large an impact in the 1920s and 1930s, nor did the airplane in the early post–World War II years. Population densities are also much higher in Europe, and cities are closer together. Thus today trains in Europe are still well patronized and offer frequent and fast service between major centers. Most trains are electrified, which adds to their cleanliness, although Britain has not yet completely electrified its main rail lines.

For the past thirty years, a network of fast trains connected the major cities in Europe. This network was known as the Trans Europ Express (TEE). These trains provided only one class of travel: first class. In 1987 TEE was disbanded, and in its place the EuroCity network was created, with both first and second class having completely air-conditioned coaches (second class costing about one-third less than first class). About two hundred cities in twelve different countries are in this system. These countries are Austria, Belgium, Denmark, France, West Germany, Italy, Luxembourg, Netherlands, Norway, Spain, Sweden, and Switzerland.

Eurailpass

A popular low-cost method of rail travel in Europe is the Eurailpass (similar to the USA Rail Pass in the United States). Travelers must purchase the Eurailpass in the United States or Canada before departing (it cannot be purchased in Europe). Prices increase with the length of time purchased (with a minimum of fifteen days and a maximum of three months). Passes may be for individuals or for two or more people traveling together. The Eurailpass provides the holder with unlimited first-class rail travel, without any fast-train surcharges, in sixteen European countries (the twelve in the EuroCity network, plus Finland, Greece, Portugal, and the Republic of Ireland). The Eurailpass also provides access to many connecting steamers, ferries, and buses, either free or at reduced prices.

For those traveling in only one European country, most of them have their own national rail passes such as the Wunder Card (West Germany), the Holland Leisure Card, and Britain's BritRail Pass. Note that Britain does not honor the Eurailpass.

European Train–Ferry Links

Where it is necessary in Europe, such as the trip from England to Scandinavia, as well as the linking of various Scandinavian countries across the Baltic and North seas and the linking of Belgium, Holland, and France with Britain across the channel, sea ferries meet the trains. However, the construction of the Eurotunnel (primarily a railway tunnel) from England to France, due to be completed in 1993, will greatly improve the cross-channel service.

Railway centers in Europe are always a great hive of activity, as any North American visitor to Europe who has used them has discovered. The trains have multilingual conductors, and crossing international borders by train causes only short delays.

European trains have excellent arrival and departure records. Stations provide complete tourist services such as tourist information offices, hotel reservation bureaus, and currency exchange facilities. Trains are scheduled to connect with bus, sea, and inland water systems to make changing from one transportation mode to another very easy. Trains, as well as railway stations, have an excellent reputation for the quality of their restaurant food. Many trains also have public pay-telephones on board.

An interesting fact about train travel is that although most governments impose a tax on air travel in order to increase revenues to help pay for the airport terminal's operating costs, a similar type of tax is not imposed on rail travel.

RECENT DEVELOPMENTS

In recent years there have been some revolutionary developments in rail travel.

Supertrains

In Japan, supertrains travel at speeds as high as 300 km/186 miles per hour and are commonly called *bullet trains*. Nevertheless, despite the popularity of these very modern trains, the Japanese government still loses enormous amounts of money on its rail system, as its costs are not covered by revenues.

Maglevs

The Japanese have also experimented with a friction-free and maintenance-free magnetic levitation (commonly known as *maglev*) system for trains. Maglev was invented in Germany in the 1930s. In Germany, the design uses electromagnets, and in Japan, it uses superconducting magnets. In both cases, the train rides slightly above the rail track, resulting in no friction and also in minimal noise and vibration.

In North America there has been a suggestion to build a maglev rail system from Los Angeles to Las Vegas, as about ten million persons a year travel between those two cities.

Trains à Grande Vitesse

In Europe the counterpart to the Japanese bullet train is the *train à grande vitesse* (TGV, or high-speed train) in France. The first TGV line was built between Paris and Lyons, with a dedicated track that is not used by freight trains. The time for the Paris-to-Lyons trip has been reduced to two hours (versus five hours by auto) as the train reaches speeds of almost 170 mph. Because of the TGV's success, its tracks now go as far as Toulon on the French Riviera and also to Lausanne in Switzerland.

Railbus

Britain is using a unique form of transportation known as the railbus. The railbus was developed to revitalize defunct railway routes and to encourage people to return to the railroads. The railbus has a highway bus body on a railway frame and is powered by a turbo-charged bus engine. It is economical because it needs less servicing and overhauling than does a regular diesel rail engine and can compete effectively against airline travel for distances up to about three hundred miles, particularly if there is a business link between the two cities to make the route profitable.

DISCUSSION QUESTIONS

1. Who introduced the first rail tour, and where and when did this occur?
2. What is a Pullman coach, and approximately when was it first introduced?
3. What was the original route of the Orient Express, and which other Orient Express route came later?
4. When did the railways start to decline in North America, and what were the causes?
5. Why is there a conflict between freight and passenger trains?
6. Describe the role of Amtrak in the United States and Via Rail in Canada.
7. Why did the train not suffer the same decline in popularity in Europe as it did in North America?
8. Briefly describe the EuroCity rail system in Europe.
9. Discuss the Eurailpass.

10. What is a maglev train, and in which country are they being built?
11. What does TGV mean, and where do TGV trains operate?
12. Describe Britain's railbus and its role in travel.

REFERENCES

Feifer, Maxine. 1985. *Going Places: The Ways of the Tourist from Imperial Rome to the Present Day*. London: Macmillan.

Galbraith, John Kenneth. 1967. *The New Industrial State*. New York: Signet.

Gee, Chuck Y., Dexter J. L. Choy, and James C. Makens. 1984. *The Travel Industry*. Westport, Conn.: AVI.

McIntosh, Robert W., and Charles R. Goeldner. 1984. *Tourism: Principles, Practices, Philosophies*. New York: Wiley.

SUGGESTED READINGS

Carper, Robert S. 1968. *Focus: The Railroad in Transition*. New York: Barnes.

Congressional Budget Office. 1982. *Federal Services for Rail Passenger Service: An Assessment of Amtrak*. Washington, D.C.: Congressional Budget Office.

Gee, Chuck Y., Dexter J. L. Choy, and James C. Makens. 1984. *The Travel Industry*. Westport, Conn.: AVI, pp. 173–175.

Page, Martin. 1975. *The Lost Pleasures of the Great Trains*. London: Weidenfeld & Nicolson.

Ship Travel

The earliest boats were made from hollowed-out tree trunks by people living on lakes and rivers. Later, when they developed more sophisticated tools and skills, they were able to build better boats. For example, the Egyptians developed a primitive kind of basket-work boat caulked with bitumen. A similar type of boat was made from the skins and hides of animals stretched over a wicker frame. These types of boats, known as *coracles*, are still made and used today in parts of Ireland, on the Euphrates, and in Alaska and Siberia.

The first boats were used by fishermen, but by about 4000 B.C. there was a fully developed sea life at the eastern end of the Mediterranean where boats were also used for trading expeditions. Because the Mediterranean is a relatively calm sea, oars were used as the main means of navigation. The first great system of transportation by sailing vessels was that of the Phoenicians, who connected caravan routes with seaports, chiefly around the Mediterranean. Sailboats remained the principal means of sea travel until the development of the steamship.

Although the first steamships were designed at about the same time as the steam engine was first used in trains, early in the nineteenth century, ship travel had already been common for thousands of years for exploration, commerce, people transportation, and even for some limited forms of leisure travel.

THE STEAMSHIP ERA

The first ocean crossing of a steamship was in 1819 when the *Savannah* journeyed from Savannah, Georgia, to Liverpool, England. The journey took twenty-nine days. The *Savannah* was a full-rigged sailing ship fitted with engines and side paddlewheels that were used only when necessary. The first crossing under steam power alone occurred in 1838 when two competing British ships journeyed from England to New York within a few days of each other. The earliest trans-Atlantic steamships were often known as *packet ships* because they carried packets of mail, as well as other cargo and passengers. The crossings in those days could take two weeks or more and were primarily for the wealthy, as passenger costs were very high. Ships also carried live animals such as chickens, pigs, sheep, and even cows which were slaughtered for food.

When emigration from Europe to North America started on a large scale, those budget travelers (known as *steerage passengers*) traveled in horrible conditions. They were kept below decks with the hatches tightly closed in bad weather and with only a few toilets available. As many as 10 percent of them died from typhus during a crossing.

Large Shipping Companies

In 1838 the Canadian merchant and shipowner Samuel Cunard started a regular cross-Atlantic steamship service from Liverpool to Halifax and then on to Boston. His fleet at one time numbered forty vessels. Other steamship companies, such as the Royal Mail Steam Packet Company (Royal Mail) and the Peninsular and Orient Company (P & O), quickly followed. During the latter part of the nineteenth century, the British dominated the trans-Atlantic steamship service. These steamships were sometimes named *liners*, as they provided a scheduled service in a straight line between two distant ports.

By the early 1900s, other companies such as the Canadian Pacific and the Holland-America had joined the competition. During this period, until the end of the 1920s, both luxury services and less expensive services were offered by the various trans-Atlantic shipping companies. Tens of thousands of people a year were crossing the Atlantic as emigrants to North America or as tourists going to and from Europe. Indeed, from the port of Liverpool alone, some seven million people journeyed across the Atlantic to North America between 1830 and 1930.

Similar ships were also traveling from Europe to Latin America, South Africa, and Australia carrying cargo, emigrants, and tourists. Indeed, travelers from Britain to places such as India and Australia coined the word *posh*—an acronym for Port Out, Starboard Home because, depending on direction of travel, those were the most favored, or posh, cabins.

The Depression Years

The Depression of the 1930s severely hurt the passenger liner business, but the technology was still improving, and by 1939, the trans-Atlantic trip had been reduced to four or five days. Many of the ships that were used in the boom days were turned into scrap during the Depression, but many other famous ships such as the *Queen Mary* survived and were used to carry troops and for other military purposes during World War II.

After the war, just as rail travel never recovered because of the inroads made by the automobile, so too did the ocean liners have major difficulties because of the new competition from air travel, the technology for which had benefited greatly from the war. But some famous cross-Atlantic liners were still built, such as the *Queen Elizabeth I*, the *Queen Elizabeth II* (still making trans-Atlantic trips today), and the *SS United States*. Indeed, the *SS United States* holds the record for the fastest crossing. But bit by bit, the airlines eroded the hold that the passenger ships had on long-distance ocean travel.

CRUISE SHIPS

Luxury ocean liners have emerged today in another form—the cruise ship. The cruise ship business is one of the fastest-growing branches of tourism, with the number of people taking cruises in the millions annually. Much of this success has stemmed from a marriage of the shipping companies with the companies that put them out of the transocean business—the airlines. This marriage came about, to the benefit of both, with the fly–cruise package concept: About 80 percent of the ship cruise business today is of this type.

The fly–cruise concept makes it cost effective for people to vacation this way, as it allows ticketed cruise passengers to fly to and from the ships' ports of call at substantially reduced rates. The cruise lines designate the air carriers to be used and, in some cases, even the flights.

The fly–cruise concept allows passengers to reach the ship embarkation point rapidly and reach home again quickly at the end of the cruise. Unlike the trans-Atlantic liners of earlier days, most of today's cruise ships offer only one class of service. However, the actual costs to the customer will differ depending on cabin size and location. Currently, costs average about $200 per day per passenger, which is a relatively low cost when compared with what a person would pay per day for transportation, hotel accommodation, all meals, and entertainment.

Large Markets

In addition to lowering their prices and offering fly–cruise packages, many cruise lines have had to repackage their product in order to attract a new type of passenger.

A recent study by the Cruise Lines International Association identified 35 million Americans as potential cruise passengers. About 80 percent of these had never been on a cruise, and 60 percent were not even aware that cruises existed as a form of vacation.

For North Americans, the most popular cruise destinations are Caribbean and Mexican ports, trips through the Panama Canal, and cruises along the northwest Pacific coast to Alaska in the summer. The Mississippi River has retained its appeal from earlier travel days and offers river cruises. In Europe, Mediterranean cruises are the most popular.

According to McIntosh and Goeldner (1984, p. 60), Florida departures have dominated the North American cruise market for the past two decades. In 1971, 60 percent of cruises departed from Florida; today that figure is 75 percent.

Self-contained Resorts

Cruise ships are basically self-contained "destination" resorts where guests are roomed, fed, entertained, and transported. In the earlier days of trans-Atlantic crossings, entertainment often consisted during the day of sitting on a deck chair, in sometimes rugged weather, reading a book. At night there was dancing with a limited choice of type of music. Today's cruise ships offer live shows, gambling, slot machines, movies, a variety of bars, discos, other dancing spots, exercise areas, shopping arcades, and sightseeing at the various ports of call. One of the best-known present-day cruise ships is the *Queen Elizabeth II*, completed in 1969 at a cost of $94 million. This cruise liner recently underwent a $130 million refit that added a shopping promenade featuring famous-name international shops, including a branch of London's famous Harrods department store. A cruise vacation offers relaxation, fun, sun, limited packing and unpacking, a variety of passengers and cultural contacts, and, invariably, superb food.

Importance of Food

The food on any ship is extremely important. Whereas land restaurants do not need to change their menus every day—they simply change customers—cruise ships, with their captive clientele, must constantly change their menus and offer consistently high-quality food to anywhere from five hundred to more than two thousand passengers per meal. Understandably, food, along with labor and fuel, is one of the high operating costs of the cruise business. A typical cruise liner menu showing dinner offerings is illustrated in Figure 11-1.

Theme Cruises

More recent is the emergence of theme cruises, which combine education and vacation experiences. Themes may be a particular cuisine, history, photography, as-

Bon Voyage Dinner

HOLLAND AMERICA LINE
ms Noordam

Captain Hans Eulderink, Commander
Mr. Henk J. de Vis, Hotel Manager

Caribbean Cruise

Fort Lauderdale — Saturday, October 24, 1987

APPETIZERS

SMOKED SALMON, *Norwegian smoked salmon, thinly sliced on Boston lettuce with onion rings, capers, crushed peppercorns and toast points.*
SEAFOOD COCKTAIL, *shredded sealegs with cocktail sauce.*
HEARTS OF PALM, *in a vinaigrette dressing.*
FRESH FRUIT CUP, *sections of fresh fruit with Benedictine Liqueur.*
CRUDITES, *crisp fresh garden vegetables with blue cheese dip.*

HOT APPETIZER

ESCARGOTS BOURGUIGNONNE, *six snails served in cocotte with garlic herbal butter.*

SOUPS

LOBSTER BISQUE, *a delicate blend of Maine lobster, brandy and fresh cream.*
GARDEN VEGETABLE, *beef broth with a bouquet of fresh garden vegetables.*
MELON SOUP, *a chilled blend of fresh cantaloupe, honeydew and cranshaw melon.*

SALADS

NOORDAM SALAD, *fresh watercress, alfalfa sprouts, orange segments and choice of dressing.*
TOSSED GREEN SALAD, *with julienne of carrots, zucchini and radishes with blue cheese dressing.*
Blue cheese, Italian, Poppyseed or *Low Calorie Dressing.*

THE PERFECT BALANCE

Based on the American Heart Association's fourth edition cookbook, Holland America Line is proud to serve:
COLD POACHED SALMON, *Alaska silver salmon presented on a bed of fish sauce with cottage cheese and cabbage salad.*

ENTREES

FRESH PACIFIC RED SNAPPER, *panfried with fresh green asparagus, pureed carrots and parsley potatoes.*
SHRIMP DEL REY, *jumbo butterfly shrimp, topped with rich del rey crabmeat and Hollandaise, served with broccoli, melon wedges and brown rice.*
GRILLED SIRLOIN STEAK, *mesquite grilled with a half stuffed tomato, Belgian endive, onion rings and a baked Idaho potato.*
GRILLED TURKEY STEAK, *charbroiled breast of turkey with fresh green asparagus, cranberries and fresh sweet potatoes.*
ALSO ON REQUEST: *baked Idaho potato with sour cream, chives and fresh bacon bits.*

FROM THE ITALIAN CUISINE

LINGUINI WITH CLAM, *tender egg linguini with chopped clams and garlic white clam sauce.*

IMPORTED CHEESE AND FRESH FRUIT

Our International selection of cheeses from the silvertray with Dutch Rusk, crackers, pumpernickel or crispbread.
Selection of fresh fruits, Calimyrna figs and dates, with stemginger in syrup.

DESSERTS

PARFAIT JUBILEE, *kirschwasser soaked cherries topped with vanilla ice cream and sliced pistachio nuts.*
CREME BRULEE, *a vanilla custard with carmelised brown sugar.*
PEAR BELLE HELENE, *a poached pear dressed on vanilla ice cream with chocolate sauce.*
FRESH APPLE TARTS, *with vanilla ice cream if you prefer.*
CHEESE CAKE, *with fresh strawberry couli.*
THE PASTRY TRAY, *an assortment of petite French pastries.*
VANILLA, CITRUS COOLER AND CREAM OR BUTTER PECAN ICE CREAM, *with whipped cream if you like.*
THE LOW CALORIE SELECTION, *fruit jello or lemon sherbet.*
Coffee, herbal teas, milk and freshly brewed decaffeinated coffee.

FIGURE 11-1. Typical cruise ship dinner menu. Holland American Line Westours Inc.

tronomy, or anything else that can draw a sufficiently large group. There have been cruises to nowhere, with passengers not knowing the destinations in advance, and cruises for closed convention groups.

One of the advantages of cruise ships is that they can move to where the market is, depending on the season of the year. For example, cruise ships on the summer run from Vancouver to Alaska might operate from the southern United States to the Caribbean or Panama Canal in the winter, or from northern Europe in the summer to the warmer Mediterranean in the winter. This mobility recently served another purpose. As a result of a cruise ship's being hijacked in the Mediterranean, the cruise line companies operating in that area found their reservations dropping drastically. Some of the ships thus were pulled out of that market and moved to other parts of the world where hijacking is less of a threat.

Specially Built Ships

Some of the earlier cruise ships were converted transocean passenger liners. But one of the problems with these liners was that they had been built for long trans-Atlantic trips and thus were deep-hulled vessels that were unable to dock in the shallow Caribbean and other ports. Passengers had to go ashore by tender. Today, most of the cruise vessels are designed specifically for the cruise market. Technological innovations have been introduced, such as stabilizers that considerably reduce the amount of side-to-side roll that a ship might otherwise encounter in rough weather. One of the more recent innovations is the introduction of a cruise ship with a garage on board large enough to carry up to 350 motor vehicles, including recreational vehicles (RVs), motor coaches, and even cabin cruisers on trailers. Similar types of car-carrying cruise ships have been common around the Baltic and North seas for some time, but most of them are not able to carry larger vehicles such as RVs and coaches.

This type of cruise ship can be marketed to people who prefer to drive, rather than fly, to the cruise embarkation point and thus save the cost of flying. The cruise company can also offer one-way cruises so that on arrival passengers simply drive off in their vehicles and continue their vacation on land before driving home.

Cruise Marketing

Cruise ship marketing has some unusual aspects. For example, researchers have discovered that for many passengers the cruise is more important than any of its destinations. However, for the ports of call these destinations are critical because of the tourists they bring in who will spend money there. The ports of departure are also important to those cities, as the cruise ship companies will spend large amounts of money there obtaining provisions and fuel.

According to Gee, Choy, and Makens (1984, p. 161), cruise lines have found that to appeal to the right market, they need to consider, first, the amount of money that people are willing to spend for a cruise, second, the amount of time they wish to spend cruising, and, third, the destinations they might want to visit.

Cruise line companies also offer special off-season rates to attract people in slow periods. These lower prices sometimes include a higher-than-normal travel agent commission to encourage travel agents to try to sell them. Most cruises are sold by travel agents, as the cruise line companies can reach a larger share of the potential market this way than they can trying to sell directly themselves.

Cruise Lines International Association (CLIA)

The Cruise Lines International Association (CLIA) represents most cruise line companies operating in North America. It is both a public relations and a promotional organization. Oddly enough, the cruise ships operating out of North America are owned mainly by Europeans. One reason for this is the high cost of operating cruise ships, with labor being one of the biggest costs. Non-American cruise ship companies can employ people at far lower wages and salaries than could a U.S. registered company. Thus, U.S. cruise shipping companies just cannot compete.

OTHER TYPES OF WATER TRAVEL

In addition to the large ocean liners and cruise ships, tourists are likely to encounter several other types of water travel vessels.

Freighter Travel

For the more adventurous, freighter travel might be the answer. Freighters carry no more than twelve passengers. This limit is used because if there are more than twelve passengers, maritime law requires a permanent doctor on board, at an additional cost to the shipping company.

Freighters do have scheduled runs, but they are subject to change and, for that reason, offer a little bit of the unknown. Freighters appeal to people with plenty of time (and plenty of money, as cabin costs are high) and to those who do not mind not having the organized entertainment and the other attractions that regular cruise ships offer.

Hovercraft

Hovercraft are seagoing vehicles lifted by propeller-induced downward air pressure on the water. Today they are commonly used across relatively narrow stretches of open sea such as the English Channel between England and France. They can carry several dozen cars and several hundred passengers and, at a top speed of about 75 mph, are considerably faster than normal ferries.

Hydrofoils

Hydrofoils (sometimes referred to as flying ships) also use their power to lift them, but rather than riding above the water like the hovercraft, they slice through the water by sucking it up and then expelling it behind them for propulsion. The foil develops lift as it planes through the water. The hull is raised above the surface, which reduces friction.

One of the more interesting hydrofoil trips is along the Danube River from Vienna in Austria to Budapest in Hungary. Hydrofoils need relatively calm waters, such as rivers, in which to operate. However, they can be used in well-protected areas of open sea, such as between Copenhagen in Denmark and Malmo in Sweden, and between Naples and the island of Capri in Italy.

Riverboat Travel

River and canal travel is far from new, as rivers and canals have been used in some cases for thousands of years to move goods and people. But it is only in the last 150 years or so that rivers and canals have been made popular for tourist travel. For example, the Mississippi River has been a popular tourist river since the United States was settled and paddlewheelers were used for gambling and entertainment on the run from St. Louis to New Orleans. Today, tourists still heavily patronize modern-day Mississippi riverboats offering two- or three-day luxury trips along the river.

In Europe the Rhine, winding through the grape-growing areas of Germany, offers similar leisurely tourist trips, as do other European rivers such as the Danube and the Dnieper.

DISCUSSION QUESTIONS

1. Why were the earlier steamships known as packet ships?
2. List three of the earlier major steamship companies. Which country predominated in the eighteenth century in ocean travel across the North Atlantic? Why do you think this was so?
3. After World War II what caused a major decline in cross-Atlantic ship travel?
4. Describe the fly–cruise concept.
5. Why are cruise ships described as self-contained destination resorts?

6. What is a theme cruise?

7. Why is food quality important on cruise vessels?

8. What is a specially built cruise ship?

9. List the factors important to marketing cruises, and explain why cruises are sold primarily through travel agents.

10. Describe freighter ship travel.

11. Differentiate between a hovercraft and a hydrofoil.

PROBLEM

Select one method of water travel (ocean liner, cruise ship, riverboat, ferry, yacht charter), and study how it has been affected in your area, either positively or negatively, by changes in tourism in the last ten years. Once you have made your selection and done your research, prepare a one-page report of your findings, addressing such questions as, Has the segment of water travel that you selected for your research been affected by other different forms of travel? What are the projections for future changes? How will they be handled?

REFERENCES

Gee, Chuck Y., Dexter J. L. Choy, and James C. Makens. 1984. *The Travel Industry*. Westport, Conn.: AVI.

McIntosh, Robert W., and Charles R. Goeldner. 1984. *Tourism: Principles, Practices, Philosophies*. New York: Wiley.

SUGGESTED READINGS

Bathe, Basil W. 1972. *Seven Centuries of Sea Travel*. London: Barrie & Jenkins.

Gee, Chuck Y., Dexter J. L. Choy, and James C. Makens. 1984. *The Travel Industry*. Westport, Conn.: AVI, pp. 160–167.

Special Report No. 43. 1982. "The Cruise Business, Part 1." *International Tourism Quarterly* 2: 41–54.

Special Report No. 43. 1982. "The Cruise Business, Part 2." *International Tourism Quarterly* 3: 68–87.

Stansfield, Charles A., Jr., 1975. "Evolving Patterns of International Sea Passenger Ports in Eastern United States." *The Tourist Review* 3:105–111.

Woon, Basil. 1927. *The Frantic Atlantic*. New York: Knopf.

Air Travel

After studying this chapter the reader will be able to

- Briefly describe the history of air travel, and state what major impact World War II had on this mode of travel.

- Explain the effect of the introduction of jet planes, and then the jumbo jets, on air travel.

- Discuss the development of charter flight travel and its status today.

- Discuss the difference between U.S. and European aircraft manufacturers.

- Discuss special aircraft types such as the Concorde and STOL and explain in what way today's new jet aircraft are more efficient than their predecessors.

- Describe hub and spoke airports.

- Explain what is meant by the term *fleet planning*, and discuss the measurement of airline profitability.

- Discuss the role of governments and airlines in Europe.

- Discuss deregulation and its impact in the United States.

- Explain frequent flyer plans.

- Translate the acronyms IATA and ICAO, and discuss the role of these two groups.

Each technological advance in a travel mode affects the other modes. The railroad replaced the horse; the automobile (and the bus) replaced the railroad; and the airplane replaced transocean ship and long-distance rail travel.

Today, the volume of air travel is huge. For example, the number of air passengers carried annually in the United States is about 450 million, and it is expected to double by the year 2000, putting the air travel system, and particularly airports, under increasing strain. One of the dilemmas in the United States is that no new major airports have been built since that at Dallas–Fort Worth in the mid-1970s. But building new airports today, even if they are desperately needed, is very difficult because of the noise problem; most people do not want them near their own communities.

AIR FLIGHT HISTORY

The first flight of an airplane took place in 1903 in Kitty Hawk, North Carolina, when the Wright brothers flew a machine for only about forty yards. Although airplanes were developed to the point of being used for military purposes in World War I, and for mail and freight purposes, the first international commercial flight was made only in 1919, from London to Paris. In the 1920s some European countries began subsidizing air travel (for example, Britain, France, and Germany), and from this their national airlines emerged.

The first U.S. regularly scheduled passenger flight was made in 1927, from Boston to New York. In that same year Pan American began service to Havana, and two years later, in 1929, the first airport hotel was built in Oakland, California.

The U.S. airlines never had as high rates of growth as did many of the European national airlines. The U.S. government was not overly interested in this new type of transportation, other than in granting mail-carrying contracts, and was not anxious to subsidize the airlines. Nor was there much incentive for the airlines, as in the early days, carrying passengers was not profitable, and the early planes were no faster than trains over the same routes and were much less reliable. The U.S. airlines thus needed the government's mail-carrying contracts to survive. Nevertheless, by 1930 there were four major airlines, which still exist today as United, American, Eastern, and TWA.

Airships

Airships had their fling also. For example, a British airship crossed the Atlantic in 1919, and a German one went around the world in 1929. People were predicting that they would be a major method of luxurious air travel. Unfortunately, there then were a series of disasters, including, in 1937, the loss of the German airship the Hindenburg, which exploded, killing many on board, while approaching its mooring mast at Lakehurst, New Jersey. As a result, the airship, or dirigible, never developed into a major vehicle for long-distance travel.

Aircraft Improvements

In the early days of flying, the planes were small and relatively slow by today's standards. For example, one of the first planes designed specifically for commercial passenger travel was the Douglas Corporation's DC-2, which carried only about a dozen passengers and flew at 150 mph.

There was considerable improvement in aircraft technology in the 1930s, but as a precaution, airline crews in the United States still carried train schedules with them so that if they had to make an unexpected landing, passengers could continue their trip by train. Stewardesses on those planes also had to be nurses to qualify for the job. In the 1930s it took up to twenty hours to fly from coast to coast in North America. The planes could not carry much fuel and so had to stop frequently.

However, by 1939 Pan American was flying across the Atlantic via the Azores, Lisbon, and Marseilles. The return fare was about $750—a lot of money in those days and the equivalent of about $4,500 today. Surprisingly, because of improvements in aircraft technology and the larger size of the aircraft, airfares for the budget traveler can be far lower than the $750 return, in terms of today's dollar.

The DC-3 Revolution

In 1935 the Model-T of the airline industry was introduced: the DC-3, or the Dakota, as it was commonly called. The DC-3 could carry twenty-one day passengers or fourteen overnight sleepers. The DC-3 revolutionized the airline industry because it was the first aircraft to make money by carrying passengers. But because its cabin was not pressurized, it flew at only ten to twelve thousand feet (compared with thirty thousand to forty thousand for today's jet aircraft) and was subject to very rough rides during turbulence.

During World War II the DC-3 was converted into a troop carrier and was renamed the C-47, although it was affectionately known by military personnel as the gooney bird.

In its peak years the DC-3 carried 80 percent of all passenger air travelers. Eleven thousand of these extremely reliable workhorses were built, and an estimated one thousand are still flying today, more than fifty years after they first were introduced. The last DC-3 was constructed in 1946.

World War II Technology

Technological improvements in aircraft and engine construction made during World War II were adopted by the airline industry after 1945, and airplane sizes and speeds were considerably increased. Servicemen had become used to traveling by plane and were not frightened of flying, and as demand grew, airports were radically improved to cope.

During the 1950s, the big airlines became interested in the mass transportation of tourists, who would change the basis of airline economics by creating a whole new area of demand—particularly across the Atlantic. In 1957, for the first time, more passengers crossed the Atlantic by air than by ship. Air traffic across the Atlantic was doubling every five years, and in 1962 over 2 million people crossed by air, compared with only 800,000 by sea.

The First Jet

In the early post–World War II period, propeller-jet (turboprop) engines were used. The pure jet engine was invented in Germany in 1939 but was not used in commercial aircraft until twenty years later. The U.S. aircraft manufacturing company Boeing introduced the Boeing 707 (B-707) in 1959 as the first pure jet-engine commercial aircraft. One B-707 could carry across the Atlantic as many people as the *Queen Mary* ocean liner could carry in the same time—by shuttling back and forth at jet speed—six and a half hours from New York to Europe.

The B-707 was quickly followed by other jet aircraft designs, having different numbers of engines and different passenger capacities for various airline routes. These jets created a surge in the growth of most international airlines, and trans-Atlantic traffic began increasing by about 20 percent a year. In the 1960s, airlines were carrying a million passengers a month across the Atlantic at a price far lower than that of a tourist fare on an ocean liner in the 1920s.

The air boom of the 1950s and 1960s also erased in many ways the borders of Western Europe. The Alps no longer cut off Italy, nor the Pyrenees Spain, from the countries to the north. Europeans could now take a fast flight to sunspots around the Mediterranean as cheaply as they could vacation in their own country. For example, the trip from London to Athens took three days by train in 1950 and four hours by air in 1960.

Jet aircraft also changed the entire economics of flying. They were cheaper and safer, and when they were introduced, they produced a large supply of used propeller planes that could be sold by the jet-owning airlines to charter companies and to new airlines in developing countries. This happened at a time when in both Africa and Asia, a number of independent countries were emerging, each of which had ambitions of operating its own national carrier.

Decline of Sea Travel

At the same time as air traffic was booming and changing travel patterns, the dominance of many of the old seaports was fading. The seaport of Southampton in England was being eclipsed by London's Heathrow airport, Hamburg in Germany by Frankfurt, Cherbourg in France by Paris, and Genoa in Italy by Milan. The old passenger shipping lines, which two decades earlier had seemed like permanent fixtures, were now dying out rapidly. Cunard was taken over by a British property company, and the beautiful liner, the *France*, was taken out of service and sold to a Norwegian tour operator.

Types of Aircraft

In the United States, planes such as the B-727, B-737, DC-8, and DC-9 were introduced. Britain had its BAC111 and the Trident, and France the Caravelle and the Mercure—but the U.S. manufacturers (such as Boeing, Lockheed, and Douglas) produced their planes in far larger numbers. For example, the production runs of the European planes were often less than one hundred, as against three hundred to five hundred for their U.S. cousins. In fact, more than eighteen hundred B-727s were constructed before production was halted.

One of the reasons for the larger quantities of the U.S. manufacturers is that the European planes were specifically designed for their own national airlines and so did not appeal to the general international airline market. American aircraft manufacturers have a major advantage: They are selling to U.S. airlines whose domestic routes carry more passengers annually than do all the rest of the airlines in the world. Their planes dominate world markets and contribute more to U.S. exports than does any other industry in that country.

The Wide Bodies

Boeing claimed another first in 1970 by introducing the B-747, the jumbo jet aircraft that, depending on its seat configuration, is capable of seating from 350 to 500 passengers. In 1965 Pan Am and Boeing had agreed on this jet; it was almost equally risky for both sides. Boeing had to invest as much as its total net capital and to build the world's largest manufacturing plant while the plane was still being designed. Pan Am agreed to pay half a billion dollars for twenty-five planes, more than all its revenues for the previous year. But the B-747 was a success and was quickly followed by other wide-bodied planes such as the Lockheed 1011 (the Tri Star), the Douglas DC-10, and, in Europe, the Airbus A300.

Oddly, even though U.S. aircraft companies produce more commercial aircraft than does any other country in the world, the A300 was the first non-U.S.-manufactured jet sold to a U.S. airline: Eastern Airlines purchased the A300 in 1977. In fact, the Airbus (now produced in several different models) was constructed by a consortium of European countries (France, Germany, Britain, and, to a lesser extent, Spain) to overcome the nationalism of European airplane manufacturers and to try to compete with the U.S. manufacturing giants.

Although jumbo jets required an extra investment in airports (longer runways, water and sewage utilities, ground transport, and communications), they also needed at the destinations new or enlarged hotels, restaurants, and other facilities. They particularly tended to reinforce the link between hotels and airlines. Sampson (1985, p. 161) described this new breed of wide-bodied aircraft:

> In the peak seasons the jumbos offered a much bleaker experience for passengers, which removed them still further from any sense of individual adventure. Four hundred people—about the same number as the slaves in an eighteenth century slaver—are packed equally closely. The passengers inside the "tin sausage," most of them far away from a window, are cut off from any sense of the earth or the sky —an experience almost opposite to that of the early aviators. As the seats crept still closer together the airliner looked still less like an ocean liner, more like a crowded cinema or fast-food counter. It became an extension of the consumer society, with

a submissive captive market all conditioned to eat, to watch films or to buy duty-free goods at the same time. The jets and jumbos brought new standards of reliability, punctuality and safety; but they also abolished almost any sense of traveling.

Newer Planes

Today, Boeing has emerged as the major U.S. manufacturer (it currently builds about 60 percent of the world's jet aircraft), and it and other manufacturers have introduced modified versions of earlier planes designed for today's market. These aircraft are far quieter and as much as 30 percent more fuel efficient than were the airplanes of the 1960s and 1970s. Boeing has also introduced newer models of the B-747 capable of flying seven thousand miles from New York to Tokyo without stopping for fuel. Larger versions, with enlarged upper decks, will soon also be on the market and will be capable of seating far more than five hundred passengers.

The Supersonics (SS)

In 1962 the governments of France and Britain signed an agreement to build for Air France and British Airways a supersonic aircraft that became one of the most politically controversial of all planes. Its manufacture was intended to cement Anglo-French unity as well as to demonstrate that European technology could sell its product to world markets.

The supersonic (SS) planes were designed to fly at speeds far in excess of the speed of sound. Although Boeing had an SS design, it never went into production. The Soviets introduced their SS, the TU144, and the Anglo-French consortium of British Airways and Air France produced the Concorde.

The Concorde can carry only about one hundred passengers, uses a lot of fuel, and requires all passengers to pay the equivalent of first-class fares, because its operating costs are extremely high. It is also limited to flying over land at subsonic speeds to avoid the noise pollution of the supersonic "boom." For these reasons the supersonics have not been a commercial success. Air France has stopped using the Concorde, although British Airways still uses a limited number on scheduled routes and also on special trips, such as from London to Moscow overnight to see the ballet, or on day trips from London to the pyramids in Egypt.

But perhaps a faster plane may eventually outdo the Concorde. In the United States and Britain, engines are being developed that are a combination of jet and space rocket for a B-747-sized airplane that will accommodate about two hundred passengers. This aircraft will fly at several times the speed of the Concorde and at heights up to 100,000 feet. It will be able to fly from coast to coast in North America in one hour, rather than the four to five hours it now takes.

Short Takeoff and Landing Airplanes (STOL)

One of the more recent introductions is the short takeoff and landing airplane, or STOL. STOL aircraft are designed to operate from small airports closer to city centers where long runways cannot be built. The advantage of these aircraft is that they can eliminate the time it takes to drive to and from distant airports from downtown areas. For short air trips from regular out-of-town airports, this driving time can be longer than the actual flying time.

Charter Flights

From 1959 to the present the airline passenger growth rate has averaged about 5 percent a year, while at the same time airfares have continued to decline in relative terms. Much of this growth resulted from the appeal of charter flights.

In the 1950s and 1960s many airline companies (some of them subsidiaries of regularly scheduled carriers) were established to handle low-priced charters, as the regularly scheduled airlines were not allowed to sell directly seats on a charter fare basis on their regular flights. Charter flight tickets could be sold only to members of groups, societies, or associations whose members all were traveling together on the same flight. As a result of these block bookings, passenger prices could be lowered.

The scheduled airlines were surprised by the success of the charters. They were used to providing scheduled routes oriented to business travelers, and it was the new charter flight companies that rapidly began to exploit the vacation travel market, either by flying their own aircraft or by contracting for blocks of seats with existing scheduled airlines. These charter companies grew up outside the "system" and could thus lower prices far below the normal fares. At first the IATA (see later in this chapter) enforced a rule (known as the affinity rule) that charter fare passengers must belong to an authentic group such as an employee organization, an ethnic group, or a hobby club. Most of these groups were authentic and had an important social role to play in returning American families to their European roots, by offering extremely low fares. But a new business sprang up to devise ways to overcome the IATA rules that qualified travelers for these low fares.

Abuses of the pure charter flights were common. For example, passengers were sometimes allowed to book and pay for seats and then sign up as a member of a group (in some cases after the flight had started!), even though they had no affiliation with it or interest in it. The affinity rule became impossible to enforce. As a result, the regularly scheduled airlines eventually gave up fighting the affinity rule and were themselves allowed to sell seats on a charter basis. These low scheduled airfares have become known as ABCs or advanced booking charters, and charter flight companies and the scheduled airlines can now sell their seats to anyone. The distinction between scheduled flights and charter flights is thus now quite blurred.

The Blue Ribbon

The United States dominates world air travel today. About 40 percent of total world travel is done within the United States and almost 15 percent more across the Atlantic to Europe. The North Atlantic route is considered by the airlines to be the "blue ribbon" run because of the large number of passengers traveling to and fro. For this reason it is a very competitive route among the airlines and offers a relative travel bargain to passengers.

Hubs and Spokes

One of the developments that occurred as airlines and airports grew larger was the concept of a major airport as a hub, with a network of spokes radiating out to surrounding regional airports that act as feeders to the hub. Sampson (1985, p. 233) described them as follows:

> The growth of hubs and spokes which had changed the American air map had still more significance in Europe, where many of the hubs coincided with the capitals. . . . Governments, airlines and labour unions all tended to favour a single centralised hub, and to resist regional pressures; . . . The hubs and spokes of Europe's air map were not fundamentally different from an old rail map whose lines converged on Paris or London, or an ancient road map with all roads leading to Rome.

GOVERNMENTS AND AIRLINES

Other than in the United States, airlines and governments have always been closely linked. From the birth of commercial air flight, the European governments were determined to use it for their own national ambitions and in particular to link their overseas colonies to the home country. The airlines had little say in the matter, as they were either owned by the government or dependent on government subsidies. The government wanted a flag carrier on which it could depend and whose routes it could control.

European passengers pay dearly for this nationalism, with high fares and a lack of regional services. A European can often fly as cheaply from Europe to North America as between two much closer European countries. However, a greater cost has been to the integration of Europe as a whole. Indeed, only three European nations (Denmark, Norway, and Sweden) have been able to join together to form an airline representing all three nations: SAS (Scandinavian Airline System).

For many countries the national airline has little relationship to the size of the country. For example, Cathay Pacific flies around the world from its base in Hong Kong with a population of about five million people and a territory of only a few hundred square miles. Similarly, Singapore International Airline operates from a country with a population of less than three million. Galbraith (1968, p. 114) summed up the government role in controlling airlines:

> It is interesting that governments which are reluctant to grant autonomy to other enterprises regularly accord it to their airline and often with good results. It seems possible that public officials, who are among the most important patrons, sense the unique dangers of denying autonomy to this industry.

FLEET PLANNING

An airline's success is a balance of its route structure, its equipment (for each jet aircraft it owns it might need as much as $1 million more in ground equipment), its aircraft scheduling, and its pricing.

Fleet planning is crucial. The airplanes must be of the right size to fit an airline's routes and the number of passengers flying them. Decisions about which aircraft to use are crucial to both the manufacturers and the purchasers of the planes. It can take five to six years from design to production for a new airframe and its engines, and a manufacturer may have to sell some four hundred to six hundred aircraft to break even. The accurate forecasting of airplane needs will be vital for a long time ahead.

Airlines also must be concerned with the price differential at which travelers will choose one mode of travel over another, as well as the airplane's comfort, scheduling convenience, and air terminal waiting time for connecting flights.

Measuring Success

Today, about 85 to 90 percent of an airline's total revenue is from passengers, and the rest is from mail, freight, and similar items. An airline's success is often measured in passenger revenue miles flown, a passenger revenue mile being one paying customer carried for one mile. Trains and buses often use this same type of measurement, but airlines also measure yield, or net profit per passenger mile.

Another measure is known as load factor, or the average percentage of seats filled on flights. This is similar to hotels that calculate their room occupancy percentage as a measure of success. But an airline flight can have a high load factor but little yield or profit, because of heavily discounted fare–paying passengers filling those seats. In North America it is estimated that about 85 percent of all airfares are discounted below the full regular economy-class fare as a result of special seat sales, standbys, and other discounted prices.

Airline Costs

Airlines also attempt to keep their planes in the air for as much of each twenty-four-hour period as possible. Obviously, an aircraft flying with paying passengers is more profitable than one sitting on the ground; even an aircraft idling its engines on the ground waiting to take off will consume vast amounts of costly fuel.

The air corridors or routes on which a plane is allowed to fly can also affect fuel consumption. These corridors are often set for political and military purposes. In Europe, in particular, planes are often required to fly tortuous routes on short-haul flights, thus adding considerably to their fuel costs.

DEREGULATION

Deregulation is the term used to signify the freeing of airlines from many government controls. This deregulation directly affects only a country's domestic airlines. International agreements must still be negotiated between two or more countries for international air travel.

The U.S. government was the first to enact airline deregulation in 1978, although until 1982 the Civil Aeronautics Board (CAB) in the United States still regulated airline fares and schedules. The CAB now no longer exists, as full deregulation allows the airlines to set their own fares and routes.

Some feared that deregulation in the United States would create an oligopolistic situation, with only a few big airlines able to control fares and routes. Their fears may have been well founded, as only a few big airlines now dominate the major U.S. airports. For example, in 1986 there were twelve major airlines with about 85 percent of all the business, but in 1988 that number had decreased to eight with about 95 percent of all the business. These eight are Texas Air (which is also the parent company of Continental and Eastern), United, American, Delta, Northwest, U.S. Air, TWA, and Pan Am. Many smaller airlines (such as People Express and Frontier) have disappeared in the process.

Deregulation has encouraged some competition and forced the major airlines to become more efficient (for example, by dropping some unprofitable short-haul routes and standardizing the planes they use, thus reducing maintenance costs). However, deregulation has resulted in severe financial problems for some of the airlines.

Many small new regional airlines have also sprung up, using dormant routes not used or no longer used by the larger airlines. In many cases these regional airlines now serve as feeders (or spokes) to the larger national and international carriers' hubs. Before deregulation there were fewer than 50 airlines operating in the United States. Now there are more than 130, for any company that can buy, or even lease, an airplane can start a new airline.

In other parts of the world, airlines are still usually regulated by government agencies, much as they used to be by the CAB in the United States. However, the Canadian government has slowly begun to introduce deregulation, as has the British government. Other European countries are more reluctant to consider deregulation, as they fear that the competition might cause the demise of their own national carriers. Sampson (1985, p. 290) described the deregulation situation:

> Certainly deregulation has brought some innovations and benefits to American passengers: more entrepreneurial leaders have challenged the old bureaucratic companies, made airlines more flexible, given new motivation to cabin-crews and ground staff, and reminded them that planes are for people. In Europe by contrast the rigid agreements between airlines and governments have too often conspired against the interests of passengers, who are only now gradually stirring themselves into protest.

Deregulation and Hubs

One thing that deregulation did was to encourage airlines to intensify the use of hubs and spokes: The more passengers that could be centralized through a few larger airports, the more easily they could fill up the seats on the longer flights from these hubs. The other side of this coin is that smaller communities have had to become more dependent on the hubs. However, this is little different from the days of the railroad when the larger cities had the main rail termini and the smaller communities were connected to them by feeder routes.

Deregulation and Safety

Deregulation does not mean the end of safe flying, as government agencies such as the FAA (Federal Aviation Authority) in the United States, the CAA (Civil Aviation Authority) in Britain, and the CASB (Canadian Aviation Safety Board) in Canada continue to control the following matters concerning their country's airlines:

- Safety standards
- Pilot skills
- Traffic control
- Aircraft certification
- Aircraft accident inspection
- Aircraft maintenance
- New aircraft certification
- Airport development and safety

Indeed, air travel is one of the safest forms of travel of any time. For example, according to Masefield (1983), if an individual is to travel ten thousand miles a year, before he was likely to be killed he would have to travel for

- 938,000 years by scheduled airline
- 760,000 years by bus or coach
- 497,000 years by train
- 220,000 years by charter or nonscheduled airline
- 78,000 years by private car

Computer Reservations

Some of the major U.S. airlines have established their own computer reservation systems (such as United's Apollo, American's Sabre, and Air Canada's Reservec). These systems allow travel agents to access them to make reservations instantaneously.

Frequent Flyer Programs

A few years ago most of the large North American airlines introduced frequent flyer programs as a marketing device to frequent travelers such as business people. The more these people travel, the more points they will earn. At various levels the points can be turned in for upgraded or free tickets and, with enough points, even for free fly–cruise packages. These frequent flyer programs have tended to create a brand loyalty to a specific airline and have also acted as a disincentive for a regular flyer to try another airline, particularly a new one starting up that is unable to introduce its own frequent flyer scheme.

INTERNATIONAL AIR ORGANIZATIONS

There are two important international air organizations: the ICAO and the IATA.

International Civil Aviation Organization (ICAO)

The International Civil Aviation Organization (ICAO) was formed in 1944 to establish technical agreements for the safety of the airlines, covering such matters as standardizing equipment, training, communication, and security and to foster cooperation among countries on airline matters. The ICAO is also the medium through which agreements are established among countries that wish to exchange airline routes. About eighty countries are members of the ICAO.

International Air Transport Association (IATA)

The International Air Transport Association (IATA) was established in 1945 to promote safe, regular, and economical air transport. The IATA's members are individual international airlines.

The IATA acts as a ticket clearinghouse and ensures the standardization of such things as prices, tickets, weigh bills, and baggage checks. The IATA's main role is setting international airfares. Any IATA agreements on fares are not binding on any individual airline until they are ratified by their national governments, which is not normally a problem. Sampson (1985, p. 93) explained the IATA:

> IATA was much more than a fare-fixer: it provided the central machinery—which ICAO could not—to coordinate and synchronise the growing network of air routes. Its timetable conferences connected up flights. Its committees on technology and safety maintained common standards. It invented the remarkable IATA ticket, which was to remain the means not only of booking seats across the world, but of changing airlines and switching currencies. A passenger could buy a multiple ticket in New York or Bangkok, unfolding like a concertina, to carry him on twenty airlines in twenty currencies to twenty destinations. Carbon copies were torn off at each stage, to be sent back to the central IATA clearing-house—an extraordinary feat of global organisation and trust.

But not everyone loves the IATA. It was described by one anonymous member as "a cartel that combines privately owned enterprises struggling for survival with state-owned enterprises operated only for nationalistic reasons."

DISCUSSION QUESTIONS

1. Briefly describe the history of air travel before World War II.
2. What did World War II contribute to air travel?
3. Explain how the introduction of jet aircraft transformed the airline industry after 1959.
4. Why did U.S. aircraft manufacturers, rather than European ones, emerge as the major international passenger aircraft builders?
5. What effects did wide-bodied aircraft such as the B-747 have on air travel, airports, and hotels?
6. In recent years which European aircraft was purchased by which U.S. airline? Who manufactures this aircraft?
7. What major advantage do recently introduced jet aircraft such as the B-757 and B-767 have over earlier models? Why is this important?
8. Who developed the Concorde; what are some of its problems; and which country is the only one currently flying it commercially?

9. Discuss the development of charter flight travel and its state today.

10. What is a STOL aircraft; where can it be used; and to what advantage?

11. What are hub and spoke airports?

12. Discuss the role of governments and airlines in Europe. What is the one European airline that represents three different countries, and what are those countries?

13. What is fleet planning, and why is it important to both airlines and manufacturers?

14. Define the terms *revenue passenger mile*, *yield*, and *load factor* as they pertain to airlines.

15. What effects did airline deregulation have in the United States?

16. What are frequent flyer plans?

17. What does the acronym ICAO stand for, and what is the ICAO's role?

18. What does the acronym IATA stand for, and what is the IATA's role?

PROBLEM

Statistics from the World Tourism Organization show that tourist arrivals to Pacific Asia have increased rapidly in the five years from 1980 to 1985. Although Europe still has the largest number of tourist arrivals, its annual growth rate between 1980 and 1985 was 2.3 percent, versus 2.7 percent for worldwide arrivals, whereas that of the Pacific Asia region was 4.3 percent. East Asia and Australia/New Zealand are the most rapidly growing areas. However, travel to the Pacific island destinations has not grown as rapidly as has the rest of the Pacific Asia area (and some have even declined in annual tourist arrivals over the last several years). These Pacific islands are American Samoa, Cook Islands, Fiji, Guam, New Caledonia, Northern Marianas, Papua New Guinea, Solomon Islands, Tahiti, Tonga, Vanuatu, and Western Samoa. The total number of arrivals to these island destinations in the south and central Pacific currently is about 1 million a year and represents a market share of less than 5 percent of the total number of annual arrivals of more than 22 million in the entire Pacific Asia area. These islands have limited economic resources yet depend on tourism more than do other countries for their economic development.

The amount of travel between these islands is limited, and most of the long-distance air travel across the Pacific from North America is oriented to Asian destinations, and vice versa. Indeed, the new longer-range jets combined with bilateral air agreements and the privatization of national government airlines are resulting in the airlines' rerouting their flights to only the highest-density and most profitable routes. As a result, many of these Pacific islands are now finding that they are no longer even intermediate stopping-off points for long-distance flights. It is not feasible for each island to have its own national airline, as economies of scale do not allow low enough fares and frequent enough flights. One suggestion is that these islands cooperate in developing a regional air system to serve their own inter-island needs and also to transport travelers to and from the islands to Asian and North American mainlands. Discuss the pros and cons of this suggestion. What might be the implications if nothing is done?

REFERENCES

Galbraith, John K. 1968. *The New Industrial State*. New York: Signet.

Masefield, Sir Peter. 1983. Paper presented at Fiftieth National Road Safety Congress, Royal Society for the Prevention of Accidents. London.

Sampson, Anthony. 1985. *Empires of the Sky*. London: Coronet.

SUGGESTED READINGS

Congressional Budget Office. 1984. *Financing U.S. Airports in the 1980s*. Washington, D.C.: Congressional Budget Office.

Garvett, Donald S., and Nawal K. Tanejo. 1974. *New Directions for Forecasting Air Travel Passenger Demand*. Cambridge, Mass.: MIT Press.

Gee, Chuck Y., Dexter J. L. Choy, and James C. Makens. 1984. *The Travel Industry*. Westport, Conn.: AVI, pp. 184–200.

Hudson, Kenneth. 1972. *Air Travel, a Social History*. Somerset, England: Adams & Dart.

Johnston, Everett E., and J. R. Brent Ritchie. 1981. "Regulation of Air Travel: A Canadian Perspective." *Journal of Travel Research* 20(2): 9.

Lane, Harold E. 1986. "Marriages of Necessity: Airline-Hotel Liaisons." *Cornell Hotel and Restaurant Administration Quarterly* 27(1): 73–79.

McIntosh, Robert W., and Charles R. Goeldner. 1984. *Tourism: Principles, Practices, Philosophies*. New York: Wiley, pp. 443–456.

Meyer, John R., and Clinton V. Oster. 1981. *Airline Deregulation*. Boston: Auburn House.

Mohnahan, Brian. 1974. *Airport International*. London: Macmillan.

O'Connor, William E. 1978. *An Introduction to Airline Economics*. New York: Praeger.

Pan American Airways. 1973. *Total Travel Planners*. New York: Bantam.

Sampson, Anthony. 1985. *Empires of the Sky*. London: Hodder & Stoughton.

Solberg, Carl. 1979. *Conquest of the Skies: A History of Commercial Aviation in America*. Boston: Little, Brown.

Taneja. Nawal K. 1976. *The Commercial Airline Industry*. Lexington, Mass.: Heath.

Taneja, Nawal K. 1981. *Airlines in Transition*. Lexington, Mass.: Heath.

U.S. Congress. 1982. *Airport and Air Traffic Control Systems.* Washington, D.C.: Office of Technology Assessment.

U.S. Congress. 1984. *Airport System Development.* Washington, D.C.: Office of Technology Assessment.

U.S. Department of Transport. 1985. *FAA Aviation Forecasts—Fiscal Years 1985–1996.* Washington, D.C.: Federal Aviation Administration.

Wyckoff, D. Daryl, and David H. Maister. 1977. *The Domestic Airline Industry.* Lexington, Mass.: Heath.

Accommodations

The earliest public houses, or hostelries, were empty huts placed at caravan stops in the Orient to shelter traders and travelers. To pilgrims, temples and religious houses gave rest and refreshment, and this custom still lingers in some alpine hospices. The Romans maintained post stations on their great highways for the use of messengers of state and other privileged travelers.

In the Middle Ages, religious groups operated roadside inns. At that time hospitality was considered a Christian virtue and was evidenced by the establishment of hospices in cities and by the entertainment of travelers at monasteries. Feifer (1985, p. 36) describes an inn during the time of the pilgrimages:

> The inn was built around a courtyard, where animals could be lodged. Inside the main hall, the floors were strewn with rushes, and there were long communal tables with benches; only the most luxurious inns had wall hangings. A single brazier provided warmth, and there was dim lighting and a want of ventilation. . . . Not

even the virtuous spent the night alone, however. Inn guests slept a dozen to a room (more in the servants' room), and two or sometimes four to a bed.

On his travels to the Orient in the thirteenth century, Marco Polo reported finding guest houses, but he should not have been surprised because in his hometown of Venice, hotels were well known and the government instructed the police to see that clean beds and other comforts were provided for travelers.

Inns kept for profit appeared in Europe about the fifteenth century and, in England, were often named after the powerful family on whose land they were established. They were usually built around a courtyard approached by a wide covered entrance.

In those days it was not difficult for a person to start a hotel. Anyone with spare beds in a house was free to offer them to travelers, although guests at such "hotels" may not have enjoyed the privacy that today's hotel guests have. Shared accommodation with strangers was the norm rather than the exception until about 1800.

MODERN HOTELS

The first hotel built as a hotel was opened in London in 1774 in Covent Garden. New York was not far behind with its City Hotel, which opened in 1794. But the first hotel complete with French cuisine was the Tremont in Boston, which opened early in the nineteenth century.

Indeed, the Tremont established a number of precedents. It had a lobby, entered from the street, for arriving room guests: Before the Tremont hotel, guests normally had to enter a hotel through the bar. The Tremont was also the first hotel to have indoor plumbing, provide a free cake of soap, and have rooms that guests could actually lock. However, even at the Tremont the toilet and bathroom were still at the end of the corridor. Guest room plumbing as we know it today has been commonly offered in hotel rooms for only the last fifty years or so.

In the last half of the nineteenth century many famous hotels were opened, such as the Palace in San Francisco and the Savoy in London in 1889.

High Standards

The high standards we enjoy in hotels today were perfected in continental Europe. Switzerland, in particular, has long been known for the quality of its hotels.

Today there are an estimated 100,000 hotels around the world, with about 50 percent of them located in North America. These hotels are large employers and contribute in a major way to the economy through salaries and wages paid to employees. In fact, in the United States it is estimated that currently about 1.2 million people are employed in hotels.

Luxury hotels of the past—and some still today in locations such as the Far East where labor is less expensive—often had a ratio of three employees to each guest room in the property. In other words, a five-hundred-room hotel might employ as many as fifteen hundred full-time staff. But because of high labor costs, most hotels in Europe and North America have had to become more efficient in their use of labor, and so that labor ratio today is more often 1 to 1. Indeed, in some less luxurious hotels that offer fewer services, the ratio might be as low as ½ to 1, or 250 full-time employees in a five-hundred-room property.

Organization Charts

The organization of a large hotel can be quite complex. Large hotels have several separate departments (such as rooms, food, and beverage), each run by its own department head. In a way each department is run like a small business within a larger one, but for efficient management there must be good communication and interaction among the departments. For example, the usage of a hotel dining room can be quite dependent on the number of people booked into the hotel through its rooms department. The dining room must therefore be aware of the number of overnight guest rooms occupied overnight. Figure 13-1 shows an organization chart for a hypothetical large hotel and the necessary lines of authority and communication.

TYPES OF HOTELS

Accommodations can be classified into various types, although any classification is purely arbitrary and can give only some indication of what the various descriptive terms mean.

Hotels

The general term *hotel* can mean anything from a ten-room boarding house to a building with a thousand or more rooms, convention and meeting facilities, recreation facilities such as swimming pools and tennis courts, and twenty-four-hour room service, along with several restaurants and bars with various types of entertainment.

Hotels can be categorized further into convention hotels, transient or commercial hotels, resort hotels, and airport hotels. Airport hotels have recently become quite popular, as they can also be convention oriented and, because they often are far from the downtown area, can offer both lower rates and fewer distractions to convention delegates, who will then be less inclined to wander off sightseeing instead of attending meetings.

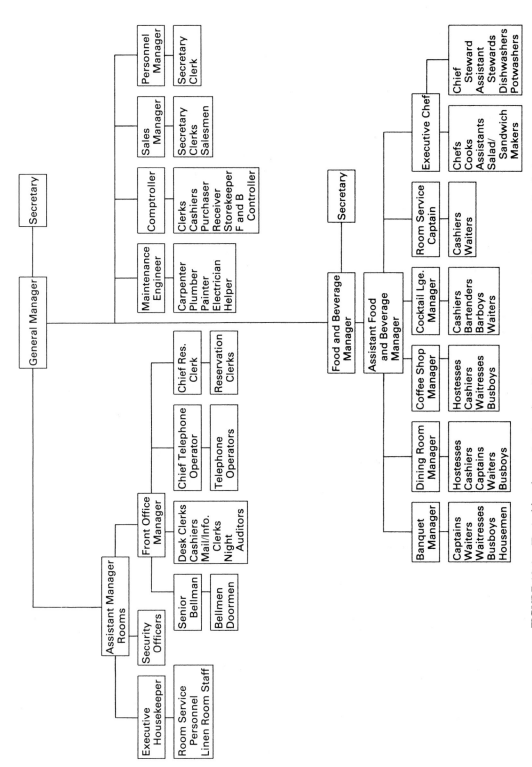

FIGURE 13-1. Typical hotel organization chart (Source: *Cost Control for the Hospitality Industry*. New York: Van Nostrand Reinhold, 1980, pp. 212–213).

Motor Hotels

Motor hotels are generally hotels that offer free parking. They normally have any-where from thirty to three hundred rooms. Motels larger than that would have difficulty providing enough free parking space. Usually motor hotels have restaurants and lounges and sometimes other services, and today swimming pools are generally expected by motor hotel guests.

Motels

In the mind of the general public, motels are simply another type of motor hotel. However, in the industry, motels offer rooms only, with no other facilities such as restaurants, although they do normally have free parking. Motels are frequently found along busy highways and cater primarily to transient, cost-conscious travelers.

Motels are often also found in locations that have many large full-facility hotels. Such locations can often support peripheral motels that cater to their own segment of the market. For example, Disney World and Epcot in Orlando, Florida, have attracted some major hotels, but that area is also well serviced by motels needed by that segment of the traveling public requiring lower-priced accommodations.

Budget Motels

A more recent phenomenon is the budget (or economy) motel for the truly cost conscious. These are absolutely no-frills motels such as Motel 6 and Days Inn in the United States and Ibis (a subsidiary of Novotel) in Europe, whose services and facilities, though still clean and modern, are pared down to minimize accommodation costs.

Resort Hotels

Resort hotels are most frequently found in destination areas that do not cater to the transient trade. They are designed mainly for recreation tourists. These hotels can range from budget to luxury and can accommodate the family trade or even the convention business. Resort hotels may be located in places with natural recreation facilities, such as beaches, or in locations where the facilities are manufactured, such as golf courses. Guest rooms in resort hotels are generally larger than those in other types of hotels and often provide kitchen facilities, as these hotels cater to families, who sometimes stay there for several weeks.

Condominium Hotels

Condominium hotels are a relatively recent innovation. They often are hotels with apartments (condominiums) instead of basic rooms. The condominium units are sold by the hotel developer to individuals who have title to the physical real estate.

The individuals then contract back to the developer, or to a third-party management company, to operate the hotel and rent the space to visiting tourists. The individual owners may have rights to visit the condominium hotel and stay in their own unit during specific and restricted periods of the year, often at a reduced room rate. The developer/management company receives a fee for managing and renting out the units. Any resulting profit (or loss) is otherwise shared among the individual unit owners. This type of hotel generally appeals to families because of the larger size of the apartments.

Timesharing

Timesharing is a specialized form of condominium ownership. Because of its phenomenal recent growth rate and potential impact on the accommodation industry, the next chapter is devoted to it.

Pensions

Pensions are found principally in Europe. They are accommodation facilities owned and operated by a family that usually lives in the building. *Pensions* have only a handful of rental units, but because of the large number of them catering to tourists, they have a large impact on the accommodation industry in Europe.

In German-speaking parts of Europe, a *pension* is referred to as a *Gasthaus*. *Pensions* and *Gasthauses* usually offer a continental breakfast but do not have facilities for any other meals.

Paradors

Paradors are unique to Spain. They are generally old castles, convents, or monasteries that have been converted into hotels by the government and are operated by the government.

Campgrounds

With a certain segment of the market, camping is a popular form of overnight accommodation in both Europe and North America. In North America it is estimated that there are currently more than twenty thousand campgrounds, some of which are owned by hotels such as Holiday Inn's Trav-L Parks and Ramada's Camp Inns.

Closely allied to the camping business are recreation vehicles (RVs), which today are one of the fastest-growing sectors of the tourism business in North America. Campgrounds and RV stopping spots are frequently found in government parks and forests.

Other Types of Accommodations

Other types of tourist accommodations are hostels and houseboats. A more recent type is the flotel, a motel made up of moored houseboats. One of the first of these is located in Fort Lauderdale, Florida.

Classes of Hotels

Although some local jurisdictions rate hotels and motels in terms of their quality, there is no internationally recognized system. In Europe, accommodations are often classified by a system of asterisks or stars. A luxury hotel is in the four- or five-star category (some are even rated with four and a half stars), and economy or basic commercial hotels have only one star.

In Australia, the word *hotel* may not mean a hotel at all but often simply a pub with a few rooms on top, as rooms are required in order to obtain a liquor license.

HOTEL TERMINOLOGY, ROOM RATES, AND PROFITABILITY

Room rates for hotels are sometimes quoted in terms that explain what meals, if any, are included in the price.

European Plan (EP) means that no meals at all are included in the price. This is the most commonly used room rate quoted by North American hotels.

American Plan (AP) means that breakfast, lunch, and dinner all are included in the quoted price. Resort hotels that have no other dining possibilities may use this rate. In Europe, AP might be known as full *pension*. Meals are normally *table d'hôte* (a fixed menu with little or no choice).

Modified American Plan (MAP) includes breakfast and dinner (but not lunch) or breakfast and lunch (but not dinner). In Europe this might be known as *demi pension*. Again, resort hotels, from which people might want to go out for lunch, often offer MAP.

A continental breakfast is offered by most European hotels and is included in the room rate. This type of plan is referred to as *hotel garni* or *pension garni* in continental Europe. Hotels that offer this arrangement often have kitchens too small to provide lunch or dinner service.

The Bermuda Plan is offered by hotels in Bermuda and some other places and includes both a room and a full English or American type of breakfast.

Bed and breakfast hotels might operate on a continental breakfast plan in continental Europe and on a Bermuda Plan in Britain and the United States.

Room Rates

Hotels normally have a maximum rate that they will charge for a room, which depends on the number of people occupying it. These rates are often referred to as *rack rates*, and in some jurisdictions the law requires that the rack rates be posted, generally on the inside of the entrance door to each guest room. But the rack rate is not always the rate that will be paid for a room. Hotels, just like airlines, have a system of tiered, or discounted, prices.

Revenue not received for a guest room (just like revenue not received for an airplane seat) is gone forever. It can never be recovered. For that reason a hotel will often offer lower (or discounted) rates to special categories of people in order to encourage them to stay at that hotel. For instance, there may be special rates for government employees, airline employees, commercial travelers, and similar groups.

For conventions and conferences, hotels will compete with one another and try to offer the lowest room rate possible to attract that type of business. They make this up with additional profits on banquet meals and liquor sales.

Rooms Occupancy

One of the simplest measures of a hotel's profitability is its rooms occupancy. This is calculated by dividing the number of rooms occupied by guests on any night by the number of rooms in the hotel and by multiplying the result by 100 to express occupancy on a percentage basis. For example, if a 125-room hotel has 75 rooms occupied on a particular night, its occupancy will be

$$(75 / 125) \times 100 = 60\%$$

Occupancy can also be calculated for a week, a month, a year, or any other period of time. In that case the numerator is the number of rooms occupied for that period, and the denominator is the number of rooms available during that period (that is, the number of rooms in the hotel times the number of days in the period). For example, if we wished to calculate the occupancy for a week in our 125-room hotel, and during that week 463 rooms were occupied, the occupancy percent would be

$$\frac{463}{(125 \times 7)} \times 100 = (463 / 875) \times 100 = 52.9\%$$

At certain peak times of the year, a hotel will run at 100 percent occupancy or very close to it. But at other times of the year, occupancy can drop considerably. Hotels are generally considered profitable if they can operate with an average annual occupancy of 65 percent or higher. According to Pannell Kerr Forster (1986), the average worldwide hotel occupancy in 1985 was 70 percent.

Double Occupancy

Occupancy percentage is not normally, however, the best measure of profitability for a hotel, as it does not show whether revenue is being maximized. If a room is occupied by either one person or two persons, this will not change the occupancy percentage, but it will change the revenue received. For this reason, many hotels calculate both the occupancy and the double occupancy rate, that is, the number of rooms occupied by more than one person.

Double occupancy is calculated by dividing the number of guests accommodated during a particular period by the total number of guest rooms occupied during that same period. For example, if during a week there were 463 rooms occupied by 713 guests, then the double occupancy would be

$$713 / 463 = 1.54$$

This 1.54 double occupancy ratio means that 54 percent of the rooms were double occupied.

Average Rate per Room Occupied

Another maximization of revenue measure is the average rate per room occupied. This average rate will increase if higher-priced rooms are being sold and/or if more rooms are double or triple occupied. The average room rate is calculated by dividing the revenue for a particular period by the number of rooms occupied during that time. For example, if our 125-room hotel had 463 rooms occupied during a week and had a room revenue for that week of $37,640 then the average room rate would be

$$\$37,640 / 463 = \$81.30$$

Average Daily Rate per Guest

Another useful statistic is the average daily rate per guest. This is calculated by dividing the total room revenue for a particular period by the total number of guests accommodated during that time. In our case, for the week, it would be

$$\$37,640 / 713 = \$52.79$$

Average Length of Stay

In order to increase their room occupancy and maximize revenue, hotels try to increase the customers' length of stay, by means of advertising and other such devices.

Break-even Point

Hotels, just like airlines, often like to know what their break-even point is. Break-even is that point at which a business will make neither a profit nor a loss. In other words, how low can the occupancy of hotel rooms drop before a hotel will start losing money? An equation for calculating this is

$$\frac{\text{Fixed costs}}{\text{Contribution margin}}$$

Fixed costs are those costs that do not change in the short run, usually a year. Fixed costs stay the same regardless of the volume of business; examples are management salaries, interest, depreciation, insurance, rent, and similar items. Contribution margin is defined as the average room rate less the variable costs of having a room occupied. The variable costs for a hotel room are primarily the costs of housekeeping (maid wages, linen, laundry, and supplies).

Suppose that the fixed costs of our previously discussed 125-room hotel were $1.95 million for a year, that its average room rate were $80.00, and that the variable costs per room occupied were $20.00. Its break-even point would be

$$\frac{\$1,950,000}{\$80.00 - \$20.00} = \$1,950,000 \, / \, \$60.00 = 32,500 \text{ rooms per year}$$

The 32,500 rooms to be occupied during the year can be converted to an occupancy figure as follows:

$$\frac{32,500}{125 \times 365} \times 100 = \frac{32,500}{45,625} \times 100 = 71.2\%$$

This does not mean that the hotel must have a minimum 71.2 percent occupancy every night to break even but that it must average this figure during the course of the year.

With any break-even calculation, it is easy to test to see whether the calculations are correct. For example, our 71.2 percent occupancy break-even requirement represents 32,500 rooms to be sold.

Total annual revenue required:

$$32,500 \times \$80.00 \text{ average rate} = \$2,600,000$$

Variable costs to sell 32,500 rooms:

$$32,500 \times \$20.00 = \$650,000$$

Profit before fixed costs: $1,950,000
Fixed costs: $1,950,000
Profit or loss: $0

Most hotels, as well as airlines, have high fixed costs relative to variable costs. For this reason they also have a high break-even point, which means they must concentrate on making enough sales to stay above this point, or otherwise they will have no profit. This is why they use tiered (or discount) pricing.

In the case of our hotel, if it can get at least $65.00 for a room, rather than $80.00, it will make an extra profit of $65.00—less its $20.00 variable cost—or $45.00. There are no extra fixed costs for selling that room at a discounted price, and if the hotel does not discount it, and thus does not sell it, it will make zero extra profit for that unsold room. In other words, it is better to discount the price and make $45.00 than not to discount it and make nothing.

Breakdown of Revenue Dollars and Expenses

According to Pannell Kerr Forster (1986), the breakdown of a revenue dollar for international hotels in 1985 was as follows:

Rooms	52.2%
Food and other income	26.2
Beverages	11.3
Telephone	4.5
Other	5.8

and expenses were as follows:

Operating expenses	36.9%
Salaries and benefits	29.0
Cost of sales	14.1
Insurance, interest, rent, and depreciation	13.0
Energy	4.4
Taxes	2.6

RESERVATIONS

Many larger hotels, and even many smaller properties affiliated with chain operations, have computerized reservation systems, many of them with toll-free customer access. But despite these computerized systems, overbooking still occurs. Hotels, just like airlines, are often given negative publicity because they overbook or sell more rooms (or airline seats) than are actually available. This is done for a reason: If hotels or airlines actually booked only to capacity, they would likely end up with empty rooms (or seats) because of "no-shows"—people who do not advise that they wish their reservations canceled. From experience, hotels and airlines know that there is a typical no-show percentage that can be compensated by overbooking.

Unfortunately, sometimes the numbers do not work out correctly, and the result is disappointed and angry customers and negative publicity.

Hotels use different methods to try to ensure that rooms are available to customers and still reduce the no-show factor. One method is for a hotel to advise that it will honor a reservation only if the customer arrives by a certain stipulated time, such as 6 P.M., unless the customer has advised that owing to airline schedules or other reasons the arrival will be later. Another method is for the hotel to ask for a deposit when a room is booked. On receipt of the deposit, the hotel will give the customer a written document confirming that the reservation has been made. Alternatively, the hotel will ask for a credit card charge number to which the room will be charged on a guaranteed basis. In other words, the hotel guarantees that the room will be available, and the customer guarantees that it will be paid (even if he or she does not show up) unless he or she cancels the reservation within a certain stipulated time ahead of the arrival date.

MANAGEMENT METHODS

Traditionally, hotels have been operated by the people who own the property. In other cases the operator may lease the hotel from the owner and then manage it. However, there are some special arrangements such as franchising and management contracts.

Franchising

Franchised hotels are usually both owned and operated by the same person or company. The hotel operator (the franchisee) simply draws up a contract with the franchisor to maintain certain operating standards and to use the franchise name on the hotel or motel.

The franchisee receives benefits such as extra business resulting from the franchisor's national or international advertising, the use of the franchisor's operating and accounting system, and a link into the franchise chain's reservation system. For these benefits the franchisee will pay a royalty and an advertising fee, which are usually calculated as a flat monthly or annual figure, plus a percentage of annual room sales or a stipulated number of dollars for each room sold. (Franchising will be covered in more depth in the Appendix.)

Management Contracts

Hotel management contracts are a fairly recent phenomenon. The first management contract is thought to have been signed by Inter-Continental Hotels in 1946, but the practice did not become widespread until the 1970s.

Under a management contract, the hotel management company has no financial interest in the hotel's real estate (land and building). The landlord owns the property but has no interest in managing it. For operating the property for the landlord, the management company receives a basic annual management fee, plus an incentive which is usually based on the hotel's gross profit and/or net profit but may also be based partly on total sales.

It was the management contract that allowed hotel companies such as Hilton International to expand so rapidly around the world. Its rate of expansion was limited only by its ability to put together capable management teams.

With a management contract, the investment risk is transferred from the operator to the property owner. The management contract also permits hotel operating companies to widen their investment base by increasing the number of rooms managed, and thus their profits. Developers with no hotel management experience will build large hotels and then turn them over to hotel management companies with the expertise to run them. Some hotel companies have also found that they could divest themselves of the high investment in properties that they owned by selling them and continuing to operate them under a management contract. The Hilton Hotel Corporation did this several years ago with six of its major hotels that it sold to the Prudential Insurance Company of America. It got out of the real estate ownership business but stayed in the hotel management business.

Chain Operations

Many hotels and motels are part of a chain operation. Chains often can, because of their size, use employee selection and training programs, buy major equipment and furniture in bulk, and conduct research on such matters as guest room layouts and productivity improvements. All of these benefits are passed along to the owner/managers of the chain units, who also benefit from chain advertising and a chain reservation system.

Referral Groups

Referral groups have become popular because the individual owner/operators can remain independent but, through voluntary membership in the referral organization, achieve many of the benefits (for example, advertising and reservation referrals) of a chain group without the disadvantage of losing their independence. One of the largest referral groups in North America is Best Western, with currently about 3,000 properties and well over 200,000 rooms.

Lodging Organizations

Most states and provinces in North America have their hotel and/or motel association, and most of these are also members of national associations such as the American Hotel and Motel Association. Most other nations have their own national associations, and many of these national associations are also members of the International Hotel Association headquartered in Paris. These various associations provide information and educational services to their members. When necessary, they also actively advocate legislation favorable to their members.

HOTELS AND AIRLINES

In earlier days there was a natural marriage between hotels and railway companies. Indeed, many hotels were built by the railway companies and were often part of the station building or were located right next door. Some hotels are still owned and operated by these railway companies.

Today, because of the changed nature of transportation, there is now a more natural link between the airline companies and hotels. One of the first links was Pan Am which tied in with Inter-Continental hotels in the 1940s, although that relationship no longer exists, as Pan Am, because of financial difficulties, sold its hotel interests to Trusthouse Forte (a British hotel and catering company) in 1982.

According to Lane (1986, p. 74), airline companies have the following three reasons for linking with hotels:

1. Their desire to protect existing business and develop future business, thus expanding their revenue and adding to profits.
2. The expectation that hotel ownership will stimulate tourism development in their home countries.
3. The desire to expand national culture.

Today there are many airline–hotel links. For example, KLM owns Hilton International. (Note that Hilton International is a completely separate company from Hilton Hotels Corporation which operates domestically in the United States. Hilton International operates in the United States under the name of Vista International, with its Vista hotels.) Other airline–hotel tie-ins are Air France and Meridien Hotels, and Aer Lingus (Ireland) and Dunfey Hotels. Sometimes these airline–hotel marriages do not work out very well. As Lane (1986, p. 79) expressed it:

> American Airlines learned a different lesson during its brief experiment with the hotel business—namely, that hotel managers should run hotels and airline executives should operate airlines. American generally built its hotels rather than acquiring them, so it often lacked seasoned hotel management.

However, even when an airline acquires a seasoned hotel chain, the relationship does not always work. For example, some years ago United Airlines and Westin hotels were part of the same organization, but recently the airline–hotel partnership was broken when Westin hotels were sold in 1987 to an outside group.

The links between hotels and airlines are not always formed by ownership or merger; there also can be only partial ownership, or even simply a working agreement.

Some major hotel chains are not owned by airlines, but by other major corporations. For example, Sheraton Hotels is owned by International Telephone and Telegraph (ITT), and Stouffers restaurants and hotels are owned by the Swiss firm Nestlé. In turn, some major hotel corporations own nonhotel businesses. For example, Marriott used to own the Great American amusement parks, although they have now been sold. But Marriott does own the Sun Line cruise shipping company as part of its hotel division. Marriott perceives the cruise liners as floating hotels. Marriott also owns airline flight kitchens around the world.

Frequent Flyer Links

Many airlines' frequent flyer programs are also linked to hotel usage; that is, the airlines award airline passengers extra mileage points for staying in participating hotels.

DISCUSSION QUESTIONS

1. Discuss employee labor ratios as they relate to different types of hotels.
2. Differentiate between a motor hotel and a motel.
3. What is a budget motel?
4. Discuss resort hotels and the market they serve.
5. What is a condominium hotel?
6. In Europe what is a *pension* or *Gasthaus*?
7. What are *paradors*, and where are they found?
8. Translate EP, AP, and MAP, and state where each is likely to be found.
9. What is a hotel rack rate? Explain why it is not always applied.
10. How is hotel occupancy calculated, and what is considered a profitable year-round occupancy level for a hotel?
11. Explain how hotel double occupancy is calculated.
12. What is an average hotel room rate, and how is it calculated?
13. What is an average daily hotel rate per guest, and how is it calculated?
14. Explain a hotel's break-even point.
15. Discuss the problem of overbooking in hotels.
16. What is a hotel management contract, and how does it differ from a franchise?

17. Differentiate a chain hotel operation from a referral group.
18. Discuss the link between hotels and airlines.

PROBLEMS

1. During one week, a 180-room hotel had 819 rooms occupied by 1,050 guests. Its total revenue for that week was $65,520. Calculate the
   a. Occupancy percent
   b. Double occupancy ratio
   c. Average rate per room occupied
   d. Average rate per guest
2. A 180-room hotel has fixed costs per year of $2.67 million. Its average room rate is $84.00, and the variable costs per room occupied are $22.00. Calculate its break-even point, and prove your answer's accuracy.

REFERENCES

Feifer, Maxine. 1985. *Going Places: The Ways of the Tourist from Imperial Rome to the Present Day*. London: Macmillan.

Lane, Harold E. 1986. "Marriages of Necessity: Airline–Hotel Liaisons." *Cornell Hotel and Restaurant Administration Quarterly* 27(1): 73–79.

Pannell Kerr Forster. 1986. *Trends in the Hotel Industry, International Edition*. Houston: Pannell Kerr Forster.

SUGGESTED READINGS

Bell, Charles Anderson. 1986. "Crosscultural Construction: Designing Hotels Overseas." *Cornell Hotel and Restaurant Administration Quarterly* 27(2): 25–28.

Brooks, Richard M. 1984. "The Technology of the 1980s in the Hospitality Industry." In *Introduction to Hotel and Restaurant Management*, ed. Robert A. Brymer. Dubuque, Ia.: Kendall/Hunt, pp. 116–121.

Cahill, Michael. 1987. "Seasonal Resorts: The Off-Season Challenge." *Cornell Hotel and Restaurant Administration Quarterly* 28(2): 87–94.

Chambers, Richard, Jr., and Elizabeth Craig. 1986. "Hotel Revenue Maximization." In *The Practice of Hospitality Management II*, ed. Robert C. Lewis, Thomas J. Beggs, Margaret Shaw, and Steven A. Croffoot. Westport, Conn.: AVI, pp. 159–170.

Dunning, J. H., and M. McQueen. 1982. "Multinational Corporations in the International Hotel Industry." *Annals of Tourism Research* 9: 69–90.

Gee, Chuck Y. 1984. "Resort Management." In *Introduction to Hotel and Restaurant Management*, ed. Robert A. Brymer. Dubuque, Ia.: Kendall/Hunt, pp. 106–115.

Gee, Chuck Y., Dexter J. L. Choy, and James C. Makens. 1984. *The Travel Industry.* Westport, Conn.: AVI, pp. 206–221.

Gomes, Albert J. 1985. *Hotels in Transition.* Houston: Pannell Kerr Forster.

Jankura, Donald E. 1986. "Why Are Hotel Management Companies Needed?" In *The Practice of Hospitality Management II*, ed. Robert C. Lewis, Thomas J. Beggs, Margaret Shaw, and Steven A. Croffoot. Westport, Conn.: AVI, pp. 179–189.

Jarvis, Lance P., and Edward J. Mayo. 1986. "Winning the Market-Share Game." *Cornell Hotel and Restaurant Administration Quarterly* 27(3): 73–79.

Johnson, Dana J., Michael D. Olsen, and Thomas L. Vandyke. 1986. "Risk Analysis in the Lodging Industry." In *The Practice of Hospitality Management II*, ed. Robert C. Lewis, Thomas J. Beggs, Margaret Shaw, and Steven A. Croffoot. Westport, Conn.: AVI, pp. 393–406.

Lane, Harold E. 1986. "Marriages of Necessity: Airline–Hotel Liaisons." *Cornell Hotel and Restaurant Administration Quarterly* 27(1): 73–79.

Lee, Daniel R. 1984. "A Forecast of Lodging Supply and Demand." *Cornell Hotel and Restaurant Administration Quarterly* 25(2): 27–40.

Lesure, John D. 1985. "1910–1985: Years of Economic Impact." *Lodging, 75th Anniversary Issue*, pp. 71–73, 130.

Lundberg, Donald E. 1979. *The Hotel and Restaurant Business.* Boston: CBI.

Makens, James C. 1986. "Don't Let Your Sales Blitz Go Bust." *Cornell Hotel and Restaurant Administration Quarterly* 27(1): 65–71.

McIntosh, Robert W., and Charles R. Goeldner. 1984. *Tourism: Principles, Practices, Philosophies.* New York: Wiley, pp. 68–73.

Olsen, Michael D. 1984. "Management Contracts." In *Introduction to Hotel and Restaurant Management*, ed. Robert A. Brymer. Dubuque, Ia.: Kendall/Hunt, pp. 60–71.

Page, Gary S. 1984. "Pioneers and Leaders of the Hospitality Industry." In *Introduction to Hotel and Restaurant Management*, ed. Robert A. Brymer. Dubuque, Ia.: Kendall/Hunt, pp. 21–29.

Pannell Kerr Forster. 1986. *Trends in the Hotel Industry.* Houston: Pannell Kerr Forster.

Pannell Kerr Forster. 1986. *Trends in the Hotel Industry, International Edition.* Houston: Pannell Kerr Forster.

Porta, Neil R. 1984. "The Management of Independently Owned and Operated Hotels and Restaurants." In *Introduction to Hotel and Restaurant Management*, ed. Robert A. Brymer. Dubuque, Ia.: Kendall/Hunt, pp. 45–56.

Powers, Thomas F. 1979. *Introduction to Management in the Hospitality Industry.* New York: Wiley.

Reichel, Arie. 1986. "Competition and Barrier to Entry in Service Industries: The Case of the American Lodging Business." In *The Practice of Hospitality Management II*, ed. Robert C. Lewis, Thomas J. Beggs, Margaret Shaw, and Steven A. Croffoot. Westport, Conn.: AVI, pp. 79–89.

U.S. Bureau of the Census. 1982. *Census of Service Industries: Preliminary Report—Industry Series: Hotels, Motor Hotels and Motels.* Washington, D.C.: U.S. Government Printing Office.

Warren, Peter, and Neil W. Ostergren. 1986. "Trade Advertising: A Crucial Element in Hotel Marketing." *Cornell Hotel and Restaurant Administration Quarterly* 27(1): 56–62.

Withiam, Glen. 1986. "Hotel Advertising in the '80s: Surveying the Field." *Cornell Hotel and Restaurant Administration Quarterly* 27(1): 32–55.

Wrisley, Albert L. 1984. "Hotel and Motel Management: The Rooms Division." In *Introduction to Hotel and Restaurant Management*, ed. Robert A. Brymer. Dubuque, Ia.: Kendall/Hunt, pp. 101–105.

Wyckoff, D. Daryl, and W. Earl Sasser. 1981. *The U.S. Lodging Industry.* Lexington, Mass.: Heath.

Timesharing

Timesharing developed out of the condominium hotel concept. The condominium hotel concept was first used with an apartment or residential hotel (an apartotel) in 1963 in Torremolinos in the Costa del Sol area of Spain. Developers later adapted the apartotel concept to the commercial hotel market.

Condominium Financing

For a condominium hotel the developer needs to pay up front about 10 percent of the total development cost and can then begin selling ownership of the individual apartments, or hotel rooms, to people willing to buy them.

These people generally have to make a 25 percent down payment and then take out a mortgage for the balance. As a result, as long as the developer is successful in making sales, he or she will receive, out of the down payment and mortgage proceeds, the full cost of development plus any profit, before the hotel is finished. Of course, this is not always the way it turns out, as developers discovered in the early 1970s when the price of oil caused the prices of many products, including construction products, to skyrocket. Real estate prices, including the prices of condominium hotels, increased dramatically, and the public stopped buying them at the inflated prices.

THE START OF TIMESHARING

Timesharing began in Europe at about the same time that the first condominium hotel was built, but the two were not linked in those early days.

Timesharing began when people found it difficult to make reservations from year to year to obtain space in a popular hotel in the summer. In order to be guaranteed space, guests began prepaying for rooms for a specified number of years ahead to ensure they would obtain the space they wanted for the one or more weeks they wanted, at the hotel of their choice.

Hapimag

As the prepayment of hotel rooms concept grew, organizations were established to handle the coordination of this between the guests and the hotels. One of the earliest of these organizations was Hapimag, which is still in business today.

Hapimag assigns to hotel rooms a certain number of points, based on the class of the hotel, the size of the room, and other factors. Purchasers then buy the number of annual points that their budgets allow. For example, for $3,000 a customer might receive twelve annual points. Each year, that customer can then stay one week in a twelve-point hotel, two weeks in a six-point hotel, or three weeks in a four-point hotel. With Hapimag, customers have a choice of hotels and destinations and may still have to make a booking early enough in order to be assured of accommodation where they specifically wish to stay and for the dates that they want.

Hapimag currently operates in about a dozen European countries, and has about fifteen hundred apartments and some thirty thousand members. With the Hapimag type of timesharing arrangement, the guest owns no real estate and has no title to the property. Guests have simply prepaid for the use of annual time for a specified number of years ahead. This is known as right-to-use timesharing, which is basically a right to occupancy.

Timesharing Leases

Although some other right-to-use timesharing organizations use a point system similar to Hapimag's, most do not. Rather, most right-to-use developers offer a lease on a particular room or suite in a specific hotel for a specified annual time period and number of years. In other words, the purchaser knows each year that the room or suite will be available in that hotel for a predetermined time period for the life of the lease.

FIGURE 14-1. The former home of Lady Alice near Balcombe, England, has now been converted into a timesharing accommodation.

Under a timesharing lease the purchaser can change the time period and the location only by using the services of one of the international timesharing exchange networks. Exchange organizations will be discussed later in this chapter.

Timesharing in the United States

Timesharing began in the United States in the early 1970s when oil prices shot up. Florida developers, unable to sell their "whole" unit condominiums, decided to adapt them to timesharing. However, they knew they would have difficulty selling the concept of right-to-use timesharing to North Americans, who were used to owning real estate, unless purchasers received a title deed showing they had some share of the real estate involved for a specific time period each year. Therefore, the early North American timeshare developers split each whole condominium unit into fifty-two individual weekly portions and sold off the portions or shares. In other words, the purchasers no longer had to pay, say, $150,000 for the entire unit, but only $3,000 for one week of ownership, or $6,000 for two weeks.

A down payment of 25 percent was required, but with the purchase came a title deed that showed that the purchaser had a financial interest in some actual real estate. This deed could be used as collateral to finance the balance of the cash required. This form of timesharing, which involves real estate ownership, is known as *fee simple*. From the purchaser's point of view, fee-simple timesharing made buying a timeshare very easy, particularly if the down payment could be paid through a credit card.

Today, however, now that the public is better educated about timesharing, North American developers are shifting back to selling only right-to-use, just as they generally do in Europe, rather than fee simple. It is up to the public to know which form of timesharing they are buying: either fee simple (real estate) or right-to-use (occupancy rights only).

PROPERTY MANAGEMENT

Who manages a timeshare property if it is "owned" by hundreds of individuals?

Management Under Right-To-Use

Under a right-to-use situation the developer will manage the property, as the developer is, in fact, still the property owner, and the individuals have only the right to use "their" units during the specified week or weeks. The developer could engage a hotel management company to operate the property, and this is often what does happen, as the developer is often knowledgeable about real estate but not necessarily about the problems of day-to-day hotel management.

Under the right-to-use situation the developer and/or management company are free to set the annual budget, hire as many employees as they deem necessary, and maintain the property as they see fit. In other words, the developer/management company is in complete control, and the timeshare owners have little, if any, input —and no third party to turn to if they do not like the way the property is being administered or if they object to the costs of operating it that are billed to and must be paid by them.

Management Under Fee Simple

Under the fee-simple timesharing arrangement, when the individual timeshare owners have title to the real estate, they have much more control over the property. The early fee-simple purchasers normally have a meeting once a sufficient number of timeshares have been sold and elect a board of directors to act on their behalf.

That board is free to decide either to have the developer manage the property for them or to hire a hotel management company to run it. A third alternative is for the board to run it themselves, but this would be most unusual and most difficult, as the board of directors, along with all other owners—other than when they use their units during their annual occupancy period—are generally located hundreds, or even thousands, of miles from the property. The board has control over the budget, the negotiated fee to be paid to the management company, and how much discretion the management company will have in hiring employees, maintaining the property, and committing the owners to other operating-cost expenditures.

Right-To-Use Versus Fee Simple

In general, the right-to-use timeshare arrangement favors the development company. The developer has the right to resell the units in the property at the end of the legal timeshare period. That period may be ten, twenty, or some other number of years and is decided by the developer when the timeshares are first offered for sale. The developer also retains any value that the property still has at the end of its useful timeshare life. The developer also controls the budget.

On the other hand, the fee-simple arrangement generally favors the timeshare real estate purchasers, as it assures them control over the property and its management and means that they will share in any capital gain or cash realized at the end of the property's useful life. They also have control over the annual budget.

Cost and Management Fees

Generally there is little difference, for developments of equal quality, between the price that a purchaser pays for each week of right-to-use or fee-simple timesharing. Today that price per week can range anywhere from $5,000 to $15,000 for each week of ownership. However, some luxury timeshares sell for considerably higher prices than that.

In addition, for each week owned, the purchasers pay an annual management fee, which includes the cost of an on-site management team, office costs, property maintenance, housekeeping, property taxes, insurance, and similar items.

These annual management fees are calculated each year through the budget process and are shared among all owners. These fees will obviously tend to rise in periods of inflation, but today they average about $150 to $250 for each week owned.

Normally, when owners arrive at the beginning of their ownership period, they have no other costs, other than for food purchases, as the timeshare unit is completely furnished and equipped. However, there are some timeshare properties, mainly in Europe, that charge a per-diem fee plus the cost of electricity used during the stay.

When the owners leave a unit, the housekeeping staff moves in to clean the unit and ready it for the next arriving owners. The ownership agreement specifies the arrival and departure day, which is usually either a Saturday or a Sunday.

In timesharing's early days, many of the properties were simply converted hotel or hotel condominium properties. Today, most new ones are specially built and designed for the family trade that needs larger units and plenty of adjacent recreational facilities.

EXCHANGE COMPANIES

One of the advantages of timesharing to purchasers is that even though the individual may "own" a period of time at a specific resort, he or she has no obligation to use it. For example, the individual can allow relatives or friends to use it or can rent it out for the week, or weeks, owned. Alternatively, owners can exchange their time at their home resort for a similar type and size of unit at another one, using an exchange company to help them arrange this.

Resort Condominiums International and Interval International

Most timeshare resorts belong to one or the other of the two major international timesharing exchange organizations. These two organizations (Resort Condominiums International or RCI, and Interval International or II) both were established in the mid-1970s in the United States to handle the growing demand by owners wishing to exchange their time at some other resort. Both RCI and II are now huge exchange companies, each with hundreds of different resorts, and hundreds of thousands of individual owners, as members. RCI and II have offices in most countries in the world where timesharing flourishes. There are also a number of smaller exchange companies, in addition to RCI and II.

Exchange companies are not resort developers or management companies but are accommodation reservation businesses helping timeshare owners wishing to exchange their home resort timeshare for a timeshare somewhere else. It is not even necessary for an owner to exchange for exactly the same time period as that owned at the home resort. The only time restriction is that an off-season timeshare cannot be exchanged for one in the peak season elsewhere. Also, a studio suite in a person's home resort cannot be exchanged for a three-bedroom unit elsewhere. In other words, the exchange must generally be "like for like."

The exchange companies make their revenue from two sources. The first is the initial membership fee paid by each resort joining the exchange organization. This fee is several thousand dollars per resort. The other source of revenue is from the timeshare owners who wish to join and use the exchange organization's services. As members they pay an annual fee (and in some cases an initial joining fee), plus a charge each time an exchange is made.

The success rate of the exchanges is quite high. As long as a timeshare owner makes a reasonable exchange request and follows the required procedures, there is generally about a 90 percent chance of having the exchange completed.

IMPACT OF TIMESHARING ON HOTELS AND RESORTS_____

Timesharing is a relatively new component of the tourism industry, but it appears to be here to stay. It has spread around the world, and today there are well over one thousand resorts and more than one million timeshare owners, each of whom owns and uses at least a week of time each year at his or her own resort or at another resort through an exchange.

One might ask what impact this has had on traditional hotel occupancies. The answer is probably very little, as timeshare purchasers are unlikely to be attracted to vacations in traditional hotels. Some major hotel companies (for example, Holiday Inns and Westin Hotels) have ventured into timesharing, but not to any great degree. Some city hotels have tried converting to timesharing (known as urban timesharing), but again the idea has not been very successful. Timesharing seems to work best at resort properties. For example, one major hotel company (Marriott Corporation) in 1984 created a new company (Marriott Ownership Resorts, Inc.) as a timeshare subsidiary and purchased a timeshare resort: Monarch at Sea Pines on Hilton Head Island. Since then Marriott has added several other timeshare resorts.

Certainly timesharing has benefited the resorts that have converted to timesharing, and the new resorts that have been built, and continue to be built, for a growing timeshare market.

Timesharing has also made profits for other branches of the tourism industry. Studies show that most timeshare purchasers live within a few hundred miles, or a comfortable driving distance, of their home resort, thereby adding to the tourist income of service stations, restaurants, and attractions en route.

But when timeshare owners make exchanges (and about 25 percent of them each year do), they will often exchange to locations distant, and different, from their own. And this likely will require air travel, to the benefit of the airline industry and travel agencies.

DISCUSSION QUESTIONS_____

1. Where and when was the first condominium hotel development?
2. From the developer's point of view, how is a condominium hotel financed?
3. Where and when did timesharing begin, and what was the rationale for it?
4. Describe how Hapimag operates.
5. What prompted North American condominium developers to adopt timesharing?
6. Differentiate between right-to-use and fee-simple timesharing.

7. Explain how the management of a timeshare property is decided under right-to-use and under fee simple.

8. Why is right-to-use generally advantageous to the developer, and fee simple to the purchaser?

9. Why should timeshare owners pay an annual management fee in addition to paying for their timeshare? What kinds of costs does this fee cover?

10. What do the acronyms RCI and II stand for, and what do these organizations do?

11. How do exchange organizations make their money?

12. Discuss the impact of timesharing on the tourism industry.

PROBLEM

A family of four has traditionally traveled to Florida for an annual two-week vacation, renting a two-bedroom hotel suite (without kitchen facilities) for their accommodation. They are now considering the alternative of buying a two-bedroom timeshared condominium (with full kitchen facilities) for an equivalent amount of time each year. Assume that they are looking ahead for ten years and wish to compare the alternative costs of continuing to rent hotel space and buying the timeshare. What information do you think they would need about the costs of each alternative in order to make that decision? What other questions might they want answered before making the decision?

SUGGESTED READINGS

Coltman, Michael M. 1981. *Resort Condos and Timesharing.* Vancouver: International Self-Counsel.

Gunnar, Peter M., and C. Starr Atwood. 1987. "The 1986 Tax Reform Act: Its Effect on Condominium Hotels." *Cornell Hotel and Restaurant Administration Quarterly* 27(4): 32–40.

Gunnar, Peter M., and Judith A. Burkhart. 1978. *The Management of Hotel and Motel Condominiums.* Ithaca, N.Y.: Cornell University Press.

Hart, Christopher W. 1986. "The Nature of the Timesharing Industry: A Descriptive Analysis." In *The Practice of Hospitality Management II*, ed. Robert C. Lewis, Thomas J. Beggs, Margaret Shaw, and Steven A. Croffoot. Westport, Conn.: AVI, pp. 103–120.

Northup, Michael, and Richard L. Ragatz. 1982. *How to Determine the Market Feasibility of a Resort Timeshare Project.* Eugene, Ore.: Timeshare Advisors.

Ragatz, Richard L. 1981. *Canadian Timeshare Purchasers: Who They Are, Why They Buy.* Eugene, Ore.: Richard L. Ragatz Associates.

Ragatz, Richard L. 1982. *Timeshare Purchasers: Who They Are, What They Buy.* Eugene, Ore.: Richard L. Ragatz Associates.

Spencer, Phyllis. 1982. *Vacation Timesharing.* Toronto: Personal Library.

Trowbridge, Keith W. 1981. *Resort Timesharing.* New York: Simon & Schuster.

Conventions and Incentive Travel

CHAPTER OBJECTIVES

After studying this chapter the reader will be able to

- Distinguish different types of gatherings such as congresses, conventions, and conferences.

- Differentiate between an on-premise and an off-premise gathering.

- List three site considerations for construction of a convention center.

- Discuss the costs of operating a convention center, and explain how exhibitions and trade shows help offset those costs.

- Differentiate a conference from a convention center, and list and describe three different types of conference center.

- Discuss the role of food services in a conference center environment.

- Define incentive travel, and describe the role of motivational houses.

- List four direct and two indirect reasons that can motivate incentive travel.

A major part of the business travel market is made up of what is called the convention business. The convention business is closely related to the demand for hotel rooms. Note that the word *convention* is often used for meetings, congresses, assemblies, conferences, expositions, and trade shows. Many people attend these various types of gatherings for both business and personal reasons. For example, the convention delegate may also be motivated to travel to the meeting's destination to see its attractions and do some shopping. The delegate's spouse might also go along and be a tourist. And both the delegate and spouse may visit that destination in the future. For this reason, many convention cities place a high priority on this kind of business.

TYPES OF GATHERINGS

Again, there are many different types of business gatherings. Lawson (1980, p. 188) defines a congress, convention, or conference as a regular formalized meeting of an association or body, or a meeting sponsored by an association or body on a regular or ad hoc basis. Depending on the objectives of a particular survey, this may be qualified by a minimum size, . . . by the use of premises, by a minimum time or/and by having a fixed agenda or program.

He further defines each of the following:

Assemblies are mainly policy-making or legislatory meetings attended by large numbers of representatives or representative groups who may formally speak and vote on the subjects of the agenda.

Congresses are usually general sessions, mostly information giving and the commonly accepted traditional form of full-membership meeting. Meetings are usually large and formal and the word "congress" carries a connotation of a serious working purpose.

Convention is a term widely used in North America and the Pacific region to describe major or total-membership meetings. Over 80% of American associations hold a major annual convention for their total membership, and many companies provide similar opportunities for their staff to meet, formally as well as socially, in attractive surroundings.

Conferences are usually general sessions and face-to-face groups with a high participation, primarily concerned with planning, obtaining facts and information, or solving organizational and operational problems. Conferences are mainly confined to members of the same company, association, or profession. Meetings are less formally organized but encourage collective participation in reaching stated objectives or goals. Numbers of delegates attending a conference may range up to 150 or more but 30–50 is more typical.

Any of these gatherings can be regional (for example, a state or province), national, continental, or international. Most of these meetings are what are referred to as *off-premises*. That is, they require the organization involved to rent meeting space in a hotel, conference center, congress hall, or convention center; to reserve hotel guest rooms and catering arrangements; and often to secure air or other travel facilities.

Many *on-premise* gatherings are held in the meeting rooms on the premises of a firm, association, or government building. The delegates and spouses who attend this type of meeting may also require hotel rooms, feeding facilities, and travel facilities. Therefore, even though they may be less visible in public meeting places (such as hotel meeting rooms), they nevertheless add to tourism revenues.

Corporate meetings (either on-premise or off-premise) form a major part of the convention business. This corporate business includes management meetings, regional sales meetings, new product introductions, national sales meetings, training seminars, professional/technical meetings, and stockholder and other meetings.

A growing part of this corporate business is incentive travel, to be discussed later in this chapter.

Tax Implications

The international convention travel business can be affected by a country's tax regulations. For example, the convention travel business of Canada and Mexico traditionally generated much of their convention business from the United States. But this business was seriously hurt in January 1977 when the U.S. government allowed a U.S. corporation to hold only two tax-deductible meetings a year outside the United States. This restrictive measure was a blow to convention organizers and very unpopular with delegates who looked forward to the possibility of international travel. Fortunately, the U.S. government relaxed the restrictions in January 1981. Now U.S. corporations and/or residents are permitted to deduct all legitimate expenses for any convention or meeting taking place in what is defined as the North American zone, which includes the United States, Canada, and Mexico.

Murphy (1985, p. 104) states that in North America "despite the economic upheaval and recessions of the 1970s, convention business boomed because face-to-face contact and up-to-date information became more important in a rapidly changing world." As a result, many cities began building special convention centers to add to the hotels' inventory of meeting-room space.

CONVENTION CENTERS

At any one time convention centers can usually house a larger number of people than can the largest meeting room in most hotels. A convention center meeting's seating capacity can be in the thousands. Because of the high costs involved in convention center construction, these centers generally must be financed by public funds with the justification that this expenditure of public funds allows more conventioneers to be accommodated, thus extending the need for more local employment. However, the need for full-time employees at a center is somewhat limited. Some permanent management and maintenance personnel are needed, but most of the employees are hired for a convention only on a part-time basis. Nevertheless, more part-time employment may also be required at nearby hotels, restaurants, shops, and attractions.

Many cities throughout the world have jumped on the convention center bandwagon over the last two decades. But particularly for the larger conventions, there is only so much business available, and filling those convention centers is now an extremely competitive business. This is further compounded by the fact that many of the largest conventions are booked years, and sometimes decades, ahead.

Convention Center Location

The convention center's location is probably the most important factor in the success of a center, particularly if it is built for the international business. It should be located with ready access to international airlines connecting potential delegate-generating areas throughout the world. After an international flight, particularly one of several hours' duration, arriving delegates are unwilling to have to wait at an airport for a domestic flight to continue the journey to the convention location. Lawson (1980, p. 185) stated:

> In the U.K. the Heathrow airport area (with a concentration of over 4,000 hotel bedrooms and aggregate meeting facilities for 6,500) has developed a substantial conference business and the trend is also evident around Gatwick (London's charter flight gateway). Chicago, with the world's busiest airport, is also a major destination for conventions and trade exhibitions.

Murphy (1985, p. 106) suggests the following five site considerations when locating a convention center:

1. Site size is critical since space varying from half- to a full city block is needed to house the main building plus possible support buildings along with delivery and service areas, parking, and entrances (which is why airport locations are often favored because the land is available at a reasonable price).

2. The site should be central and accessible to quality accommodation and major inter-city transportation terminals for domestic delegates.

3. The site should be close to major shopping and entertainment districts (which is why downtown convention centers are not uncommon) or regional shopping centers.

4. Plenty of parking is necessary within the center, or close by, again because many domestic delegates will drive there, and international delegates, as well as domestic air arrivals, will often rent cars at the airport.

5. Proximity to recreation facilities and attractive surroundings is important.

Costs

The largest cost to the convention center community is the high capital investment in building a new center. In addition, there are high operating costs for energy and maintenance, as well as marketing. There are also increased community costs (for example, police) when conventions are being hosted, and extra demands on public facilities and services.

Few convention centers can make a direct profit. But the argument in their favor is that they generate extra revenue for hotels, restaurants, shops, and attractions;

contribute to the financial success of those enterprises which will then pay extra taxes; and allow these businesses to hire employees who will also then spend more in the community as well as pay more in personal income taxes.

To be more profitable or, rather, to lose less money, many newer centers are becoming more than just one-purpose convention facilities to accommodate meetings. They are built as multipurpose facilities allowing trade shows or fairs (exhibitions) where the revenue generated by the exhibitors in rental fees paid to exhibit their goods and services can be considerably higher than the income from renting out an equivalent amount of space solely for a large meeting. To increase revenue further, these exhibition or trade centers may contain public restaurants, theaters, and other facilities, such as libraries and art galleries, as well as facilities for cultural and education uses that can be used by the community at large.

In order to participate in the convention business, some communities have considered scaling down the size of convention centers and have opted for conference centers, as the funding for these can often be borne by private enterprise.

CONFERENCE CENTERS

A conference center differs from a convention center by the considerably smaller size of its operations. Conference centers developed from the corporate retreats and remote lodges of earlier days. This new market was created by a corporate desire for continuing education and/or training for their employees and by the fact that this need demanded rather specialized types of facilities.

Types of Centers

A number of different types of conference centers have emerged. One of these is the executive center designed to handle the specialized requirements of top corporate management. Such facilities feature sophisticated audiovisual equipment and similar conference aids run by highly professional conference coordinators.

Another type is the corporate conference center used primarily for a company's in-house use, although sometimes this type of center will be rented out to others.

A third type is the nonprofit center, usually part of a university campus where the emphasis is on adult (not necessarily corporate) continuing education. This type of center may offer dormitory accommodations only to those attending.

The final category is the resort conference center at which there is more emphasis on recreation than is typical of the other three types. Resort centers, during the off-peak time for conferences, will often try to draw transient guests. Recreational facilities generally are tennis courts, a swimming pool, and an indoor games room.

Centers' Environments

Conference centers need to create the right environment for their market, that is, an environment for learning. Apart from any recreational facilities they may have, they will need to avoid any distractions that nightlife and nearby shopping and other attractions might create. They are thus often located in remote, rustic places far enough away from the corporation's offices that attendees are not readily inclined to go back to the office to catch up on work. Their remote locations thus require good efficient transportation routes and possibly transportation facilities (limousine pickup) to nearby airports.

Because these centers have a captive market, usually for two or three days, that cannot usually dine elsewhere, both the food facilities and the quality of the food must be first class. These food and beverage operations also must be based on the conference schedule and not the center's schedule. Buffet food service is often found at these centers.

Specially Built Centers

Although many conference centers have been created from existing lodges and resorts, the conversion of bedrooms and meeting rooms does not always fit what is required. Today, therefore, many new conference centers are being specially designed and built for educational and/or business conferences. These conferences can range from less than fifty to as many as three hundred attendees. If a group is larger than this, the size of hotel required will begin to detract from the needs of the typical conference group.

International Association of Conference Centers (IACC)

The International Association of Conference Centers (IACC) was founded to address the specialized needs and interests of the conference center segment of the tourism industry.

INCENTIVE TRAVEL

Incentive travel is the lure of a travel trip to motivate employees at work. Incentive travel has become increasingly popular with North American corporations in the last few years, with trips to popular destinations such as Bermuda, the Caribbean, Mexico, and even Europe as the carrot. Even destinations within the United States, such as Las Vegas and Hawaii, attract some employees.

Motivational Houses

The fast growth of incentive travel led to the creation of several organizations (sometimes referred to as *motivational houses*) that specialize in arranging incentive trips for the companies involved. Many of these travel–organizing firms belong to their own association: the Society of Incentive Travel Executives (SITE). SITE defines incentive travel as a "modern management tool used to achieve extraordinary goals by awarding participants a travel prize upon attainment of their share of the uncommon goal."

Incentive travel–organizing firms negotiate with suppliers such as airlines, cruise companies, hotels, and car rental companies to establish a total cost per trip, to which they add a markup (usually 15 to 20 percent) that they charge to the company. This markup covers the organization's costs and provides them with a profit. The organization thus acts as a tour wholesaler that acts on behalf of the company so that it does not have to be involved in all the details of arranging the incentive trips for its employees. In many cases the organization will assist in promoting incentive programs to motivate the companies' employees.

Types of Incentive Organizations

There are several different types of incentive organizations. Gee, Choy, and Makens (1984, p. 153) identify the following three types:

1. A full-service organization that specializes in incentive travel and is able to offer a client assistance in developing and managing the incentive program within the client's company, and in planning, organizing, and directing the travel.

2. A fulfillment type of organization that is usually a smaller company that may have been started by a former executive of a full-service firm. A fulfillment company tends to specialize in the sale of the travel portion of the package and does not offer fee-paid professional assistance in planning the incentive program. Compensation comes from normal travel commissions. Compensation for the work of a full-service company is usually received on the basis of professional fees, expenses, and normal commissions on the sale of such travel services as transportation and hotel.

3. Travel agencies that have established special incentive travel departments. These firms may or may not be able to offer a client professional assistance in the incentive planning portion. If they do, they will often charge on the same basis as a full-service firm.

Incentive Travel Motives

Companies that offer their employees the possibility of an incentive trip are generally motivated by one or more of the following direct reasons:

- Increasing sales volumes and/or employee productivity.
- Selling new accounts and/or slow-moving items.
- Introducing new products.
- Offsetting competitive promotions.
- Bolstering slow-season sales.
- Helping in sales training.

In addition, there may be indirect benefits to a firm using incentive travel in such areas as

- Improving employee morale and goodwill.
- Improving attendance.
- Reducing accidents.

The concept of incentive travel is that it should be self-liquidating to the company. In other words, the incentive program should pay for itself through increased sales or reduced company costs.

DISCUSSION QUESTIONS

1. Differentiate congress, convention, and conference.
2. Contrast an on-premise with an off-premise gathering.
3. List three site considerations regarding the construction of a convention center.
4. Discuss the costs of operating a convention center.
5. Describe how exhibitions and trade shows can offset some of the costs of operating a convention center.
6. Differentiate a conference center from a convention center.
7. List and briefly discuss two types of conference center.
8. Discuss the role of food services in creating the right conference center environment.
9. Define incentive travel.
10. Explain the role of motivational houses in incentive travel.
11. List four direct and two indirect types of incentive that a company can use to promote incentive travel.

PROBLEM

You have been asked to advise the local chamber of commerce of a winter ski resort about constructing a new convention or conference center. The ski resort currently has a permanent resident population of about five thousand. For the winter season there are now about two thousand guest rooms available in a variety of hotels, condominiums, and timesharing developments. These have about 90 to 95 percent occupancy during the five-month ski season. The chamber of commerce wishes to bring in various types of meetings during the seven-month off-season and is unsure whether to construct a full-scale convention/exhibition center or a smaller conference center.

Advise, giving your reasons, the chamber of commerce which one would be preferable. Also answer, with your justifications, the following questions:

1. Should the center be attached to an existing hotel or be built as a separate facility? What are the pros and cons of one versus the other?

2. Should the center provide and operate its own catering facilities, or would catering be better provided by an existing hotel with an established foodservice operation?

REFERENCES

Gee, Chuck Y., Dexter J. L. Choy, and James C. Makens. 1984. *The Travel Industry*. Westport, Conn.: AVI.

Lawson, Fred R. 1980. "Congresses, Conventions and Conferences: Facility Supply and Demand." *International Journal of Tourism Management*, September, p. 188.

Murphy, Peter E. 1985. *Tourism—A Community Approach*. New York: Methuen.

SUGGESTED READINGS

Astroff, Milton T., and James R. Abbey. 1978. *Convention Sales and Service*. Dubuque, Ia.: Brown.

Berman, Frank W., David C. Dorf, and Leonard R. Oakes. 1978. *Convention Management and Service*. East Lansing, Mich.: Educational Institute of A.H. & M.A.

Fortin, P. A., and J. R. Brent Ritchie. 1977. "An Empirical Study of Association Decision Processes in Convention Site Selection." *Journal of Travel Research*. 15(4): 13–20.

Fortin, P. A., J. R. Brent Ritchie, and Jules Arsenault. 1979. *A Study of the Decision Process of North American Associations Concerning the Choice of a Convention Site*. Vol. 1:9: *Final Report*. Quebec: Quebec Planning and Development Council.

Gee, Chuck Y., Dexter J. L. Choy, and James C. Makens. 1984. *The Travel Industry*. Westport, Conn.: AVI, pp. 152–154.

Hosansky, M. 1983. "The $27.8 Billion Meetings Industry." *Meetings and Conventions*, December, p. 28ff.

Lawson, F. R. 1980. "Congresses, Conventions, and Conferences: Facility Supply and Demand." *Tourism Management* 1: 184–188.

Lewis, R. C. 1984. "The Basis of Hotel Selection, 1984." *Cornell Hotel and Restaurant Administration Quarterly* 25(1): 54–69.

Murphy, Peter E. 1985. *Tourism—A Community Approach*. New York: Methuen, pp. 104–108.

Pizam, A., and P. B. Manning. 1982. "The Impact of Inflation on Convention Site Selection." *International Journal of Hospitality Management*, Spring, pp. 65–66.

Renaghan, Leo M., and Michael Z. Kay. 1987. "What Meeting Planners Want: The Conjoint-Analysis Approach." *Cornell Hotel and Restaurant Administration Quarterly* 28(1): 67–76.

Stavro, Lisa, and Thomas J. Beggs. 1986. "Buyer Behavior and the Meeting Planner: An Exploratory Study." In *The Practice of Hospitality Management II*, ed. Robert C. Lewis, Thomas J. Beggs, Margaret Shaw, and Steven A. Croffoot. Westport, Conn.: AVI, pp. 515–523.

Tideman, M. C. 1982. "Cost–Benefit Analysis of Congress Tourism." *Tourist Review* 37(4): 22–25.

Thompson-Smith, Jeanie M. 1988. *Corporate and Business Travel*. Albany: Delmar.

Williams, Judy. 1987. *How to Plan and Book Meetings and Seminars*. Berkeley, Calif.: Ross.

Food Services

Restaurants, in one form or another, have existed for a longer period of time than has any other sector of the tourism business. Even in the days of the Greek and Roman empires, restaurants, or taverns, were common. But their operators were often considered to be in an inferior occupation, and for that reason many of the taverns and restaurants were run by slaves. Perhaps that is one aspect of restaurant operations that has not changed over time, as many still consider that one has to be a slave today to operate a restaurant!

In the sixteenth century, British inns and taverns began to serve one meal a day at a fixed time and price and at a common table. The meal was known as the *ordinary*, and these dining rooms were called *ordinaries*. Some of the more famous ordinaries in London were the Castle and Lloyd's—the latter a meeting place for merchants and those with shipping interests. In the seventeenth century the ordinaries became fashionable clubs and gambling places, as well as centers for political discussion.

The word *restaurant* was first used in the late eighteenth century for a Paris dining room serving light, or restoring (thus restaurant), dishes.

Early U.S. taverns and inns were much like those in England; a well-known one in New York City was Fraunces Tavern. In 1834 the famous Delmonico's was opened in New York, and it is no coincidence that the first U.S. railroad dining car was named The Delmonico.

Classifying Restaurants

It is difficult to classify restaurants, for there are so many different kinds. Even a hotel may offer several different types of restaurants, such as a coffee shop, a dining room, and a buffet, other food services such as room service and banquets, and even food service in its cocktail bar, lobby, and by the pool. A hotel's food and beverage revenue can account for as much as 50 percent of its total revenue and thus is critical to its success.

Nonhotel food services can be broadly classified as multiunit corporate restaurant chains or franchises, such as McDonald's and Kentucky Fried Chicken, and the independents that may operate only a single foodservice outlet.

RESTAURANT TYPES

Within each of these broad categories of restaurants are included the following.

Family or Commercial Restaurants

Family-style restaurants offer a wide menu of "meat and potatoes" selections within a medium price range that appeals to an average family income. If they have a liquor license, it will usually be restricted to beer and wine. The decor is bright, and a combination of counters, tables, and booths is common. Parking is a necessity, as the customers (the family unit) generally arrive by car. Location is thus important, with proximity to a residential area with good highway access the best.

A family restaurant's operating hours are usually from early evening to midnight. Chain and franchise restaurants, whose reputation attracts repeat business, are often successful family operations. The staff is friendly and efficient, but not necessarily highly trained. The initial investment is medium to high.

Coffee Shops

Coffee shops are characterized by fast-food service and high seat turnover, the latter often limited to counter service. The decor is simple, and prices are relatively low. The best location for a coffee shop is an office building or shopping mall with a high pedestrian traffic volume. But as a result, the rent may also be high. The staff are often minimally trained. A coffee shop's peak periods are lunch and coffee breaks, with some breakfast business. Hours may run from early morning to early evening or later. A takeout service may be offered.

Cafeterias

Cafeterias require large traffic volumes, and so their location is critical. Shopping centers and office buildings are likely locations. Self-service is typical, with somewhat limited menus of soups, entrees, desserts, and beverages.

Cafeterias often require large preparation areas. Their staff are minimally trained; beer and wine may be offered. The speed of service is essential to handle the traffic volume. Cafeterias' hours will depend on the location (for example, school, office building, airport, highway).

Gourmet Restaurants

Gourmet restaurants generally require a higher initial investment than do the others discussed so far, as they require an expensive ambience and decor. This type of restaurant caters to those who want a higher standard and are willing to pay for it, and it depends on establishing a reputation that will attract repeat business.

The prices are higher at a gourmet restaurant because of the investment required and the slow seat turnover. The menu and wines must be carefully planned, and the staff must be highly trained.

Even though the lunch trade is important to such restaurants, the evening period is often their main emphasis. The location of such restaurants may be important but not critical, as discriminating diners will seek out quality gourmet restaurants. Word-of-mouth advertising and repeat business are keys to success.

Ethnic Restaurants

Ethnic restaurants feature the foods of a specific region or country. Ethnic restaurants can be family (Chinese) to gourmet (classical French) cuisine. A decor fitting the ethnic motif is important, as is menu design, staff uniforms, and training.

To be successful, ethnic restaurants must serve authentic food, which means that the food preparation staff must be well trained and knowledgeable. Prices range from budget to elevated. Beer, wine, and liquor may or may not be served. The initial investment may be high because of decor and staff training. The location can be variable, with the main hours being in the evening, although a luncheon business with lower prices may also be feasible.

Fast-Food Restaurants

Fast-food restaurants have mushroomed in the past twenty years as people have become more mobile. Franchising is prevalent in this type of restaurant. Fast-food restaurants can be eat-in or takeout or a combination of both. Their menu is limited, with relatively low prices. The menu need not be limited to hamburgers and related items. For example, ethnic food can be sold in a fast-food format. Because of low prices, a high traffic volume (pedestrian and/or automobile) is important.

Fast-food restaurants must stay open long hours and generally seven days a week. Alcoholic beverages are not usually offered. A well-trained staff may not be important unless it is a franchise fast-food operation whose franchisor sets standards of service and food quality that must be maintained at all times.

Chain fast-food restaurants have been successful in the past two decades mainly because they have offered only a limited menu. This has given them greater purchasing power, less waste, more portion control, and lower labor costs and other costs (for example, by using disposable paper, plastic, and styrofoam containers which saves all the costs associated with dishwashing). These restaurants have become pioneers in creating more efficient food-operating systems.

Deli Shops

Delicatessen food service, combining traditional delicatessen cold meats and cheeses with takeout sandwiches, salads, and similar items, is now quite popular. Some deli shops may also have limited seating. They are generally located in traditional shopping areas or office buildings and, for that reason, usually are open from 9 A.M. to 5 P.M. or 9 P.M. Takeout selections are limited, and the capital investment is relatively low. This type of restaurant has low labor costs, as only one or two owners/employees may be involved.

Buffet Restaurants

Buffet restaurants are usually established as a completely self-serve operation. However, if liquor, beer, and wine are offered, table service for these beverages may be necessary.

The food buffet is usually an "all you can eat" hot and cold food, one-price operation. Food preparation and service staff can be kept to a minimum. Buffet restaurants cater primarily to the family trade and therefore must offer reasonable prices. Although a luncheon trade may be feasible, the principal business is from 5 P.M. to 11 P.M.

Location is important, as plenty of nearby parking must be available. Banquet and catering facilities may also be part of the restaurant operation. Buffet feeding also is often used by hotels for large banquet groups.

Transportation Feeding

There is a natural tie-in between transportation and food service. Restaurants of all kinds are commonly found along auto and bus transportation routes, but they also are found at bus, rail, and air transportation buildings, as well as on the transportation vehicles themselves, such as trains, ships, and airplanes.

Some restaurants specialize in catering to tour groups, particularly bus tour groups, for although the needs of these groups often conflict with those of other clientele, these restaurants can be quite profitable if they can maintain their market. These restaurants require special cafeteria or buffet facilities so that arriving groups can quickly be fed and continue on their travels.

FRANCHISING

Franchised restaurants are a major component of the foodservice industry, particularly in the fast-food sector. Because of the importance of franchising to this sector, as well as to other participants in the tourism business, franchising will be discussed in some depth in the Appendix.

RESTAURANT PROFITABILITY

The restaurant business has a high mortality rate. It is an easy business to get into, and it is an even easier one to fall out of. In North America, about one-third of all restaurants in business today will turn over within a year, and within three years, 50 percent of them will be out of business. Only 20 percent will survive to a fifth year. One reason for this is that the typical restaurant's ratio of profit to sales is quite low. For the industry generally, it is about 3 percent, which means that out of each dollar of sales, only three cents is profit. As a result, it does not take much loss of control over two of the major costs of operation, food and labor, for this profit margin to be completely eroded.

Food Costs

Food costs are often used to measure the success of a restaurant operation. They are calculated by dividing the food cost for a particular period (a day, a week, a month) by the sales for that same period and then multiplying that figure by 100. For example, if the cost of food for a month were $40,000 and sales were $100,000, the food cost would be

$$(\$40,000 / \$100,000) \times 100 = 40\%$$

In fact, many restaurant operators believe that they should strive for less than a 40 percent food cost, as this will make the restaurant more profitable. Indeed, it is common for some fast-food establishments to operate at a 20 percent food cost. However, a restaurant can also operate successfully at a food cost much higher than

40 percent, because the gross profit is more important than is the actual percentage figure.

Gross Profits

Gross profit is the selling price of an item less its food cost. Consider the following simple illustration of the importance of gross profit when comparing two possible menu items:

Item	Cost Price	Selling Price	Cost Percentage	Gross Profit
1	$4.00	$8.00	50%	$4.00
2	$1.00	$4.00	25%	$3.00

In this illustration, all other things being equal, it would be better to sell item 1 rather than item 2. Item 1 has a higher food cost percentage, but it also has a higher gross profit, and therefore a greater contribution to net profit, than does item 2. For each of item 1 sold with a 50 percent food cost, there is a $4 gross profit, versus only $3 with item 2, even though item 2 has only a 25 percent food cost. There is a saying in the restaurant business that it is net profit that goes into the bank, and not the cost percentage.

Labor Costs

Labor costs are often also controlled by expressing them as a percentage of sales on a daily, weekly, or monthly basis and comparing the actual cost with the standard desired and watching for undesirable changes in the trend of this ratio.

Rather than treating labor costs as separate from food costs, many successful restaurants look at these two control measures as a combined cost. In other words, they set a standard of, say, 75 percent above which food costs plus labor costs must not rise. As long as the operation maintains the combined costs below this level the restaurant will be profitable, and it will not matter how much one goes up as long as that increase is compensated by a decrease in the other.

In a large restaurant the organization of the labor force is important to labor cost control. An organization chart for a large restaurant is illustrated in Figure 16-1.

Average Guest Check

Another profitability measure used in restaurants is the average guest spending, or average check. Average guest spending is calculated by dividing the total revenue

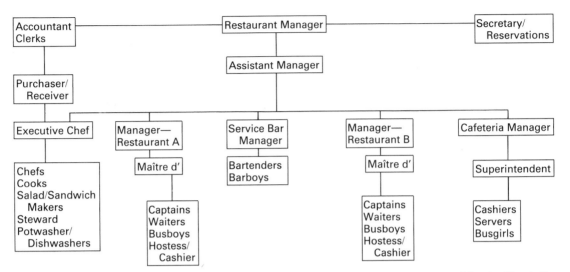

FIGURE 16-1. Typical restaurant organization chart. (Source: *Cost Control for the Hospitality Industry*. New York: Van Nostrand Reinhold, 1980, p. 210.)

received for a particular period (a meal, a day, a week, a month, or a year) by the total number of guests served during that period. For example, if 350 guests are served at dinner and the total revenue received is $3,610, then the average spending will be

$$\$3,610 / 350 = \$10.31$$

Break-even Points

If one knows what a restaurant's average check is and what its fixed and variable costs are, it is possible to calculate a restaurant's break-even point in terms of the number of guests that must be served during the year. The concept of fixed and variable costs and the break-even equation were discussed in Chapter 13.

For example, suppose that a restaurant has annual fixed costs of $125,000 and an average guest spending of $10.00 and that its variable costs (food, labor, and other) are 75 percent of revenue, or $7.50 per guest served. Its break-even point can be calculated using the following equation:

$$\frac{\text{Fixed costs}}{\text{Contribution margin}}$$

The contribution margin is average check less variable costs, or $2.50 ($10.00 less $7.50) in our case. The break-even number of customers is therefore

$$\$125,000 / \$2.50 = 50,000$$

The proof of this is

Total revenue: 50,000 x $10.00 = $500,000
Variable costs: 50,000 x $7.50 = (375,000)
Fixed costs: (125,000)
Profit or loss: 0

MENUS

The menu is the basic planning document for any successful restaurant. Many aspects of the restaurant's operation depend on the menu. The menu creates the first impression about what is offered, the range of offerings, and the selling prices. Therefore the menu's design, printing type, size, and colors all are important. The menu must reflect the style and theme of the restaurant. But note that the menu alone will not do this: It can attract customers, but it is the sense of satisfaction, of having received value for one's money, and the service received that keep customers returning.

The menu is important in several other ways. For example, it can determine the equipment needed and thus the investment required. Generally, the more extensive the menu is, the more varied the equipment needs will be. If a restaurant sells only such items as hamburgers, hot dogs, fries, and soft drinks, its equipment requirements will be minimal compared with those for a restaurant with twenty or thirty menu items requiring a variety of different cooking methods and possibly even some specialized equipment.

The menu can also determine a restaurant's labor costs. In a cafeteria or fast-food takeout operation, the customers expect to provide their own pickup service. But in a family, commercial, or gourmet restaurant, customers expect to be served at their tables, and the more items that are on the menu, the more complex this service can be. For instance, a group of four seated at a table, each having a three-course meal and each ordering a different appetizer, entree, and dessert, requires twelve different items to be ordered, prepared, served, and cleaned up. In other words, the menu can determine the number of staff required and the cost of staff training for food preparation and service.

The menu can also have an impact on costs, such as those for uniforms, purchases, storage and space, and actual food costs. The menu also helps emphasize (by means of bolder print, for example) which menu items have the greatest gross profit and which the restaurant would prefer customers to order.

AIRLINE CATERING

Around the world, airlines spend billions of dollars each year on food purchases. The average spending per airline passenger, depending on journey length, is somewhere between $1.00 and $7.00. On short routes, this amount is less, as passengers may be offered only a nonalcoholic beverage and a light snack. On longer routes, on which two or three meals may be offered—including the free alcoholic beverages that some airlines offer on international routes—the amount obviously will go up. Indeed, about 3 to 4 percent of an airline's total costs is spent on food—not a large amount when compared with the costs of fuel and labor. But for the airlines it is not just a matter of cost but also of food variety and quality.

Food Quality

An airline's main problem is producing a meal on the ground and serving it several hours later as much as seven miles high in an extraordinarily dry cabin atmosphere to a varied group of people, with their own food likes and dislikes and whose prime motivation for being there is to travel rather than to eat.

Airline passengers were first served a sandwich and coffee from a thermos on a flight from London to Paris in 1922. In the more than sixty years since then the airlines have found that a cold-food box lunch is still the best type of food to serve on today's jets, despite all the advances in foodservice equipment and research into food production. Unfortunately, particularly on long flights, passengers expect hot meals.

Logistics

In order to produce hot meals the airlines have to link menus, materials, labor, airplane movements, and passenger loads, all in order to minimize costs. They must prepare specifications for recipes, ingredients, yields and portion sizes, cooking methods and temperatures, and labor for each separate flight. All this requires a forecast using the actual passenger reservations for each flight, less a no-show allowance, plus an allowance for standbys and last-minute reservations, in order to have the correct raw materials, equipment, and food production staff for each shift. Preliminary meal counts are normally prepared from twenty-four to seventy-two hours ahead so that food supplies can be purchased.

Menus also must be selected for each flight so that a passenger is unlikely to be served the same meal on two succeeding segments of a trip or on a round trip. In addition, trays and other serving utensils and supplies must be in the kitchen as the meal is prepared. Some airlines actually travel with a complete set of clean trays and utensils (as well as all the dirty ones from that flight), so that the clean ones will be available to the flight kitchen on arrival.

Airplane Galleys

The first airplane galley was designed in 1936 by Douglas for its DC-3. Meals prepared on the ground were kept hot or cold in insulated containers on the aircraft. After World War II the introduction of larger airplanes allowed them to have warming ovens and refrigerators on board in their galleys. The removable ovens were filled with hot entrees in the ground flight kitchen, moved to the aircraft, and then plugged into electrical outlets.

Flight Kitchens

The first airline flight kitchen opened in the late 1930s near the Washington, D.C., Hoover Field airport. A gentleman named Marriott had a restaurant (known as the Hot Shoppe) near that airport, and he noticed that passengers would stop at his restaurant to eat before boarding their flights, on which no meals were served. He approached Eastern Air Transport (now known as Eastern Airlines) and offered to prepare box lunches in his restaurant for Eastern's passengers. Eastern agreed, and the first flight kitchen was born. Today Marriott In-Flite Services has about 100 flight kitchens around the world catering to 150 different airlines serving 100 million meals a year.

Some airlines have their own flight kitchens, preparing meals for their own passengers. Other airlines are not in the catering business at all. Some will contract with airlines that do run their own kitchens. Others will contract with an outside catering company (such as Marriott) that specializes in airline food preparation.

The trend today is for airlines to turn over their catering to outside caterers, mainly because many of the airlines' own kitchens are just not large or efficient enough. Another problem is that flight kitchens must be designed differently to serve the three different types of in-flight food service: The "international gateway" kitchen must produce relatively small quantities of many different menu items for a large number of customers of different nationalities, each with their own ethnic food desires. The "hub" airport kitchen must turn out vast volumes of food in short periods for banks of dozens of flights. The "spoke" kitchen, which services connecting flights going to a major hub airport, must produce small volumes of meals economically.

Another trend today is for flight kitchen operators not to own their own large inventories of trays and other dining service components but to lease them from firms that specialize in supplying trays, glasses, dishes, and utensils as needed by the flight kitchen.

Differences

Airline catering is not like the normal restaurant in which the cooks are on the other side of the door to the diners and can make last-second adjustments. For example, a steak might be prepared in the flight kitchen and be accompanied by a sauce and vegetables to be served two hours later. During this time it must be kept hot. If there is a flight delay of only an hour, the steak will be so well done that it will be stringy; the sauce will be congealed; and the vegetables will be mushy. In a normal restaurant a meal like that would not be served, but on an airline the serving crew usually has no other alternative.

The logistics are extremely complex, but airlines go to enormous effort to get good meals into the air and even to respond to the needs of passengers on special diets if given enough notice. A sample airline menu is illustrated in Figure 16-2.

B A R   M E N U

WHISKY	JOHNNIE WALKER
	CUTTY SARK
	HAIG
	TEACHERS
	DEWARS
	JACK DANIELS
GIN	BEEFEATER
	GORDONS
VODKA	WYBOROWA
	SMIRNOFF
BRANDY	CHATEAU TANUNDA
RUM	BEENLEIGH WHITE
	BUNDABERG GOLD
BEER	AUSTRALIAN
	including light ales
CHAMPAGNE	AUSTRALIAN
WINES	Specially selected red and white wines from renowned Australian wine producing areas
MINERAL WATER	
JUICES	Orange, Tomato
MIXERS & SOFT DRINKS	Cola, Lemonade, Dry Ginger, Diet Cola, Tonic, Soda
CORDIAL	Lemon, Lime

VANCOUVER–HONOLULU 5 HOURS 40 MINUTES

DINNER

Shrimp Salad
Turkey Cordon Bleu
served with buttered noodles
or
Fillets of Ocean Perch
Orange Grand Marnier
Cheese
Coffee   Tea

HONOLULU–CAIRNS 8 HOURS 55 MINUTES

MIDNIGHT SNACK

Chicken Salad and Papaya
Carrot Cake
Coffee   Tea

BREAKFAST

Tropical Fruit Cocktail
Tomato and Mushroom Omelette
or
Apple Pancakes with Maple Syrup
Danish Pastry
Coffee   Tea

CAIRNS–BRISBANE 2 HOURS 10 MINUTES

REFRESHMENT

Fresh Fruit Cocktail
Yoghurt
Hot Savoury Croissant
Banana Muffin
Coffee   Tea

Due to aircraft space limitations
not all brands listed may be available.

Please accept our apology if, owing to the
previous passenger selections, your choice is not available.
Y 26 TH. SA/9.7

FIGURE 16-2. Sample international airline menu. Used by permission of Qantas, Australia's international airline.

ORGANIZATIONS

Most provinces and states have restaurant associations that represent their members' interests. In the United States the members of the state associations generally also belong to the National Restaurant Association (NRA), and in Canada the provincial association members generally also belong to the Canadian Restaurant Association (CRA).

DISCUSSION QUESTIONS

1. List the various food services that a large hotel might need to offer its customers.
2. Discuss family or commercial restaurants and the market they serve.
3. Discuss gourmet restaurants and the market they serve.
4. Discuss fast-food restaurants and the market they serve.
5. Discuss buffet restaurants and the market they serve.
6. Discuss transportation feeding.
7. How is a restaurant's food cost percentage calculated?
8. Explain the importance of gross profit in a restaurant's food costing.
9. How is a restaurant's average guest check calculated?
10. What information is required to calculate a restaurant's break-even point in terms of the number of customers to be served?
11. Explain the menu's role in a restaurant's success.
12. What is the airlines' major problem in serving meals in an enclosed cabin at a high altitude? How does this affect the food?
13. Discuss the logistics of preparing a meal in a flight kitchen.
14. Who started the first flight kitchen? How and when did this happen, and with which airline?
15. List the three types of airline flight kitchens and the problems of each type in preparing meals.
16. What trends seem to be occurring in flight kitchens today?

PROBLEMS

1. A restaurant currently offers the following four items on its menu, with item cost, selling price, and average daily sales as indicated:

Item	Cost	Selling Price	Average Daily Sales
1	$2.25	$5.20	55
2	$1.70	$4.80	60
3	$1.55	$3.55	125
4	$2.55	$6.00	70

The restaurant is considering replacing the present menu with a new one. Information about the new one is as follows:

Item	Cost	Selling Price	Average Daily Sales
1	$1.80	$5.30	50
2	$2.05	$5.45	65
3	$1.90	$3.75	130
4	$2.30	$5.00	65

    a. For each of the menus, calculate the cost percentage, the total gross profit, and the gross profit per guest. Which menu would be preferable? Why?

    b. On the new menu, suppose that item 1 is removed and a new item 1 is substituted, with a cost of $2.00 and a selling price of $6.00. If the substitution is made and the same quantities are sold, will your answer to (a) change?

2. A restaurant has an average guest check of $12.00. Its variable costs are 80 percent of each sales dollar, and its fixed costs are $175,000 a year. In terms of the number of customers to be served, what is the restaurant's break-even point? Prove your answer.

SUGGESTED READINGS

Berger, Florence, Denis H. Ferguson, and Robert Woods. 1986. "How Restaurateurs Make Decisions." *Cornell Hotel and Restaurant Administration Quarterly* 27(4): 49–57.

Berlinski, P. 1980. "Foodservice: A View from the Corporate Boardroom." *Restaurant Business*, May, pp. 177–197, 304, 306.

Feltenstein, Tom. 1986. "New-Product Development in Food Service: A Structured Approach." *Cornell Hotel and Restaurant Administration Quarterly* 27(3): 63–71.

Gee, Chuck Y., Dexter J. L. Choy, and James C. Makens. 1984. *The Travel Industry.* Westport, Conn.: AVI, pp. 224–239.

Go, Frank M. 1986. "The Restaurant Presentation Mix and Its Relationship to Positioning

Formulation." In *The Practice of Hospitality Management II*, ed. Robert C. Lewis, Thomas J. Beggs, Margaret Shaw, and Steven A. Croffoot. Westport, Conn.: AVI, pp. 363–375.

Greenberg, Carol. 1986. "Analyzing Restaurant Performance." *Cornell Hotel and Restaurant Administration Quarterly* 27(1): 9–11.

Kasavana, M. L., and D. S. Smith. 1982. *Menu Engineering: A Practical Guide to Menu Pricing*. Lansing, Mich.: Hospitality Publications.

King, C. A. 1980. *Professional Dining Room Management*. Roselle Park, N.J.: Hayden.

Lundberg, Donald E. 1979. *The Hotel and Restaurant Business*. New York: Van Nostrand Reinhold.

Martin, William B. 1986. "Measuring and Improving Your Service Quality." *Cornell Hotel and Restaurant Administration Quarterly* 27(1): 80–87.

Miller, J. 1980. *Menu Pricing and Strategy*. Boston: CBI.

Ninemeier, Jack D. 1987. *Planning and Control for Food and Beverage Operations*. East Lansing, Mich.: Educational Institute.

Ninemeier, Jack D., and Raymond S. Schmidgall. 1986. "Budgeting Practices in Multi-Unit Foodservice Organizations." In *The Practice of Hospitality Management II*, ed. Robert C. Lewis, Thomas J. Beggs, Margaret Shaw, and Steven A. Croffoot. Westport, Conn.: AVI, pp. 307–316.

Olsen, Michael D. 1984. "Management Contracts." In *Introduction to Hotel and Restaurant Management*, ed. Robert A. Brymer. Dubuque, Ia.: Kendall/Hunt, pp. 60–71.

Pajella, Franco. 1984. "Fundamental Food Preparation." In *Introduction to Hotel and Restaurant Management*, ed. Robert A. Brymer. Dubuque, Ia.: Kendall/Hunt, pp. 83–87.

Pavesic, David V. 1986. "Cost/Margin Analysis: A Program for Menu Pricing and Design." In *The Practice of Hospitality Management II*, ed. Robert C. Lewis, Thomas J. Beggs, Margaret Shaw, and Steven A. Croffoot. Westport, Conn.: AVI, pp. 291–305.

Porter, Neil R. 1984. "The Management of Independently Owned and Operated Hotels and Restaurants." In *Introduction to Hotel and Restaurant Management*, ed. Robert A. Brymer. Dubuque, Ia.: Kendall/Hunt, pp. 45–56.

Ricca, Thomas D. 1984. "The Full Process of Restaurant Design." In *Introduction to Hotel and Restaurant Management*, ed. Robert A. Brymer. Dubuque, Ia.: Kendall/Hunt, pp. 230–234.

Stefanelli, John. 1985. *The Sale and Purchase of Restaurants*. New York: Wiley.

Swinyard, William R., and Kenneth D. Struman. 1986. "Market Segmentation: Finding the Heart of Your Restaurant's Market." *Cornell Hotel and Restaurant Administration Quarterly* 27(1): 89–96.

Ware, Richard, and James Rudnick. 1984. *The Restaurant Book*. Toronto: Methuen.

Wilson, Ralph D. 1984. "Restaurant Lease Basics." In *Introduction to Hotel and Restaurant Management*, ed. Robert A. Brymer. Dubuque, Ia.: Kendall/Hunt, pp. 71–78.

Wyckoff, Daryl D., and W. Earl Sasser. 1978. *The Chain-Restaurant Industry*. Lexington, Mass: Heath.

Economic Impacts

Tourism is an invisible export; other invisible exports are banking, insurance, consulting, and shipping. Invisible exports sell a service rather than a physical product, but tourism differs from other international exports in a number of ways:

- The purchaser (the tourist) visits the exporting country to "collect" the product.
- The exporter adds no freight costs (although there are invariably travel costs for the tourist).
- The tourism demand is frequently subject to noneconomic factors such as changes in popularity or fashion of tourist destinations, local political troubles or disturbances, and even positive or negative media coverage of a destination.
- The vacation tourism demand (much more so than business travel) is also highly subject to changes in its product cost and tourists' disposable income. It is what economists call highly price and income elastic, which

means that changes in either one or both of these factors can cause more than a proportionate change in demand for tourism products.

- Tourism is not delineated so much by the nature of the product as by the characteristics of its purchasers.

- Tourism is not one industry but a multifaceted product that cuts across many industries, such as accommodations, food services, shops, attractions, transportation, and entertainment. It also affects many secondary suppliers such as utility companies and furniture and equipment manufacturers.

- Tourists can often buy some tourist products at a lower cost—at duty- or tax-free prices—than can the local residents.

- Tourism has environmental and social/cultural costs that most other types of export do not have.

ADVANTAGES AND DISADVANTAGES OF TOURISM

There seems little doubt that tourism offers both significant economic benefits, or advantages, and disadvantages to a city, area, or country.

Advantages

One advantage of tourism is that it provides income to an area. In the case of a country it is an earner of foreign exchange that helps a country's balance of trade and helps finance its growth. Because tourism is highly labor intensive compared with many industries such as manufacturing, it is also a major employer. For example, in Britain it is estimated that each two new tourism jobs create another job elsewhere (such as in manufacturing or farming). If tourism's growth continues in Britain at its present rate, 70,000 new jobs a year can be created. A report prepared in 1986 by the Institute of Manpower Studies for the English Tourist Board stated that more than one million people are now employed by Britain's tourist industry, that the number of jobs in the industry has risen by more than 300,000 since the mid-1970s, and that 90 percent of those jobs are in the hotel and catering sector. This is due to the development of tourism, the growing business and conference trade, and people's changing leisure activities.

Similarly, Canada, a country with only half the population of Britain, has one million people, or 10 percent of its work force, working in tourism jobs, according to the Canadian Government Office of Tourism (1982). Indeed, the tourist business in Canada is the seventh largest earner of foreign exchange.

In the United States over the past two decades, travel has created jobs at twice the rate of the rest of the economy. According to the U.S. Travel Data Center, tourism jobs provide more than 5 percent of total payroll employment, representing well over five million jobs.

As long as the suprastructure (airports, and roads, for example) is in place, tourism also helps stimulate the development of needed infrastructure elements, such as hotels, restaurants, and shops, that the local people can also patronize. Because of the small scale of many of these businesses, the initial capital investment is relatively low, yet this investment brings in a further investment in supporting industries. As a result of this added infrastructure development, local property values can increase to the benefit of both businesses and houseowners.

Tourism creates government revenue in the form of taxes, which can be direct (such as a sales tax on hotel rooms or restaurant meals, airport taxes, airport departure fees, customs duty, and visa charges) or indirect (such as higher employee earnings and thus increased income taxes paid by those employees). New money brought in from tourism also has a multiplier effect.

Disadvantages

Tourism is often seasonal, which means that local businesses must be able to survive on less revenue than if they had year-round tourism. Similarly, employees may have jobs for only part of each year. Tourism also can increase local property values, which may be good for the seller but can be disastrous for a potential purchaser of a home or business.

In some societies tourism can also increase the cost of daily necessities, such as when local agriculture is no longer able to meet the demands of both residents and tourists. Food items must then be imported at higher costs, which will also force up the prices for locally produced goods. In addition, imported foods may not be the same as local ones, which could affect the local residents' health.

Some local materials may no longer be available, as agricultural workers and others may leave their trade to work in tourism. Those goods then will also have to be imported at higher cost. Local crafts people, who previously sold to other local people whom they knew, now have to try to also sell to tourists to increase their business. To do this they may have to sell through a middleperson who, in effect, skims off what would otherwise be the craftsperson's profit.

In some cases, particularly in less developed countries, the government may direct funds into tourism development that would be better spent on social services such as education or health care. When this happens, the country becomes more dependent on tourism for its economic survival.

Although tourism has immense potential in the development of an area's economy, it cannot cure many of its ills. Governments of developing countries must be aware of the costs imposed by too rapid a development of tourism. In the developed countries this is not as big a problem, as their stronger economies are better able to absorb these costs.

MULTIPLIER EFFECT

One frequently quoted advantage of tourism is its *multiplier effect*. To understand this effect, consider the money spent in a restaurant by tourists: To be in business, a restaurant operator had to buy equipment and furniture and decorate the restaurant. The payments for those items will be made to equipment and furniture manufacturers who in turn will pay their employees, who in turn will spend that money in the local economy. The restaurant operator must hire cooks, servers, cashiers, and possibly other employees, who also will spend their money in the local economy. The restaurant buys food, liquor, and other supplies from suppliers who may have to buy their products from other sources. The suppliers also will have employees who have to be paid and who in turn will also spend their money in the local community. Some of the money paid out by the restaurant will be put in banks by some of the people receiving it. This money will be lent by the banks to other people who need to borrow it to finance the purchase of homes and cars. The banks will pay interest to depositors and profits to shareholders.

In other words, in this simple illustration, the money paid by restaurant patrons will pass through several sets of hands, or layers of the economy, and this is known as the multiplier effect. The more layers or levels that the money passes through, the higher will be the multiplier effect. The multiplier effect is illustrated in Figure 17-1.

Some people benefit from tourism money's multiplier effect without realizing it. Consider the dairy farmer who sells his milk to a cooperative that processes it and sells it to wholesalers that sell it to restaurants. Although that dairy farmer would probably not know it, he is gaining from tourism's multiplier effect.

Multiplier Size

The size of the multiplier depends in part on how closely the various sectors of the economy are linked, or how diverse their activities are within the tourist area. When these sectors purchase for their own needs from other sectors within the local area, there will be less need for goods to be imported, and the multiplier will be larger than if the reverse were the case.

In general, tourism's multiplier effect is higher (and therefore more beneficial) to a local economy than a manufacturing plant's multiplier effect would be. One reason is that tourism is much more labor intensive than is manufacturing and thus produces more employee income for local spending. Also, manufactured goods are generally shipped out, and the retail sales are made in other towns or areas, benefiting the businesses and employees in those communities rather than in the community where the manufacturing actually occurs.

Tourism also comprises many relatively small businesses. The revenue from tourists is quickly filtered down to a broad cross section of the population, thereby

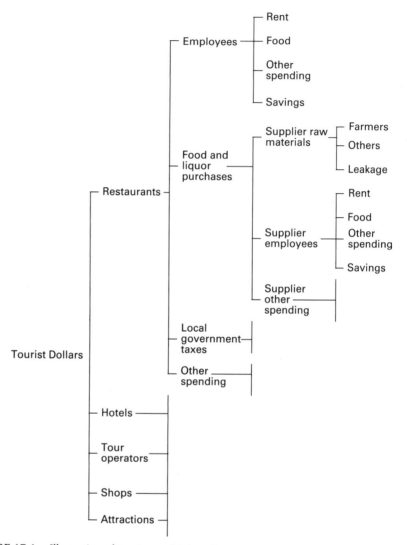

FIGURE 17-1.   Illustration of tourism multiplier effect.

increasing the multiplier effect. In this way the entire community shares the economic benefits derived from the visitors.

In summary, the importance of the multiplier to a tourism area is reflected in the impact of tourism on its economy. The multiplier is an indication of how many times each tourist dollar circulates through the area before disappearing through leakage (to be discussed in the next section). The factors that dictate the number of times that each dollar circulates are the base and size of the local economy, the need to import goods for consumption by both tourists and local residents, and the local residents' habits with regard to how much they save, rather than spend, from any tourist earnings they receive.

Multiplier Equation

Lundberg (1976, p. 157) provides the following equation for calculating the tourism income multiplier (TIM):

$$TIM = \frac{1 - TPI}{MPS + MPI}$$

where

1 = Tourist dollar

TPI = Tourist's propensity to import (or buy imported goods or services)

MPS = Marginal propensity to save (by residents)

MPI = Marginal propensity to import (by residents)

Leakage

The multiplier effect is not completely advantageous, however. Some money brought into an area by tourists will leave that area, in a process known as *leakage*. For example, if a tourist area has to import goods from another area, then money will leave the local area to pay for those goods, which reduces the multiplier effect on a local area. Nonetheless, local warehouses, trucking companies, and possibly importers all will be creating local-area jobs to move these goods, which will help offset the leakage.

Other forms of leakage are

- Commissions to travel agents or tour operators whose businesses are outside the local area.
- Advertising and promotion expenditures paid to businesses outside the local area.
- Rent paid to absentee landlords.
- Interest and profit paid to "outsiders."
- Tourists' use of credit cards and travelers' checks that do not benefit local banks.

The more solid the economy's base is in an area, the less it will need to import goods, and the larger its multiplier will be, as the less leakage there will be. For example, most national multipliers are relatively large, for, at least in developed nations, their economy is generally self-sufficient. Less developed nations have a lower multiplier, as they have to import most of the goods that the tourists and residents demand. At the state or provincial level of a developed nation, the multiplier will be lower than the national one. The reason is that their economies are not as broadly based and they have leakage, through tax payments, to the national government. The multipliers of cities and other smaller communities are lower still, as their economies may be very narrowly based and they pay taxes to two or more higher levels of government.

Multiplier Effects and Accommodation/Travel Modes

The multiplier is also affected by how tourists travel and the types of accommodations they use. Tourists who are on a VFR trip tend to be low multiplier tourists, as they often do not use local accommodations and may not eat at local restaurants. But if they use the local public transportation, this will add to the multiplier. Campers have a notoriously low multiplier effect, as they often bring all of their food and other supplies with them, spend nothing on hotel or motel accommodations, and do not normally patronize local restaurants. Hotel tourists who spend money in local restaurants and use a local car rental add to the multiplier. Finally, airlines flying into a tourist area can add significantly to the tourist multiplier as they buy fuel and supplies, as well as hire employees, locally. In addition, their crews often have to be accommodated and fed locally.

Unanswered Questions

Multiplier effects indicate only some of the gains and losses from tourist income dollars. They do not show the costs of receiving that income (economic, environmental, and cultural costs). Nor do they show the advantages to communities outside the multiplier area's immediate boundaries. For example, a multiplier may be lowered by leakage from importing goods from another region. But what is lost from leakage in one community is a gain to another. Multipliers also do not show that a high multiplier for one region may seem advantageous to that region but may conflict with the goals of a higher level of development planning, for example, the national level.

TOURISM EMPLOYMENT

Tourism is highly labor or employment intensive. This employment is either primary or secondary. Primary, or direct, employment refers to those employees directly involved in tourism businesses such as hotels, restaurants, and sightseeing. Secondary, or indirect, employment is the employment created in the construction of tourist infrastructure and suprastructure or in agriculture as a result of tourists' demand for food. This indirect employment depends on how closely the tourism is linked to the local economy. The closer the link is, the more secondary or indirect jobs will be created.

Tourism Dollars and Jobs

Employment is sometimes measured in terms of how much tourist income is needed to create one new job in a local economy. For example, in a particular area, $12,000 in tourist income may be needed to create one new job. If it is forecast that a new tourist area will generate $12 million per year in tourism income, this will translate into one thousand new local jobs.

Another measure is the amount of tourism spending needed to create each new job, what economists refer to as the *employment–output ratio*. Because the tourism business is not only labor intensive but also capital intensive, a high cost of new tourism supra- and infrastructure can translate into a high cost for each tourist job created. For instance, luxury tourist facilities often cost more to build, but they often also create more primary jobs after they are built, which benefits the local community if the employees are locally hired.

Seasonal Labor

Tourism is also frequently seasonal, although some areas have both a winter and summer season, creating a more stable labor force. One of the solutions to a highly seasonal tourism labor situation that is disruptive to an otherwise stable local labor force is for the tourist businesses to import outside seasonal labor. This, however, creates a new problem of having to provide more local housing. Imported labor also adds to the multiplier effect–leakage problem, as employee savings will likely go out of the local area.

Another solution to the seasonality problem is for an area to build a convention center that will draw conventions and conferences during the off- and shoulder seasons to compensate for the seasonality of vacation tourism.

Other possible solutions are lowering prices and increasing advertising for the off-season or creating special off-season attractions. A more drastic solution is to limit the number of tourists in the peak season, although it is doubtful that the revenue lost from this action would make it an economically viable long-run solution.

Ranking Employers

Which types of employers in the tourism business hire the most employees? The following list ranks various businesses, with the highest employer at the top:

Foodservice

Accommodation

Public transportation

Entertainment

Automobile transportation

Travel arrangers

Tourism employers are in the service business—the segment of industry and business that has grown faster than any other in the last thirty years and that is predicted to grow faster than any other in both Europe and North America in the foreseeable future.

Most tourist enterprises also fit into the category known as small businesses. Small businesses have always been the backbone of most economies, because as a group they are large employers and produce a high multiplier effect. There is no reason to think that this will change in the near future.

TOURISM GROWTH AND ECONOMIC EFFECT

Among economic planners are many supporters of balanced growth, who believe that tourism should be viewed as only one element of a broadly based economy. In other words, these planners suggest that the tourism supply (the hotel rooms to be provided, the restaurants to be built) needs the support of other businesses and that these other businesses (for example, food suppliers to the restaurants) should be local ones. This requires a great deal of economic planning, with the objective of integrating all the various sectors so as to increase the tourism multiplier.

On the other hand, there are those who support unbalanced economic growth, who believe in expanding tourist demand so that the supply will follow. These people think that creating tourist demand will spark surrounding economic growth in the form of creating tourist supply and peripheral businesses. As demand is created, both the tourist industry and other industries will see the need for their products and services and so will supply them, thus expanding the area's economic base.

Coordinated growth is a compromise between balanced and unbalanced growth, and it is often easier to achieve when a viable tourist base already exists and is then supplemented as the need arises. An example of this is building a convention center in a larger city that already has the hotel accommodations available to cope with the peak-season tourist demand but has spare capacity (that is, empty rooms) during the off-season that could be marketed at reasonable rates to convention groups.

Social Impacts

Governments must decide which strategy of economic growth to pursue (balanced, unbalanced, or coordinated) and also the social impacts of tourism development. Indeed, economic impacts really are social ones, as they usually relate directly to the creation of new jobs in the area and to the generation of new cash inflows.

For example, the creation of a tourist base provides new jobs for local residents and also attracts to the area new people from outside who may be seeking employment. These "outsiders" will compete with local residents for the jobs but also will make demands on rental accommodations for their own living needs, all of which will put social pressures on the local community. Therefore, the potential rate of population growth must be considered when developing an economic tourism strategy. The faster this rate of growth is, the greater the strain will be on the community's present facilities and services. The arrival of new people in a community may also have a social impact on the surrounding communities. There are many instances of this in which a healthy tourist industry is created in a primarily agricultural area. Farm laborers are attracted into better jobs in tourism and thereby deplete the supply of labor available to the agricultural industry.

As a tourist base matures, it also changes the skill levels required of those working in it. The number of professional and managerial jobs tends to grow faster than do many other types of jobs, as stated in a recent report of the English Tourist Board: "The need for hotel managers is expected to grow faster than for most other occupations in the 1980s." Unfortunately, for a community starting to build a tourist base, as these skills do not exist locally, many of the better-paying jobs will be offered to outsiders. This implies that in tourism planning some consideration should be given to training and educating local residents for these managerial positions, in order to avoid creating local frustration and resentment.

ECONOMIC OBJECTIVES AND INCENTIVES

The overall economic objective for most tourism development is to maximize tourism revenue and job creation and minimize leakage and other effects on a community. A local government can often do this through incentives and controls so that tourism supply grows in a balanced way as an integral part of the local economy and not in a way that emphasizes tourism growth without regard to the other factors in the local economy.

Controls may be imposed on such things as the removal of cash from the host country to a foreign country, foreign exchange rates, the use of foreign labor, and import substitution to prevent leakage. Incentives are sometimes necessary to help tourist business projects that, without incentives, would not proceed or would be delayed. These incentives can be either direct or indirect.

Direct Incentives

Direct incentives may be

- Nonrefundable government grants that reduce a project's initial capital cost.
- Government loans that will be forgiven or canceled. These are really phased nonrefundable grants.
- Low-interest government loans that reduce a project's ongoing operating costs.
- Loans from an outside financing company that the local government guarantees.
- Working capital loans from the government to meet the project's working capital needs.
- Infrastructure assistance in which the government pays for part of the infrastructure costs that would normally be borne by the project developer.
- Outright, or low-cost, land donations by the government.
- Leasebacks, in which the government buys the land, or land and building, from the developer and then leases them back.
- Equity investment or financial participation by the government for which it receives an ongoing share of the project's profits.
- Nonrefundable training grants from the government to train local employees.

Indirect Incentives

Indirect incentives include

- Tax holidays, in which the government defers the payment of the project's income taxes or other taxes for a stipulated time period.
- Tax reductions, in which the government lowers the normal tax rates that the project would otherwise pay.
- Increased depreciation allowances that are, in effect, a reduction of income taxes.
- Removal or reduction of import duties by the government on goods and/or services needed by the project.
- Government guarantees of stable tax conditions or tax rates for the project for a stipulated number of years.
- Government guarantees of minimum levels of such things as hotel occu-

pancies or the project's profits. If these levels are not reached, the government will then subsidize the project.

- Free or unrestricted repatriation of all or part of a project's invested capital, profits, interest, and dividends.
- Government guarantees against appropriation or nationalization of the project.

Methods Used

The method used to attract foreign investment will have varying economic impacts. Foreign investment will shift the financial risk to that foreign investor. For example, if a new hotel is to be built in a developing country by an international hotel group and the hotel chain handles all the financing, then it will suffer all the losses if the hotel's occupancy is not sufficient. Of course, in this situation, the developing nation may have little control over the size and scale of the new hotel being developed, the room rates to be charged, the number of local people to be employed, and the level of service to be provided. Furthermore, any profits from the hotel will likely flow directly back to the hotel chain's head office (causing leakage). For a developing nation, one alternative is to borrow the funds from an outside source (such as an international development bank). In this case the advantages and disadvantages would be the opposite of those outlined. A third alternative is to have a mix of borrowed money and external financing. The actual financing method that a developing nation chooses will depend on its economic and political objectives.

MEASURING THE VALUE OF TOURISM_____

The economic impacts of tourism are not easy to measure because the various components of tourism on both the supply and the demand sides are closely linked to other segments of the economy. For example, a meal can be purchased in a restaurant by both a local resident and a tourist, and the revenue from it cannot be separated into tourist revenue and resident revenue. Similarly, if a tourist buys an item from a local shop, that shop will also probably be selling to local residents.

Some communities conduct consumer expenditure surveys to separate local and tourist purchases of goods and services. Others measure tourism prices (for example, for the average restaurant meal or room rate) and calculate tourism revenue figures based on visitor counts. Others hand out tourist questionnaires at border points. Another method, using hotel guest room sales tax as a base, was illustrated in Chapter 7. The objective of these measuring methods is to determine the net economic benefit of tourism to the community and to measure this benefit against previous tourism growth decisions.

Any actions resulting from economic decisions regarding tourism growth will affect direct revenues and costs differently and will have different social, cultural, and environmental impacts. Too often plans for tourism development emphasize the use of "free" resources such as unused land, available scenic attractions, and the local culture as if they will not be affected. The cost to these of tourism development is often hard to calculate, as are the additional social costs for community services such as traffic control, police protection, and health.

On the other hand, local residents frequently use facilities provided by tourism from both public and private investment. What are their benefits to the community? It would be useful for any community planning tourism development to ask appropriate cost–benefit questions to determine whether the community as a whole would be better off with the development than without it. This question requires the community to consider the long-term consequences and to acknowledge that tourism is a consumer of land, labor, funds, and other resources.

In this cost–benefit equation, certain factors are easy to quantify, such as revenue to be earned (sometimes in the form of foreign exchange), employment, and taxes, but there also are intangibles that are virtually impossible to quantify, such as community pride. The value of a cost–benefit analysis will often depend on how appropriate the assumptions are. Also, after the event, it is often not possible to analyze the actual results against those forecast, as these results are often based on value judgments.

DISCUSSION QUESTIONS

1. List four factors that differentiate tourism from other exports.
2. Discuss some of the economic benefits of tourism.
3. Discuss some of the economic disadvantages of tourism.
4. Explain the multiplier effect of tourism.
5. Discuss leakage as it pertains to the multiplier effect.
6. Describe some of the ways that users of different types of tourist accommodations can affect the tourism multiplier.
7. What three questions do tourist multipliers leave unanswered?
8. Give three examples of direct and three examples of indirect employment as a result of tourism.
9. What are some of the solutions to the problem of seasonal labor demand in tourism?
10. Define balanced, unbalanced, and coordinated tourism growth.
11. Discuss the social impacts of economic growth through tourism.
12. What sorts of economic controls can a government impose to maximize tourism revenue and job creation, while minimizing leakage?

13. Give five examples of direct government incentives for tourism development.

14. Give four examples of indirect government incentives for tourism development.

15. Discuss the cost–benefit analysis of tourism's value.

16. Some Caribbean tourist countries impose a high import duty on everything coming in to the country. Why do you think they do this?

17. Why do you think that high-spending tourists sometimes benefit the local community the least?

PROBLEMS

1. The tourism minister of a small developing country has asked your advice on ways in which it could attract external funding to construct needed accommodation facilities. Suggest to him what you think might be the three most useful direct and the three most useful indirect incentives, and for each incentive cite possible advantages and disadvantages.

2. Assume you have been recently appointed as the tourism minister of a newly formed ministry of tourism in a developing country. As a new ministry it must compete vigorously with other long-established ministries for available government funds. List and discuss the reasons you would use to argue in favor of funding and government support for your new ministry.

REFERENCES

Canadian Government Office of Tourism. 1982. *Tourism Is Important to All of Us*. Ottawa: Canadian Government Office of Tourism.

Institute of Manpower Studies. 1986. *Jobs in Tourism and Leisure*. London: English Tourist Board.

Lundberg, Donald E. 1976. *The Tourist Business*. Boston: CBI.

SUGGESTED READINGS

British Tourist Authority. 1981. *The Economic Significance of Tourism Within the European Community*. London: British Tourist Authority.

Butler, R. W. 1974. "The Social Implications of Tourist Developments." *Annals of Tourism Research* 2(2): 100–111.

Dearden, P. 1983. "Tourism and the Resource Base." In *Tourism in Canada: Selected Issues and Options*, ed. P. E. Murphy. Victoria: University of Victoria Western Geographical Series 21, pp. 75–93.

De Kadt, Emanuel. 1979. "Social Planning for Tourism in the Developing Countries." *Annals of Tourism Research* 6(1): 36–48.

Diamond, J. 1977. "Tourism's Role in Economic Development: The Case Re-examined." *Economic Development and Cultural Change* 25: 539–553.

Farrell, Bryan H. 1977. "The Social and Economic Impact of Tourism on Pacific Communities," a paper produced for the Center for South Pacific Studies. Santa Cruz: University of California.

Gee, Chuck Y., Dexter J. L. Choy, and James C. Makens. 1984. *The Travel Industry.* Westport, Conn.: AVI, pp. 106–113.

Jafari, Jafar. 1973. *Role of Tourism on Socio-Economic Transformation of Developing Countries.* Menomonie: University of Wisconsin at Stout.

Lesure, John D. 1985. "1910–1985: Years of Economic Impact." *Lodging, 75th Anniversary Issue*, June, pp. 71–73, 130.

Mak, James, and Edward Nishimura. "The Economics of a Hotel Room Tax." *Journal of Travel Research* 17(4): 2–6.

Mathieson, Alister, and Geoffrey Wall. 1982. *Tourism: Economic, Physical and Social Impacts.* London: Longmans.

McIntosh, Robert W., and Charles R. Goeldner. 1984. *Tourism: Principles, Practices, Philosophies.* New York: Wiley, pp. 189–201, 225–231, 395–435.

Murphy, Peter E. 1985. *Tourism—A Community Approach.* New York: Methuen, pp. 77–103.

Pizam, A. 1978. "Tourism's Impacts: The Social Costs to the Destination Community As Perceived by Its Residents." *Journal of Travel Research* 16(4): 8–12.

U.S. Travel Data Center. 1985. *Impact of Foreign Visitors on State Economies.* Washington, D.C.: U.S. Travel Data Center.

World Tourism Organization. 1981. *Tourism Multipliers Explained.* Madrid: WTO.

World Tourism Organization. Annual. *Economic Review of World Tourism.* Madrid: WTO.

18

Environmental Impacts

CHAPTER OBJECTIVES

After studying this chapter the reader will be able to

- Discuss possible solutions to minimize tourism's environmental stress.

- Discuss the arguments for and against tourism's effect on the environment.

- Discuss the environmental impact as tourism radiates out from a central core.

- Explain environmental terms such as the *intensity of tourism development*, the *time horizon of the developer*, and the *resiliency of the environment.*

- Give two examples of areas that should be completely protected from tourism.

- Differentiate between protecting the environment for tourism and protecting it from tourism.

- Discuss some of the special problems of trying to protect parks from too much tourism.

- Define the term *carrying capacity* with reference to environmental protection.

- Select a tourism area of your choice, and discuss its effect on its environment.

Tourism communities often perceive tourism as a relatively nonpolluting growth industry that creates many supporting businesses and is highly labor intensive. However, there is no question that tourism changes the environment. Rather, the question is whether tourism developers improve the natural environment or impose on it an undesirable transformation. But this problem is not unique to tourism. For example, creating a new industrial area or logging a forested area also can have an environmental impact.

∪THE PROBLEM

The competition for tourists is keen and has resulted in the governments' and others' becoming more aware of tourism's effect on the environment and more concerned that the tourist product protect local resources for the continued enjoyment of both tourists and residents. When the number or intensity of tourists exceeds an area's physical ability to cope with them, there is bound to be a deterioration in basic natural resources such as land and water. Frequently this deterioration can be forecast by earlier events that are indicative of strain. For example, when conflicts or hostilities arise between locals and tourists over the use of local facilities, then the overcapacity of tourism is beginning to show. This can occur when local people start to complain vigorously about such matters as traffic congestion and lack of parking spaces, but it can also be manifested in complaints about the lack of park or beach space.

Some Solutions

Sometimes these complaints can be resolved by having a number of nearby tourist destinations work together to help disperse the tourists. Another tactic is to increase the supply of facilities at a destination area so as to spread out the demand and reduce crowding. Another method is to use zoning within a destination area to help separate tourists from locals and guide tourists to specific zones where there will be less conflict with local residents and any environmental stress can be restricted to those zones.

Finally, when automobile congestion is severe because of too many "windshield" tourists, those automobile tourists can be encouraged to park their cars in designated areas and then walk or use public transportation to reach local attractions. Many parks, in particular, use this method to minimize environmental impacts.

Matching Supply to Demand

An initial logical reaction by tourist planners when signs of environmental stress begin to show is to increase the tourist capacity. When private sector entrepreneurs are free to build more hotels, condominiums, restaurants, and attractions, this is a natural response. But when governments can control capacity, they can limit it.

PROS AND CONS OF TOURISM'S EFFECT

One of the arguments in favor of tourism is that uncontrolled urbanization, modernization, and other forms of industrialization do great damage to the natural environment and the people living in it. This is particularly true of uncontrolled urbanization in developing countries that have a poor water supply, inadequate sanitation and sewage, and other problems that create sickness, disease, and even malnutrition. Controlled tourism development can help avoid these problems. But many of these developing countries lack both the incentive and the money to preserve their natural environment and/or their historic sites. Indeed, some controlled modernization and urbanization may be necessary to attract tourists.

If tourism is planned properly, then the problems of uncontrolled modernization may be avoided, and tourism can provide the motive to preserve natural settings and historic buildings, as well as provide the economic benefits outlined in the previous chapter. Controlled tourism can also make the local population appreciate their environment, their culture, and/or their historic buildings.

Arguments Against Tourism

Arguments against tourism are that it requires a physical infrastructure of roads, airports, sewers, and other facilities, as well as a suprastructure of hotels, restaurants, and entertainment places that normal growth would not require. These structures do damage the natural local environment, as suprastructure developers, in particular, race to build on the best sites without concern for the environment. In this process tourist sites may be drastically changed.

Tourists also often expect more amenities than do the local people, which requires more infra- and suprastructure development than would otherwise be necessary. There is also environmental noise pollution from jet aircraft and other traffic that deprives an area of its former tranquillity.

Can We Cope with Tourism?

An example of how the environment can survive and even be enhanced by tourism is the restoration of colonial Williamsburg in Virginia. Examples of major environmental preservation include the Serengeti Park in East Africa, and the Galapagos Islands, which are six hundred miles west of Latin America and owned by Ecuador. Ecuador has imposed a form of controlled tourism (by limiting the number of tourists who may travel there) to ensure that damage to the islands' environment is minimized.

Control is the critical element. Tourism development generally starts with a core and then moves slowly outward with its commercialization. This can destroy the environment but can also, in some cases, help restore historic sites. For example, forty years ago the Castle of Chillon near the tourist town of Montreux, Switzerland, was visited by no one. It was just a moldy, uninhabited, decaying building that would have cost a fortune to renovate for no specific purpose. The castle, built between the ninth and the thirteenth centuries, had been made famous in Byron's poem *The Prisoner of Chillon* but since had been forgotten. With the expansion of Montreux as tourism increased, a new highway was built that passed near the castle, and today the castle is a government museum visited each day by busload after busload of tourists.

Urbanization causes villages to become towns, and towns to become cities, and the original urban-core buildings and attractions can become something other than what they originally were. An extreme example of this is in Hawaii, where Waikiki has been converted in the last fifty years from a relatively peaceful beach area with one or two Hawaiian-style hotels into an overcommercialized, noisy center of contrived activity that is as different from the Hawaiian life-style as could be imagined.

FIGURE 18-1. The Castle of Chillon near Montreux, Switzerland, was "saved" by tourism.

But Hawaii has had land development laws for longer than any other state in the United States. The state is divided into four areas: conservation, agriculture, rural, and urban. Most tourism and other development is allowed only in the compact urban areas, such as Waikiki, so as to protect the other three areas. Controls have now also been placed on any further growth of tourism in Waikiki.

FIGURE 18-2. Hotels crowd Hawaii's Waikiki beachfront.

FACTORS AFFECTING ENVIRONMENTAL IMPACT

Several factors influence the degree to which tourism will affect a local environment.

Intensity of Tourist Development

One factor is the intensity or amount of tourist development, which is dictated by the number of tourists, how long they stay, the facilities available to them, and the things they want to do. If tourists can be spread over a larger area without damaging it, then the tourism will be less intense. In Austria, the majority of tourists are German, who, because they enjoy walking and hiking, like to stay in *Gasthauses* in the numerous smaller towns and villages in the Austrian Alps. At night they generally stay in or go for a stroll and make no demands for nightlife. The German tourists are well dispersed throughout the country, need little in the way of infrastructure, and demand little in the way of suprastructure. Even though they stay in an area for a week or two, the intensity of development they require is extremely low.

At the other end of the intensity scale is Waikiki where controlled high intensity is allowed within certain boundaries: the ocean on the south, the zoo and Kapiolani Park on the east, and the Ala Wai canal on the north and west. Another example of permitted intense tourism is Innsbruck in the Tyrolean Alps of Austria. In Innsbruck virtually all tourists are confined to an area in and immediately adjacent to the eight-hundred-year-old city core. This area is bounded to the west by a residential area, to the south by the main intercity railway station and trackage, to the north by the Inn River, and immediately to the east of the old city by a park and other green areas. Most of the hotels, shops, restaurants, historic sites, and other tourist attractions are within this one-square-mile area. The park next to the core is hidden behind a high brick wall and is not revealed to tourists who do not accidentally wander into it. Indeed, a stroll through this peaceful park shows that it is patronized primarily by local families out for a walk, a peaceful afternoon reading on a park bench, or a game of outdoor chess. Seldom are tourists seen, and the local people are well protected from the masses of passengers who are disgorged daily from the endlessly arriving tour buses that park immediately outside the park gates.

Rapid and intense tourist development can cause a short-term local boom. It can attract migrant workers from the surrounding countryside who, after the boom, are unable to find work and may become slum squatters. An example of this can be seen in Acapulco, Mexico, where in effect there are now two Acapulcos—the tourist one and the ghetto.

A tourist area can, however, undergo rapid development without doing great harm to the environment. An example of this is Disney World/Epcot in Orlando, Florida. Developed in an area that previously was a swamp, Disney World has, obviously, changed the environment, but only minimally and not in a way that is displeasing to most people. The development is well spread out and is far enough away from the city of Orlando that it is not attached to that city.

This type of unintensive tourist development can be organized only with careful cooperation between the developers and several levels of government to ensure that no striking natural attractions are spoiled.

Time Horizon of the Tourist Developer

The time horizon of the tourist developer also can affect an area's environment. Speculative developers who care little for the local environment and are interested only in making the most money in the least time do the most damage. They will grab the most desirable development sites, build on them high-rise hotels that block the view and access to the beach of those farther back, and often end up creating an environment that is not attractive even to tourists.

Resiliency of the Environment

The third effect that tourism can have on the environment is on its resiliency. Big tourist-oriented cities such as New York, London, and Paris seem best able to absorb hordes of tourists in the peak season and to return to their normal way of life in the off-season. But even these large cities are often overcrowded in the high season. Furthermore, if city planners allow tourism to continue to grow unchecked, with more and more residences converted into bed and breakfast places, and more and more sites turned over to hotel construction, then even in these large cities life may never be able to return to normal in the off-season.

Some areas do not have any resiliency at all; intensive tourism development in a previously tranquil countryside or beach area can cause irreversible damage. Accordingly, some areas should be completely protected from tourism. Consider the Great Barrier Reef in Australia. Coral is a living animal, and if unchecked tourist development is allowed in this part of Australia, and tourists are given uncontrolled access to the reefs, they can end up killing the very thing that attracted them in the first place. Coral reefs, small islands, and other areas have extremely delicate ecosystems that have to be protected from tourism, as they do not have the ability to recover from major damage.

MANAGEMENT OF THE ENVIRONMENT

Management of the environment is required for its own protection and can occur only at government levels. The government's task is to make people, including developers, more aware of their environmental responsibilities and, when necessary, to impose controls. These controls can be general protective measures such as the protection of rare or endangered plants and animals and the preservation of public amenities such as beaches, parks, and wilderness areas while still allowing the tourists to use them. The objective of this approach is to protect the environment *for* tourism.

A stricter level of government involvement is regulation to prevent tourism's growth, with the objective of protecting the environment *from* intensive tourist use and short-range environmental exploitation by developers. But environmental management has a high cost, for it requires a great deal of planning and implementation. Some people suggest that revenue from tourism should help pay for this planning, but setting up a financial mechanism to do this would be difficult.

Environmental Costs

In summary, the environmental costs of tourism can be any or all of the following:

- Increased levels of general congestion and pollution and the costs of controlling them.
- Changes in the natural environment and ecological balance.
- Lessening of the environment's natural attraction and even the loss of wilderness areas.
- Resulting costs of creating new conservation or wilderness areas or other environmental enhancement areas.
- Resulting costs of taking retroactive measures, if it is not too late, to preserve historic and cultural sites.

PROTECTION FOR PARKS

Perhaps the need for environmental concerns and controls is best illustrated by a discussion of park planning. The greatest demand on parks' natural tourist resources occurs when they have great scenic attractions, recreational opportunities, and good road access. Tourist growth in parks must be controlled to prevent their being overrun. Without control, tourist activities will change the landscape and wildlife as trees are cleared for parking areas, campsites, and trails and the land is used for unnatural purposes, compacting the soil and changing ground cover vegetation. The growth in the number of government-operated parks in North America has been impressive, but it has failed to keep up with demand, especially in the eastern states and provinces. The signs of the parks' physical deterioration are clear.

Parks Dilemma

The dilemma for those who control the parks is whether to preserve the parks' integrity or natural environment or to concede to demand and make them even more accessible to tourists. Reconciling these two conflicts is difficult enough, but often there is another conflict with businesses that wish to use the parks' resources, by logging trees or mining minerals. The loss of revenue in government taxes if commercial interests are prohibited simply adds to the extremely high costs of operating these parks.

In other cases, wilderness parks face a further problem. This has occurred, for example, in Alaska and British Columbia where the competition for the wilderness areas by both commercial interests and tourists has become so intense that native Americans have started to make demands to exclude both parties so as to protect their heritage.

Defining the Purpose of Parks

What governments must do with regard to parks is first to define the role they must play and what part tourism will take in this role. The decision is between conserving the wilderness for future generations and developing it for tourists today. If the decision is solely in favor of tourist development, it can be based only on the assumption that tourism is a nonconsuming activity. But tourism can cause an environmental deterioration (that is, consumption) of the wilderness if it exceeds the park's capacity to cope with it. Parks Canada in 1980 established the following objectives for Canada's national parks:

> To protect for all time those places which are significant examples of Canada's natural and cultural heritage and also to encourage public understanding, appreciation and enjoyment of this heritage in ways which leave it unimpaired for future generations.

One strategy for achieving such a goal and reducing the potential environmental damage to parks is for the government to expand recreational opportunities elsewhere. The Canadian government has done this by taking over the administration and promotion of historic parks that were previously operated by others.

In Britain where a relatively large population is concentrated into a small geographic area compared with that of the United States or Canada, the demands on parks have been even more intense. For this reason, areas of unique natural beauty, which include both inland parks and coastal areas, receive special consideration and are added to the country's inventory of recreation areas to be conserved in as natural a state as possible. The government also instituted a policy of creating "honeypot" parks, or small regional country parks designed to divert automobile tourists away from major parks needing more protection. These honeypot parks are designed with a variety of attractions for family recreation. They are located mainly near larger urban areas so that they can provide a day's outing without requiring families to drive longer distances and to use a campsite for an overnight stay before returning home. But because the demand to use parks is constantly increasing, such buffer parks can only slow down the demand for park space.

An alternative solution is to keep as many vehicles as possible out of parks. For example, Yosemite National Park in California instituted a park and ride system. Day visitors are required to park at the entrance to the park valley's narrow gorge and view the gorge and falls by using a shuttle bus system. Only campers and other overnight guests who have reservations are allowed to take their vehicles into the park.

Park Zoning

Another way of preserving parks is to use the same strategy of zoning used in urban areas. In other words, some park areas are set aside for complete preservation and other parts for recreation. Zoning is a useful method for separating parks into specific areas to reduce the conservation-versus-tourism conflict. It is possible that —as in some situations in urban planning—the zoning can become an end in itself rather than the means to an end. This might then cause an inflexible park classification that cannot be changed when change may be necessary. A need for change may be caused by such things as altered wildlife migration patterns, natural "disasters" such as forest fires, or changed tourist patterns such as more campers and fewer bus tours.

Parks and Skiing

Parks are particularly vulnerable when they are also popular ski destinations. During the winter months there *appears* to be little environmental damage, as the ground is covered with snow. But to create ski runs, trees may have had to be cut down, and under the ski runs there can be substantial vegetation damage and soil erosion where the runs have been packed down. This deterioration becomes visible only during the summer months.

Governments at all levels must also cooperate in environmental protection. There is little point in a national government's imposing restrictions or controls on tourist growth within the parks that come under its jurisdiction if that simply imposes more tourist pressures on parks administered by lower levels of government.

A SOLUTION TO CARRYING CAPACITY

Finally, Murphy (1985, p. 66) suggested a carrying-capacity approach to help identify and assess the environmental compatibility of tourist areas in both parks and other tourist destinations. There are three steps:

First, to facilitate tourists' satisfaction a destination has to review visitor needs and activity patterns. This will develop different experience zones for different visitor types. Second, to establish or maintain a high quality environment requires information relating to the physical and biological carrying capacity of the experience zones, particularly the sensitive and more popular ones. Third, combining the first two steps into environmental experience zones will indicate the degree of compatibility between visitor group desires and the natural environment. The level of compatibility will help to determine which groups a destination should pursue in the tourism market, and which would fit in with the long-term goals of a renewable resource industry.

DISCUSSION QUESTIONS

1. Discuss possible ways to minimize environmental stress caused by too much tourism.
2. Discuss the arguments in favor of tourism development, despite its impact on the environment.
3. Discuss the arguments against tourism development because of its environmental impact.
4. Discuss the environmental impact of tourism as it radiates outward from a central core.
5. How does the intensity of tourism affect the environment?
6. What is meant by the time horizon of the tourist developer?
7. It is stated that cities are generally resilient to mass tourism. What does this mean?
8. Why must some areas be completely protected from tourism? Give two examples.
9. Discuss the need to protect the environment *for* tourism, compared with the need to protect it *from* tourism.
10. List three environmental costs of tourism.
11. Discuss some of the special measures that can be used to protect parks against too much tourism.
12. What is the carrying-capacity solution to protecting the environment from too much tourism?
13. Select a tourist area with which you are familiar, and explain how the environment has been negatively affected by tourism.
14. Select a tourist area with which you are familiar, and explain how the environment has been positively affected by tourism.

15. In regard to the environment, what do you think would be the costs of creating a recreational vehicle campsite in a wilderness area?

PROBLEM

A ski resort area is some seventy-five miles from its closest international airport. The ski area caters to those in higher income brackets. To avoid the time of driving by narrow mountain road from the airport to the ski resort, the ski resort's chamber of commerce is lobbying the government to build a nearby airport that would allow smaller commercial jet planes to land even in bad winter weather and also to come in the summer, as the resort plans to add golf courses and a conference center to extend its tourist season. The location of this new airport would be about fifteen miles from the ski resort in a flat valley. The valley is a farming area that has a resident population of about two thousand people who are petitioning strongly to keep out the airport, as they see no need for it for their own community and do not want their environmental peace disturbed by jet plane arrivals and departures. How might the ski resort's chamber of commerce argue in favor of the airport and overcome the valley community's objections?

REFERENCES

Government of Canada. 1980. *Parks Canada Policy*. Ottawa: Ministry of the Environment.

Murphy, Peter E. 1985. *Tourism—A Community Approach*. New York: Methuen.

SUGGESTED READINGS

Bosselman, F. 1979. *In the Wake of the Tourist*. Washington, D.C.: Conservation Foundation.

Budowski, G. 1977. "Tourism and Conservation: Conflict, Coexistence and Symbiosis." *Parks* 1: 3–6.

Dearden, P. 1983. "Tourism and the Resource Base." In *Tourism in Canada: Selected Issues and Options*, ed. P. E. Murphy. Victoria: University of Victoria, Western Geographical Series 21, pp. 75–93.

Eidsvik, H. K. 1983. "Parks Canada, Conservation and Tourism: A Review of the Seventies—A Preview of the Eighties." In *Tourism in Canada: Selected Issues and Options*, ed. P. E. Murphy. Victoria, University of Victoria, Western Geographical Series 21, pp. 241–269.

Gee, Chuck Y., Dexter J. L. Choy, and James C. Makens. 1984. *The Travel Industry*. Westport, Conn.: AVI, pp. 116–120.

Government of Canada. 1980. *Parks Canada Policy*. Ottawa: Ministry of the Environment.

Howard, Dennis R., and John L. Crompton. 1980. *Financing, Managing and Marketing Recreation and Park Resources*. Dubuque, Ia.: Brown.

Mathieson, Alister, and Geoffry Wall. 1982. *Tourism: Economic, Physical and Social Impacts*. London: Longmans.

Murphy, P. E. 1985. *Tourism—A Community Approach*. New York: Methuen, pp: 41–51, 60–76.

19

Cultural Impacts

```
CHAPTER OBJECTIVES_____

After studying this chapter the reader will be able to

• List eight ways in which culture is reflected in a nation.

• Differentiate between the anthropologist's and the economist's definition of culture.

• Define the term acculturation.

• Explain why developed countries risk less loss of their culture from tourism than do developing ones.

• Discuss concentration versus dispersion tourism as methods to minimize culture loss.

• List three causes of polarization between tourists and local residents.

• Give three examples of positive effects of tourism on local culture.

• Describe how the Polynesian Cultural Center in Hawaii operates.

• List four of the cultural costs of tourism.

• Define social carrying capacity, and list five ways in which this can be used to protect a community's culture.
```

The basic dilemma of tourism's cultural impact is that people at home do not want their local culture influenced by tourists, but when they themselves become tourists they often feel it is their right, because they have paid for a trip, to impose themselves on other cultures. McIntosh and Goeldner (1984, p. 113) state that

> the highest purpose of tourism is to become better acquainted with people in other places and countries. This furthers understanding and appreciation. Travel thus provides knowledge and communication, which are so important to building a better world for all. Tourism presents unexcelled possibilities for people to learn of other cultures. Causes of harmony or (alas) conflict among peoples lie much deeper than questions of understanding.

Unfortunately, in too many cases, it has been lack of harmony that prevails, and the result, according to Murphy (1985, p. 31), is evidence of growing hostility towards visitors in the more popular tourist destinations which are becoming overwhelmed by the volume of business. In some areas it is evident in a growing antipathy toward tourists, as in Cornwall where they are referred to as "emmets" (ants), in southern England where they are called "grockles" (a commercially worthless shellfish). In Hawaii those tourists dressed in outrageous Hawaiian shirts or mu-mu's, complete with sunburn and the ever-present camera, are referred to as "howlies" [more accurately *haoles*, a Hawaiian (and pejorative term) for foreigners].

CULTURAL ASPECTS

The science of anthropology defines culture as an integrated system of meanings by which the nature of reality is established and maintained by people. In other words, culture is what a society wishes it to be in order to cope with life. Culture can be seen in many aspects of a nation's life, such as

- Music. All forms are included.
- Dance. The costumes, music, setting, and skill of the dancers are what differentiate the dances of various nations.
- Fine arts. This includes architecture (including landscape architecture), painting, sculpture, and graphic arts.
- Language. Many people become tourists in another country because the culture embodied in its language appeals to them.
- Literature. This includes books, magazines, and newspapers, or the lack of them in some countries, which may reflect the restrictions of the political system.
- Education. The general level of education of a nation's people often shows how developed the country is. Its historic university buildings are often a tourist attraction in their own right.
- Science. The state of a nation's science is generally reflected in its scientific displays and museums.
- Handicrafts. These are considered cultural only if they are made by local people in the country where they are sold.
- Agriculture, business, and industry. These all are reflections of how a nation has developed and what its economic base is.
- Government. The method of government is sometimes a reflection of its culture, and many government buildings are popular tourist attractions that many people visit to learn about the country's governmental culture.
- History. The history of a country can often be absorbed through visits to its museums and historic preservation areas.

- Religion. Many people travel for religious motivations and also the desire to see how a religion is practiced in a foreign culture or to visit the center of that religion, such as the Vatican in Rome.
- Gastronomy. Food and drink are a reflection of a country's cultural heritage. Unfortunately too many tourists never seek out, or wish to try, a foreign nation's food specialties.
- Traditions. For example, handshaking in Japan is not often used as a form of greeting. Instead, one bows, and the older or more important the other person is, the deeper the bow will be.

Authenticity of Culture

The degree to which tourists seek authentic cultural experiences in a foreign nation obviously differs from tourist to tourist. But it can also depend on the degree of authenticity of the culture in the host country. Less developed countries' culture is often more authentic than that in more developed ones that cater to mass tourism. One of the reasons for this is that as a destination caters to more and more visitors, its planning must be modified to cope with a larger tourist market, which affects its social and cultural habits in the densely used tourist areas. For example, traditional local events may have to be "staged" in an unnatural environment in order for more tourists to be able to see them. However, this is sometimes taken one step further when the host area stages an event and leads the tourist to believe that it is much more authentic than it really is. This can also be seen in heritage museums that have been built to condense the history and traditional way of life in a way that can be taken in by the tourist in a one-hour visit rather than an all-day tour, or even to show a traditional way of life that no longer exists because tourism has extinguished it.

Economists' Viewpoint

Economists say that anything for sale must be produced by a combination of land, capital, and labor, which they refer to as the *factors of production*. If we accept what the economists say as true, we can then ask, Where does an intangible culture fit in, as culture is sold as part of what tourists pay for in their tourism experience? The economists would answer by defining culture as a natural resource. In other words, it is part of the land factor of production, or a commodity like any other.

But if a commodity or attraction is used in advertising to lure tourists to a destination, what are the local residents being paid for their culture, and did anyone ask them if they wanted to sell it? If they are not being paid, is this not a form of exploitation?

And culture is being sold. Pick up any tourism brochure, and you will likely find that culture is being packaged, priced, and sold like fast food in a restaurant, often without the consent of the participants and in a way that changes the way in which they must cope with life. This creates a conflict between the anthropological and the economic definitions of culture, as well as between those who are tourists and those who are not.

ACCULTURATION

Nevertheless, anthropologists agree that when two cultures come into contact for any length of time, each becomes a little bit more like the other through borrowing, a process known as *acculturation*. Ever since people first began to travel and came into contact with other people, acculturation has taken place. It is inevitable. For example, when tourists visit a foreign land, they often expect the host-area people to use the tourists' language. The host nation thus needs desk clerks, foodservice workers, tour guides, and police who speak the tourists' language. As a result, they frequently borrow words from the tourists and use them in their own language; they also borrow mannerisms and dress.

Acculturation is most obvious in the growing standardization of hotel accommodations built for the mass tourists, in the restaurants that provide food to those same tourists who want things just like home, and in the use of English as the standard language around the world. Indeed, the extent to which a local language is still in use is often a good indicator of the degree of local acculturation.

Two-Way Borrowing

But this borrowing or acculturation is a two-way street. Any visitor to Hawaii will notice that male tourists wear brightly colored "Hawaiian" shirts, and women wear *muumuus*, whereas many of the local people are the ones with the T-shirts and blue jeans. Tourists often also change their behavior when away from home. The middle-class resident at home becomes the rich tourist abroad and often changes his or her attitude to adapt to this changed role. Similarly, the former local agricultural worker who becomes a tour guide adopts the role of an expert on local history.

Acculturation is unavoidable wherever two different cultures come into contact, and so because it is inevitable, then perhaps there is nothing wrong with a host area's culture being affected by an influx of tourists. Culture is always changing. Tourism simply affects the rate of change. Perhaps, like environmental change, it just needs to have some controls applied to it. It may be the only alternative.

McIntosh and Goeldner (1984, pp. 140–141) listed the following possible negative social/cultural effects on a host society:

1. Introduction of undesirable activities such as gambling, prostitution, drunkenness, and other excesses.

2. The so-called "demonstration effect" of local people wanting the same luxuries and imported goods as those indulged in by tourists.

3. Racial tension, particularly where there are very obvious racial differences between tourists and their hosts.

4. Development of a servile attitude on the part of tourist business employees.

5. "Trinketization" of crafts and art to produce volumes of souvenirs for the tourist trade.

6. Standardization of employee roles such as the international waiter—same type of individual in every country.

7. Loss of cultural pride, if the culture is viewed by the visitor as a quaint custom or as entertainment.

8. Too rapid change in local ways of life due to being overwhelmed by too many tourists.

9. Disproportionate numbers of workers in low-paid, menial jobs characteristic of hotel and restaurant employment.

CULTURAL CHANGES IN DEVELOPED COUNTRIES

Tourism development's effect on local culture is easier to minimize in developed countries, particularly those that have a long history of acculturation. The best evidence of this is in Western Europe.

Western Europe has had a massive exposure to North American culture since World War II. But it has been able to adapt to it, adopt some forms of it, and still maintain its own cultural identity. Even from country to country in Europe we see cultures retained and maintained and demonstrated in such things as music and dance. It is true that these cultural traditions are often performed for pay for the sake of tourists. But those performances in turn tend to reinforce the culture in the local people's minds.

At times there is a conflict between cultural protection and economic necessity even in developed countries. Consider France, a country whose government has been most protective of its culture over the decades, even to the point of officially banning the use of English words in the language. And yet France is importing a massive amount of U.S. culture with the soon-to-be-opened Disney theme/amusement park near Paris to be known as EuroDisneyland. A political decision to do this was made because the development of the park will inject two billion dollars into the French economy, will create thirty thousand new jobs during construction, and will employ ten thousand people when finished. This will be France's biggest construction project for two decades. The finished park is to respect both French and European traditions, and even Donald Duck will have a French accent, for as one official stated, "Disney culture is universal!" An opinion poll commissioned by the greater Paris region council showed that 85 percent of French people approve of the project.

Saturation Levels

But this is not to imply that tourism cannot overwhelm the local culture in developed countries. For example, this occurs when cultural performances are put on only for the tourists and are never participated in and enjoyed by the local people themselves when the tourists are absent. In other words, the performance becomes more important than the performers. This lack of traditional ceremonial participation will eventually break down cultural traditions. We also see this occurring when historic sites are virtually turned over to tourists and their original meaning is forgotten. An example of this is Westminster Abbey in London which is visited by stream after stream of tourists, most of whom look at it from everything but a religious perspective.

Cities too can change their culture. London is so full of tourists in the summer that one can sometimes walk along some of the main shopping areas, such as Oxford Street, and seldom hear anyone speaking English. The shops are there primarily for the tourists, with the local people a secondary consideration. In turn this changes the local residents' shopping and transportation patterns, as they tend to go elsewhere to shop in order to avoid the crowds of tourists.

Concentration Versus Dispersion

There are generally two ways to plan tourism, at least in developed countries, to help cope with culture shock. Either the concentration or the dispersion of tourists can be used, depending on the local situation, and it may even be appropriate to use both of them in a larger area or nation.

Concentration is often a useful strategy in cities, where the central core area can be specifically zoned for tourism development, with appropriate hotels, restaurants, attractions, shops, and parking. Planning can even go so far as to isolate the tourist area (except for transportation corridors) from other areas around it frequented by local residents for their specific shopping and other needs. This kind of development has been used to rebuild city core areas that had been vacated by the movement of businesses and shops to the suburbs. For example, Atlanta's run-down core area has now been replanned as a convention tourist area, complete with major hotels and a convention center. This in turn has created a new business center and many new job opportunities (even though many of these new jobs may be low paying) for both that city center and the residential areas immediately surrounding it. In other words, tourism has created a beneficial economic option that has had major local environmental and social/cultural advantages.

In taking this concentrated approach to tourism planning, care must be taken that the new high-activity core does not spill over into surrounding residential areas in the form of high traffic densities and shortage of parking that can cause tension between the core-area tourists and the local residents and upset the cultural balance. If this is likely to happen, then a dispersion strategy, either independent of or along with a concentration strategy, must be considered.

Dispersion tourism is directing and diverting tourists to surrounding areas. Dispersion spreads the impacts of tourism over a much wider area of a community, and so it is less likely to have a major negative effect. Dispersion allows tourists to be easily absorbed into the local environment without changing land zoning from residential to commercial, and it often uses existing transportation corridors (road or rail) so that new ones do not have to be built.

When a large city reaches its cultural capacity for concentrated tourism planning, it can often then use a dispersion strategy to complement it so that the benefits of tourism in the concentration area are maintained at an appropriate level and not reduced, thereby depriving it of its economic base.

Care also must be taken in dispersing tourists that small rural or agricultural communities do not lose their cultural identity through the growing pressures of tourism. This can happen if access to those areas that need protection is made too easy, because of, for example, new or improved highways. These communities can often better retain their cultural and social values if they remain out of the tourism mainstream. Residents of smaller communities will consider tourism as less of a threat to their life-styles if the rate of change is slow and local resources (for example, labor) are used.

CULTURAL CHANGES IN DEVELOPING COUNTRIES

Rapid change in culture is most obvious in developing countries, because they often must have tourism for their economic survival. This dilemma is often compounded in developing nations as tourism modernization programs often perpetuate the local people's status quo, with the rich getting richer and the poor people no better off than before. The growth of tourism in developing countries often has a sociological cycle. In the early stages, there is a relatively low volume of visitors, and the local people welcome them, often seeing them as an economic salvation.

Full Development

In the full-development stage, the local people still welcome the tourists, as they seem to be making a visible economic contribution. Also during this stage, agricultural workers have become waiters or taxi drivers, and fishermen have become tour boat guides. This work-force migration actually begins the process of breaking down the traditional family unit that is part of local culture. However, the migrant tourist workers do not yet see this as a problem, as they may have gained economic wealth and independence. Indeed, their relative wealth means that they can afford to buy more products, possibly even imported ones, at higher costs. Those workers not involved in tourism begin to resent this, as their wealth has not improved, and they may now be paying higher prices than before.

Tourist workers may also now be able to afford to buy land, pushing up the prices beyond the reach of nontourist employees. Land may also be taken from local agriculture, and landownership patterns may change as well. In addition, tourists may "raid" (steal) local historical or archaeological art and other assets.

Tourists may even demand that local restaurants serve food completely alien to local traditions. For example, Puerto Rico has replaced much of its traditional food with imported food from Florida. And in highly visited areas of Spain, where the British tourists are predominant, the fish and chip shop has replaced the local bodega.

Crime

In the later stage of tourism development, crime may become a problem, as seen in muggings and robberies. This may lead to a kind of segregation in which the tourists are socially and geographically distanced from the local people. Golden ghettos of hotels and tourist attractions may be created only for the tourists.

Polarization

Finally, the tourists and the locals and the local haves and have-nots may become polarized by the tourists demanding goods and services that are not available or affordable to the local residents. In addition, untrained local employees, unable to cope with the service levels demanded by the tourists, may be replaced by imported, more highly skilled employees.

Cultural Conflicts

At the last stage, a cultural conflict has been reached. Local people are hostile toward visitors. They may compete for local resources, such as beaches and other recreational areas, where tourists are no longer welcome or where the locals are prohibited from going. In the workplace there will be low employee morale and, as a result, low productivity, poor service, delays, absenteeism, and even strikes. At the very worst there may be organized opposition to the tourists, even leading to revolts (as has been the case in some Caribbean countries), as well as sabotage, insecurity, crime, and eventually the demise of the tourism business. The degree of this conflict between locals and tourists depends on such things as the similarity of their normal living standards, the extent to which the two societies can adopt some of the other's norms, and the intensity of the tourism or the volume of tourist traffic.

CULTURAL LOSS WITHOUT CONFLICT

Some developed areas may experience a major cultural loss without any conflict at all, as has happened to the Lapp area of Finland. Tourism in Finland has interfered in the Lapp culture to the point that many of the local occupations such as reindeer herding have been seriously damaged.

The Amish

Another example is the Amish area of Pennsylvania. The Pennsylvania Dutch country is about 150 miles from New York and, for the Amish, has stayed firmly rooted in the eighteenth century. The Mennonites and Amish are the "Dutch" people of Pennsylvania. "Dutch" is a distortion of the word *Deutsch* (or German) and has nothing to do with the Dutch of Holland. The Mennonites have gone with the flow of the twentieth century, but the Amish have not. Most of the Amish live on a piece of land twenty miles long and ten miles wide, in a very simple world where the horse and buggy predominate as transportation. The Amish have an entrenched love of the land and a close sense of community.

It is not easy for strangers to get to know the Amish, as their way of life sets them apart in time as well as customs. They are a religious sect (much like the Quakers) who originally left their German homes because they opposed war. This is evidenced by the absence of buttons on their clothes, as buttons predominate on military uniforms.

Relationships between the tourist and the Amish can be difficult, mainly because of the tourists' cameras, as the Amish forbid taking photos. Clearly, too much tourism could destroy the Amish culture, and once it is gone, it cannot be replaced.

Research

What is required, particularly for developing areas, is research into the social and cultural consequences of tourism and the active involvement of the local people in planning and developing tourism so that they can have some say about how they want their culture affected. For example, should a hotel developer be allowed to build a high-rise hotel, or must it be a smaller hotel using a local architectural style and local, rather than imported, materials?

POSITIVE ASPECTS

Tourism does not always have a negative impact on local culture, however. For example, it can remind a local area of its history and culture. It can result in the return of local people to some of the arts and crafts they had forgotten and reawaken their interest in their own heritage. Much of the native American culture was lost in the United States as the railroad pushed west. However, the railway was slower to make inroads into the southwest, and the Cherokee and Navajo people in those areas did not lose their skills. These preserved skills now serve them well as they cater to the tourists' desire to buy and treasure their traditional handmade pottery and ceramics. Likewise, London's live theaters could not survive financially today if the tourists did not patronize them.

The Polynesian Cultural Center

A good example of created cultural preservation is the Polynesian Cultural Center (PCC) in the small town of Laie in Hawaii. The center was started by the adjacent Brigham Young University (BYU) operated by the Mormon church.

The center employs more than five hundred students and subsidizes their education, as well as helping finance BYU's operations. These students and other workers hold many different jobs in the various cultures that are part of the PCC. The PCC also pays the local Polynesian workers incomes that allow them to send money home. The PCC handles more than one million visitors a year, without opening on Sundays and without having changed the nearby town of Laie. Indeed, the local Laie community is prospering. Most important, the PCC has created an environment in which the Tongan, Tahitian, Samoan, and other cultures are kept alive and shared with tourists who can leave Hawaii with a better understanding of others.

Social Carrying Capacity

One way for planners to understand tourism's cultural implications is to be aware of what d'Amore (1983, p. 144) refers to as social carrying capacity, or "that point in the growth of tourism where local residents perceive on balance an unacceptable level of social disbenefits from tourism development." This concept provides a basis for assessing the social and cultural impacts of tourism development. D'Amore identified nine guidelines for planners:

1. Promotional campaigns should be used to advise local residents in tourist destinations of the socioeconomic significance of tourism to that area.

2. Development should be based on overall goals and priorities identified by those residents, as they, and not the tourist industry, should decide the rate of change they want.

3. The residents should approve promotional endeavors for the tourist area, as that promotion helps decide what kind of visitors, and how many, will be attracted.

4. There should be coordinated public and private efforts to maintain the

integrity and quality of local opportunities for recreation and relaxation.

5. If the indigenous people are affected (as is often the case in North America), they should be included in the planning process so that their culture and values will be respected.

6. Local capital, labor, and entrepreneurial ability should be invested in local tourism development so as to preserve a greater degree of local control over tourism development.

7. Opportunities for community involvement and participation in tourist events and activities should be broadly based.

8. Tourist destination areas should use themes and events that reflect their history, life-styles, and geographic setting.

9. More effort should be put into reducing local growth problems before any tourism activities are begun.

These social carrying-capacity guidelines are an attempt to balance the local residents' wishes with the rate of tourism development. They offer a framework for reducing tension and creating greater compatibility between visitors to and residents of a tourist destination area.

SUMMARY

Tourism is a medium for social and cultural change (it has always been so) and is not the cause of it. Cultural change, good or bad, is in the eyes of the beholder and often is a matter of judgment rather than precise measurement. Tourism is not the only vehicle of change, although it is often the most visible one. It can also be used as an agent to prevent change if it is properly planned, marketed, and managed. In this regard, it is important for a community to retain those aspects of its culture that differentiate it from others, but still to attempt to make this protected culture valuable to visitors.

A nation's cultural heritage can cope with a tourist-introduced culture, and both can gain from it. Their success will depend on maintaining a proper balance between the two different cultures, and those in tourism planning must be constantly aware of the cultural and social costs of tourism development. Tourism's economic decisions will affect the economy, but they also will have a direct influence on environmental as well as social and cultural costs, some of which are

- Additional demands on social services.
- Cost of creating new jobs.

- Loss of privacy in rural areas affected by tourism.
- Stress on family life of workers' unanticipated changed life-style.
- Cost of creating and retaining a positive community attitude.
- Psychological costs to local people because of the difference in wealth between them and tourist workers, and between local people and tourists.
- Friction between locals and tourists over shared use of local recreational land.
- Friction caused by spending limited local funds on tourism infrastructure rather than on resources that would more directly benefit the local residents.
- Cost of changes to local cultural ceremonies and traditions.

DISCUSSION QUESTIONS

1. List eight ways in which culture is reflected in a nation.
2. What is the anthropological definition of culture?
3. According to some anthropologists, history and culture are commercialized by tourism. Explain what you think this means.
4. To an economist, what are the three factors of production, and which factor includes culture?
5. Define the term *acculturation*.
6. Why are developed countries, such as those in Western Europe, not as vulnerable to cultural loss through tourism as are the developing countries?
7. Discuss concentration versus dispersion tourism as strategies to minimize local residents' cultural losses.
8. What is the major cause of cultural loss from tourism in developing countries?
9. Give three causes of polarization between tourists and local residents.
10. Give three examples of the positive effects of tourism on local culture.
11. Describe how the Polynesian Cultural Center in Hawaii has had a positive effect on Polynesian cultures.
12. List four of the cultural costs of tourism.
13. Define *tourist social carrying capacity*, and list five examples of it.
14. Give an example from your own knowledge of tourism in a particular area where tourism has had a positive effect on the local culture.
15. Give an example from your own knowledge of tourism in a particular area where tourism has had a negative effect on the local culture.

PROBLEMS

1. A major hotel chain has a property on the Mediterranean coast of Algeria in North Africa. When the Algerian government agreed to the hotel, it insisted that the local residents continue to be given access to the beach area (for fishing and other reasons). The hotel caters primarily to residents of Europe, who consider it normal to have an outdoor cocktail lounge on the beach/pool area to serve them while they relax. But most of the local residents are Muslims who do not consume alcohol and have come to resent its ready availability on what was "their" beach. This has created a cultural conflict between the tourists and the local residents. Discuss any possible way(s) in which you think this conflict could be resolved to the satisfaction of both parties.

2. A popular mountain resort has both a winter and a summer tourist trade. The local community has a base population of about five thousand, borders a national park, and is located in an area with a great deal of historic interest. One of the community's dilemmas is that in the summer, the tourist trade is very transient because although there are many daytime outdoor activities (fishing, golf, horseback riding) for visitors, there is nothing at night for them to do other than visit the local tavern. On rainy days there also are no local attractions for them to visit, and so they move on. Local retail outlets would like the local government to try to extend the visitors' length of stay during the summer months but does not want to "import" big-city events that would not reflect the local culture. What suggestions do you have for solving this problem?

REFERENCES

D'Amore, L. 1983. "Guidelines to Planning Harmony with the Host Community." In *Tourism in Canada: Selected Issues and Options*, ed. P. E. Murphy. Victoria: University of Victoria, Western Geographical Series 21.

McIntosh, Robert W., and Charles R. Goeldner. 1984. *Tourism: Principles, Practices, Philosophies*. New York: Wiley.

Murphy, Peter E. 1985. *Tourism—A Community Approach*. New York: Methuen.

SUGGESTED READINGS

Bell, Charles Anderson. 1986. "Crosscultural Construction: Designing Hotels Overseas." *Cornell Hotel and Restaurant Administration Quarterly* 27(2): 25–28.

Buck, Roy C. 1977. "Making Good Business Better: A Second Look at Staged Tourist Attractions." *Journal of Travel Research* 15(3): 30–32.

Butler, R. W. 1974. "The Social Implications of Tourist Developments." *Annals of Tourism Research* 2(2): 100–111.

Cohen, E. 1979. "Rethinking the Sociology of Tourism." *Annals of Tourism Research* 6(1): 18–35.

Collins, L. R. 1978. "Review of Hosts and Guests: An Anthropology of Tourism." *Annals of Tourism Research* 5: 278–280.

De Kadt, Emanuel. 1979. "Social Planning for Tourism in the Developing Countries." *Annals of Tourism Research* 6(1): 36–48.

Farrell, Bryan H. 1977. "The Social and Economic Impact of Tourism on Pacific Communities," a paper produced for the Center for South Pacific Studies. Santa Cruz: University of California.

Gee, Chuck Y., Dexter J. L. Choy, and James C. Makens. 1984. *The Travel Industry.* Westport, Conn.: AVI, pp. 110–115.

Graburn, Nelson H. H. 1976. *Ethnic and Tourist Arts.* Berkeley and Los Angeles: University of California Press.

Mathieson, Alister, and Geoffrey Wall. 1982. *Tourism: Economic, Physical and Social Impacts.* London: Longmans.

McIntosh, Robert W., and Charles R. Goeldner. 1984. *Tourism: Principles, Practices, Philosophies.* New York: Wiley, pp. 113–133, 137–142.

Murphy, P. E. 1981. "Community Attitudes to Tourism: A Comparative Analysis." *International Journal of Tourism Management* 2(3): 189–195.

Murphy, P. E. 1985. *Tourism—A Community Approach.* New York: Methuen, pp. 127–133, 134–151.

Nunez, T. A. 1977. "Touristic Studies in Anthropological Perspective." In *Hosts and Guests: The Anthropology of Tourism,* ed. V. L. Smith. Philadelphia: University of Pennsylvania Press, pp. 207–216.

Pearce, P. L. 1982. *The Social Psychology of Tourist Behaviour.* Oxford, England: Pergamon.

Pizam, A. 1978. "Tourism's Impacts: The Social Costs to the Destination Community As Perceived by Its Residents." *Journal of Travel Research* 16(4): 8–12.

Ritchie, J. R. Brent, and M. Zins. 1978. "Culture As a Determinant of the Attractiveness of a Tourist Region." *Annals of Tourism Research* 5(2): 252–267.

Smith, Valene L. 1977. *Hosts and Guests: The Anthropology of Tourism.* Philadelphia: University of Pennsylvania Press.

Smith, Valene L. 1980. "Anthropology and Tourism: A Science–Industry Evaluation." *Annals of Tourism Research* 7(1): 13–33.

Turner, Louis, and John Ash. 1975. *The Golden Hordes.* London: Constable.

Young, George. 1973. *Tourism: Blessing or Blight?* Harmondsworth, England: Penguin.

Planning

After the end of World War II many governments recognized tourism's development potential as a method of economic expansion. Entrepreneurs also were not slow to see the potential profits to be made in the building phase of tourism. In the early years after the war, growth was the prime motivation behind the expansion of tourist facilities; management of the environment and control over culture erosion were secondary considerations. Tourism was often perceived as a renewable resource. Tourists were not viewed as consumers of this resource but, rather, as visitors who came to tourist destinations only to see and enjoy the natural landscape and other attractions or to participate in the local customs as an educational experience.

Today, as tourism has matured and become an enormous industry, those involved in its development are more and more conscious that it competes for scarce resources and money for which there are alternative uses. Governments have also recognized that it is a consuming industry and not simply a passive one that generates economic benefits. In other words, tourism needs careful initial planning and subsequent effective management. Murphy (1985, p. 153) states the case as follows:

> More emphasis is needed on the interrelated nature of tourism development, in terms of its component parts (physical, economic, and social considerations), its spatial implications (accessibility, routing, and intervening opportunities), and evolutionary pattern (development stage and competitiveness). More balance in the decision-making process is required between those with the funds (governments, big business, banks) and those who have to live with the outcome and are expected to provide the hospitality. . . . Finally, the new approach to tourism development must combine planning (the initial goal and development strategy) with management (day-to-day, season-to-season operational decisions), because the ability to adjust to changing market or seasonal conditions is of paramount importance in such a competitive business.

A POSSIBLE SCENARIO

What motivated the early postwar developers? Why did they want to develop areas for tourism? Perhaps the reason was political patronage to favor a specific group who owned some property in a good location. Perhaps it was that a government could have a fancy hotel to house and entertain distinguished guests or to serve as a monument to someone's ego or pride. Or it might have been to provide a quick profit to a developer through land appreciation or to increase the value of the surrounding land. Or perhaps it was that the government did want to raise employment levels or that tourist developers were looking for solid long-term profits rather than fast speculative gains.

Consider the following hypothetical scenario of a developing country as it introduces tourism:

Stage 1: A Country Needs Foreign Exchange

    a. A developing country grants extensive tax advantages to hotel entrepreneurs.

    b. Import duties are waived for them.

    c. Tax holidays on profits are also allowed for ten years.

    d. Land is cheap for the hotels, as there is as yet no local speculation.

    e. The locals are happy to have hotel work, and the hotels are happy to have the cheap labor.

    f. The locals view the tourists as benefactors.

Stage 2: The First Few Years

a. Hotels do well financially, with labor costs 15 percent of sales, versus a normal 30 to 40 percent elsewhere.

b. Local food is available for the hotels' restaurants at low prices.

c. Hotel profits are not taxed, and cash can be taken out of the country.

Stage 3: Storm Clouds on the Horizon

a. The locals begin to resent tourists because fewer locals than expected are benefiting.

b. Land speculators move in and are getting rich as land prices shoot up.

c. An agricultural society has been changed into an urban/tourist one.

d. Local radicals are saying that they have simply changed one kind of servitude for another and begin pressuring the government to act.

e. The government starts to take a hard line on tourism, as 80 percent of its benefits are going outside the country.

Stage 4: Trouble Is Brewing for the Hotels

a. The end of the tax holiday period arrives.

b. The hotels' local fixed costs are now rapidly rising out of control, and local food prices are inflating quickly.

c. Local unions are insisting on external wage levels.

d. Employees' resentment causes a decline in productivity.

e. Tourists are treated with indifference and insults.

f. Negative word-of-mouth publicity means declining arrivals.

g. The government panics and increases the advertising budget.

h. The government bans importing skilled labor and insists on locals' becoming managers.

i. The government opens a hotel management training school (with few applicants) instead of a vocational training school that could provide far more jobs.

Stage 5: Serious Problems Surface

a. There are now too many hotel rooms for the number of arrivals.

b. Many hotels were built on uneconomic, high-priced land after the tourist boom had started.

   c. No planning has been done, and so there is a random development of high-rise hotels and blocked views.

   d. Beauty spots have been closed to the public.

   e. Marginal independent hotels are sold to chains that have international marketing and can regain business at the expense of other independents.

   f. Other smaller properties are now looking run-down, as they have not been maintained; they must lower their rates to attract business.

Stage 6: Maturity and Decline

   a. The area has matured . . . but with unanticipated political and psychological problems.

   b. There are now many unprofitable smaller hotels (probably owned by local entrepreneurs).

   c. The government must step in and run the unprofitable properties or provide financial aid.

   d. There is widespread local resentment and perhaps riots, as have occurred in Jamaica and Curaçao under similar circumstances.

NEED FOR PLANNING

To prevent this scenario from taking place, planning is needed in areas such as

- Conducting market research.
- Establishing tourism policies.
- Ensuring adequate long-term financing for proposed tourism projects.

At one end of the scale in tourist planning are improvements in the economic and social situation for an area, and thereby net benefits. At the other end of the scale are changes that lead to an overdependency on tourism that does provide economic growth but also leaves an underplanned and underdeveloped social situation that ends up reinforcing many local residents' poverty. A few developers and others involved in tourism gain, but most people do not.

According to Murphy (1985, p. 120), how a community views tourism and the opportunities it provides depends to a large degree on its attitude toward tourism as indicated by the type of contact between local residents and visiting tourists, the relative importance of tourism to both the community and the local residents, and the local residents' tolerance threshold in regard to the volume of business that a tourist destination can handle.

Contact Situations

Common contact situations between local residents and tourists occur when the tourists purchase goods or services or when both the locals and the tourists participate in enjoying the same attraction such as a beach or a restaurant. However, these are generally transitory contacts and do little to foster an understanding of customs and cultures between people. They are simply a by-product of most tourism planning. Many of these contacts tend to develop strong ideas in the minds of the local people about tourism. Those directly involved in tourism (such as those employed in it and receiving direct financial benefits) tend to feel positive about it. Those who feel negative about tourism often do not have any direct contact with it. They tend to become negative as the result of poor planning that creates tension, frustration, and hostility as the local people compete with the tourists for scarce beach or parking space. Such negative attitudes are further reinforced by traffic congestion, the growth of strip development for motels and restaurants, litter and vandalism, increasing property values, and local governments' preferential treatment for businesses involved in tourism.

Anticipating Negative Attitudes

With good planning, such negative situations can be anticipated and avoided, often by limiting tourism growth to minimize stresses. It is difficult to determine the stress level because it is intangible. Stress tends to be lower in larger metropolitan areas, particularly if there is a core of tourism development. Stress is often higher when tourism enters smaller communities.

What is often left out of planning, and is much more difficult to plan, are encounters that increase understanding between tourists and residents.

Master Plan

Planning can involve specialists in planning, as well as experts in architecture, finance, marketing, economics, sociology, and even archaeology, in order to provide an intelligent direction for the extent and quality of tourism growth and to prevent the misuse of land, undesirable environmental change, and stress between different cultures.

A master tourism plan should be prepared that allows gradual development, each stage blending in with earlier ones. If possible, the master plan should allow modifications, if needed, as subsequent stages are introduced.

Without planning, tourist facilities end up becoming part of a construction jungle —and this can occur in both developed and developing countries. Witness the motel rows that lead into most North American cities where motels compete with one another to erect larger and more garish advertising billboards directing potential customers to their properties.

Around the world we notice that access to the sea has been largely unplanned, with each multistory hotel close to the next one, preventing public access to the beaches because the rich have had their hotels built on the choice sites and sometimes confine the beaches to themselves. This type of undesirable development can be seen in Waikiki in Hawaii, in Mexico, in Costa del Sol in southern Spain, and at Copacabana in Rio de Janeiro.

In this era of mass tourism, planning is even more imperative as areas and countries compete with one another for tourist dollars. This planning translates into a problem of attracting the maximum number of desirable tourists with a minimum amount of negative impact.

Community Involvement

One problem that often surfaces in tourism planning—after the event—is that local residents are not aware of the economic benefits of tourism development to their community. Thus a good plan should include some method, or methods, to communicate this information. This is mainly a public relations problem that is vital if tourism is to win the cooperation and goodwill of the entire community.

Questions to Ask When Planning

Most of tourism's problems are due to

- Too many tourists.
- Too much adverse visitor impact.
- Too much tourism infrastructure.

Some of the planning questions that need to be answered to avoid these problems are

- How large is the tourism to be?
- How intensive or dominant in the area is it to be?
- Should it be concentrated or dispersed?
- What will its impact be on the local economy, environment, and culture?
- What undesirable elements of a foreign culture might it bring in?
- How much foreign capital will it bring in or be allowed to bring in?

Planning Goals

The reason for asking these questions is to establish goals to provide a general direction, rather than strict, rigid requirements, for planning. These goals must be achievable and have the support of the community. They must complement the community's overall goals, and the wider the support is, the more credible the tourist product will be. Note that to achieve this support, one goal might be to reduce tourism, as when a tourist destination is so dependent on tourism that the community would be at real risk in an economic downturn. Unfortunately, too many goals are established with the sole aim of commercial and economic growth. McIntosh and Goeldner (1984, p. 353) state that tourism goals should aim at

1. Providing a framework for raising the living standard of the people through the economic benefits of tourism.
2. Developing an infrastructure and providing recreation facilities for visitors and residents alike.
3. Ensuring types of development within visitor centers and resorts that are appropriate to the purposes of those areas.
4. Establishing a development program consistent with the cultural, social, and economic philosophy of the government and the people of the host country or area.

TOURISM PLANNING IN DEVELOPED AREAS

Tourism planning in developed areas is not as difficult as that for undeveloped areas, as much of the infrastructure will already be in place. Tourism planning in developed areas differs little from normal planning for a city or region, for which the two major problems are a consideration of the alternative uses for the land (as well as avoiding visual monotony, unnecessary leveling, and uniformity of building construction), and the health and welfare of the local residents.

Land development in this context implies more than just real estate development: Real estate development means the best possible use of the land for the developers' profit, and land development means development for both the community at large and the developer. The development of a new resort destination from scratch, in an otherwise developed area, may require a greater commitment to ensure that all the final tourism elements will harmonize with one another, be economically viable, and draw visitors.

Proper land development includes the people affected as part of the planning process. Improperly conceived plans can fail, but more often than not they fail because there was not adequate consultation with those affected and their support was never gained. As a result, they will feel that the proposals were imposed on them, rather than being the result of consultation.

Obviously, it is not feasible for every affected local resident to be involved in all the planning details, but through a series of meetings there can be local input, feedback, and review so that all points of view are tabled and considered. Communication is vital to developing cooperative attitudes and discussing alternative tradeoffs and situations in which compromise is required, so that the end result of planning is a tourist product that is economically, socially, environmentally, and culturally viable.

DETAILED PLANNING CONSIDERATIONS

One of the most important aspects of a tourism plan is the preparation of a strategy to determine tourism development opportunities and to take advantage of the strengths, minimize the weaknesses, and aid in the maximization of potential tourist markets. Successful strategies are a combination of concepts and ideas drawn up by local planning personnel and consultants, and the experience and expertise of those already involved in the tourism industry. The success of a plan results from the willingness of the private sector and tourism organizations to cooperate and participate. This approach encourages the extensive and direct involvement of these people and increases the opportunities for successful planning. It also encourages commitment to the implementation of the plan and provides the basis for an ongoing and effective development process. There are five areas that require information for analysis before a tourism plan can be prepared.

1. Preparing a Resource Inventory

A good tourism plan must maximize the community's resources. Some communities already have a base of tourism, and some attractions and events may already be extensively developed. The resource inventory provides a basis for assessing the significance of the tourism resources in the area to determine the possibilities (both existing and potential) for tourism development. The ability to create a tourist demand needs to be judged on the quality, uniqueness, and capacity for the development of local assets. Although special events such as festivals are important to attracting tourists, so too are accommodations, food services, shops, entertainment, and other resources.

Both strengths and weaknesses in terms of contribution to tourism should be listed and assessed. A major problem in most resource assessments is the peaking of activity during the summer months (or winter months in a ski area). It is important to analyze tourist resources in regard to operating-season length, carrying capacity, and competitiveness to determine whether there are enough resources to carry out the plan.

The following should be considered when evaluating the strengths and weaknesses of attractions and services:

- Type and number
- Seasonality

- Quality
- Profitability
- Value for money spent by tourists

In assessing resources where a tourism base already exists, any current marketing programs for those resources should be evaluated. The following might be some of the factors to use in this evaluation:

- Information provided to tourists and potential tourists.
- Quality of advertising material used (such as brochures).
- Creativity and originality of this advertising material.
- Duplication of any advertising efforts.
- Value for money spent on existing marketing programs.

The resource inventory should be summarized by identifying:

- Improvements required to increase the satisfaction of existing tourists.
- Any "gaps" in the current situation.
- Any improvements to existing attractions and services, or creations of new ones, to expand the current tourist base.
- Any ways in which the season of a tourist base can be lengthened.
- Any ways in which new markets can be encouraged.

In preparing a resource inventory it is useful to separate this list into those resources that are marketing oriented and those that are operationally or functionally oriented.

Marketing-Oriented Resources

Some marketing resources are easy to identify and list. Others are more difficult, as they are intangible. Harder still is the problem of deciding what action to take to protect and retain each resource. A possible list might include:

- Natural resources:
  Landscapes
  Parks
  Lakes
  Rivers
  Streams
  Mountains
  Cliffs
  Gorges

    Flora and fauna
    Seashores
    Harbors

- Cultural/historic attributes:
    Archaeological sites
    Traditional architecture
    Native crafts
    Native foods
    Ceremonies
    Rituals
    Customs
    Dances

- Recreation areas:
    Parks
    Golf courses
    Camping areas
    Picnicking spots
    Swimming locations
    Ski areas

- Tourist facilities:
    Entertainment and events
    Accommodations
    Restaurants
    Shopping
    Information centers
    Reservation systems

- Climate

- Other natural resources

- Psychological appeal:
    Scenic beauty
    Pleasant local attitude

Operationally/Functionally Oriented Resources

The operational or functional resources might include

- Land availability

- Planning and zoning

- Transportation:
    Roads
    Airlines/airports

Railways
Buses
Boats
Underground/subways
- Utilities:
  Water
  Power
  Sewer
- Support industries:
  Police
  Fire
  Health
  Churches
  Banks
  Food supplies
  Laundries
  Other support services
- Labor force:
  Availability
  Skills
  Language training
  Technical training
- Capital
- Local government attitudes

2. Conducting an Economic Impact Analysis

Direct economic impacts must be explored in some depth in a tourist plan. Indirect economic impacts also need to be investigated. For example, if the building of a major hotel necessitates changing local water and sewer lines, the costs of this must be determined. If a convention center is to be built, the costs of extra support services such as policing must be calculated. What adjustments will there be to traffic flows and parking? What extra taxes will be necessary?

3. Conducting an Environmental Impact Analysis

There are many examples around the world in which careful environmental impact studies were not undertaken when developing tourism. These can be seen in attractions surrounded by garish neon lights, displeasing architecture, and traffic congestion. Environmental analysis requires a careful assessment of the area directly affected and also the surrounding areas. The difficulty of this type of analysis is often compounded when various closely located destinations must combine their efforts in an overall environmental review.

The government may also need to coordinate environmental plans in order to resolve any differences. This dilemma is made more difficult by tourism's diverse and fragmented structure, with numerous individual enterprises each wishing to extract the maximum revenue out of their own developments. Also, environmental changes are not always apparent before they appear. The environment can change very slowly, and some changes can be initially desirable but detrimental in the long run. By this time, it may be too late to reverse the damage or to reorient the tourism plan to eliminate further damage.

4. Conducting a Social/Cultural Impact Analysis

Many tourism plans in the past have ignored social and cultural factors; the emphasis instead has been on the customers and their needs. But this has changed, as resentment by local residents to tourism plans without local input have become known among planners. Local people's concerns about the effect on them of traffic congestion, noise, loss of recreation areas, and acculturation can no longer be ignored. Tourism is often referred to as the hospitality industry, and to generate hospitality, it must look beyond the customers and consider its social and cultural impacts on the total community.

D'Amore (1983, p. 144) talked about "that point in the growth of tourism where local residents perceive on balance an unacceptable level of social disbenefits from tourism development." In other words, every destination can accept only so much tourism because resources are limited, and an awareness by tourist planners of this capacity will ensure that they consider the tolerance level in their plans.

5. Preparing a Marketing Analysis

Information about potential tourist markets can often be collected at the same time that resources are being inventoried. Marketing analysis should collect data on the following six areas of the tourism plan:

- Past and present tourist trends, if any.
- Present and potential tourist sources, numbers, and profiles.
- Present and potential tourist preferences and habits.
- Market position.
- Competitive destinations' strengths and weaknesses.
- Destination image desired.

The information about existing visitor markets should be analyzed to categorize markets by type and origin. The most important influences on tourism trends include

- Demographics, such as the age, sex, and income of visitors.
- Economic, such as the cost of travel to the destination, the general state of the economy, and inflation levels.
- Life-styles, such as recreation needs, work ethic habits, and food demands.

Marketing analysis also entails assessing the tourism base in relation to competitive destinations. This assessment must consider the competitiveness in nearby tourist destinations and future opportunities.

Even though an area's visitors may have traditionally visited that area, it is important to determine why they have done so. It may also be useful to question these visitors to see whether they might increase their length of stay. To help produce information, interviews could be conducted at visitor information centers to ascertain market characteristics of the area.

Potential markets need to be considered. History has shown us that despite such setbacks as recession and inflation, new markets can develop from changing demographics, attitudes, and life-styles. For a tourist destination, these new markets can either add to or replace existing traditional markets.

The advertising programs of all those promoting the destination should also be evaluated. This advertising includes printed literature (pamphlets and brochures), public relations, and any other types of advertising carried out by individual suppliers (hotels, attractions), tourism associations, chambers of commerce, governments, and others.

Finally, profiles need to be prepared of the types of potential visitors to reflect which types of travel markets have the highest tourism potential for the area.

POLICIES, PLANS, AND PROJECTIONS

The end result of this detailed five-part analysis is the preparation of a set of policies, plans, and projections guiding the decision makers in their planning decisions. The final part of the planning process has five steps.

1. Determine Strategy Goals and Objectives

The first step is to draw up goals and objectives. As much as possible these goals should be quantifiable (for example, to attract an average of one thousand new visitors per week to the destination). In establishing these goals and objectives, planners need to keep in mind the overall tourism development and marketing strategy, the potential for new opportunities, the availability of funding from both public and private sectors, timing, and the roles and responsibilities of all those involved.

2. Identify New Development Opportunities

The second step is to identify any new development opportunities, through a master plan which should include the location of proposed visitor facilities such as hotels, food services, attractions, any required infrastructure, and traffic flows.

The master plan must be supported by economic projections showing such things as anticipated visitor demand, hotel occupancy rates, availability of labor, required investment, availability of investment funds, sales volume required to support the investment, and direct and indirect returns on that investment. These economic plans are often put into a feasibility study. (A suggested outline for a feasibility study for a proposed new hotel will be presented in Chapter 21.)

The opportunities with the highest return on investment are often those that appeal most to private entrepreneurs. However, the opportunities with lower direct returns may provide other benefits, such as more visitors to the destination area in general. In such cases, government subsidies or financial incentives might be considered to encourage private investors.

3. Develop an Organization Plan

The third step is to develop an organization plan, which initially requires a review of the policies and budgets of those involved in organizing tourism, such as local governments, chambers of commerce, convention and visitor bureaus, and hotel, restaurant, and attraction associations. The idea is to see where each of these is supporting or constraining the overall organization so that strengths can be maximized and weaknesses eliminated or minimized. Organizational recommendations cover such matters as structure, funding, and performance review.

4. Establish a Marketing Plan

The fourth step is to establish a marketing plan. A review of current resources and markets will provide information for determining target markets and their future potential. These markets, and advertising programs to reach them, must be evaluated in regard to available budgets in order to maximize visitor arrivals.

Marketing objectives should reflect the current marketing plan assessment and help create the right image for the area. They might even include an overall theme for uniting all the different sectors involved in tourism at the destination.

An outline of a marketing plan might include any or all of the following:

1. Marketing goals and objectives
2. Competitive evaluation summary
3. Market strategy
   a. Target market segmentation by type

  b. Present market position
    i. Financial resources
    ii. Stage of development
    iii. Competition
    iv. Other
  c. Market mix
    i. Product
    ii. Price
    iii. Promotion
    iv. Promotion distribution channels

4. Action plan
  a. Tourism literature production
  b. Public relations plan
  c. Market penetration objectives
  d. Use of supplier associations
  e. Market research proposals
  f. Local education programs
  g. Action plan evaluation programs

5. Develop an Implementation Strategy

The fifth step is to devise an implementation strategy that describes the actions, efforts, and funds required to implement the overall tourism plan recommendations and develop the area's tourism potential. Delivery methods should be discussed, evaluated, and recommended to show how the development and marketing opportunities can be introduced, promoted, and implemented to gain the greatest possible support of both public and private sectors. Before any final action is taken, the implementation responsibilities of all participating groups must be determined. Any potential problems and constraints must be identified so that action plans can include contingency alternatives.

DESTINATION LIFE CYCLES

The assumption is often made in tourist plans that tourist destinations will always remain tourist destinations. Very few plans consider the expected life cycle of an area or its attractions (life cycles were discussed in Chapter 4). It is often difficult to locate tourist areas on a life cycle because different sectors of an area are sometimes at different stages of this life cycle, and appropriate information is often not always available. However, planners should address this matter and at least consider the area's potential life cycle relative to the competition, as well as comment about the long-term implications of life cycles in the development and marketing process.

Postimplementation Review

Finally a postimplementation review of a tourism plan is recommended. Keiser and Helber (1978, p. 231) describe this process as follows:

> After the project phase of a tourism development program is complete, there should be a planned, coordinated program of data gathering, reporting, evaluation, and decision making aimed at determining how successful the program has been and how successes can be used as building blocks and failures or weaknesses overcome. This process is, in effect, a reporting and surveying exercise like the one which preceded entry into the tourism development endeavor. Its purpose is to report on achievement as compared with objectives and to produce recommendations on where the tourism industry should go in the immediate, intermediate, and long-range future.

> In other words, a tourism master plan should not be rigid and inflexible. It should be an integrated continuous process embracing development, monitoring, and constant revision of future plans.

SUMMARY

In summary, the goals of proper planning are to avoid undesirable results such as

- Hostile competition among individual tourism plant operators.
- Hostile and unfriendly attitudes between locals and tourists.
- General overcrowding and traffic congestion.
- Loss of local traditions and cultural identity.
- Permanent damage or unnecessary alteration of local natural features and attractions.
- Various kinds of pollution.
- Too great a seasonality in tourism.
- General lack of awareness by local people of the benefits of tourism.
- Lack of awareness in potential tourists, through poor marketing, of the attractions in the area.
- Lack of education of tourism employees in the skills of hospitality.
- Lack of sufficient attractions and events, resulting in too short a length of tourist stay.

- Inadequate advertising and travel information services.
- Failure to capitalize on new marketing opportunities.
- Erosion of market share owing to the actions of competitive destinations.

DISCUSSION QUESTIONS

1. Who are some of the specialists who should be involved in tourism planning?
2. What are some of the key questions that must be posed before a tourism plan is prepared for an area?
3. The chapter states that most of tourism's problems are caused by three factors. What are they?
4. List three of the purposes of planning goals.
5. In tourism planning in a developed area such as a city, what are the two main problems that must be addressed?
6. Why is it necessary in tourism planning for the planners to consult with the people to be affected?
7. Before preparing a tourism plan, information is needed in five major areas. What are they?
8. Differentiate between marketing-oriented and operationally oriented resources, and give five examples of each.
9. What are the five steps in the final planning process?
10. The objective of proper planning is to avoid certain undesirable end results. What are four of them?
11. Discuss the importance of being aware of life cycles in the tourism destination–planning process.
12. What is a postimplementation planning review, and what purpose(s) does it serve?
13. From your own knowledge about tourism planning in a specific area, describe the results of some good planning.
14. From your own knowledge about tourism planning in a specific area, describe the results of some poor planning.

PROBLEMS

1. You are a planning adviser to a developing nation, which has carried out a resource inventory that shows a positive potential for tourism planning. At present it has no tourism base. The nation's tourism ministry is anxious to

prepare a policy for tourism development. List ten recommendations that you would want to be included in this policy. Support each.

2. An established tourist destination wishes to expand its tourism base. Private suppliers (hotels, restaurants, attractions) have indicated their willingness to make investments to expand this base if the current zoning restrictions are relaxed. Some members of the local government are in favor of this, but others are vehemently opposed. How would you recommend that this dilemma be resolved? Support your reasons.

REFERENCES

D'Amore, L. 1983. "Guidelines to Planning Harmony with the Host Community." In *Tourism in Canada: Selected Issues and Options*, ed. P. E. Murphy. Victoria: University of Victoria, Western Geographical Series 21.

Keiser, C., Jr., and L. E. Helber. 1978. *Tourism Planning and Development*. Boston: CBI.

McIntosh, Robert W., and Charles R. Goeldner. 1984. *Tourism: Principles, Practices, Philosophies*. New York: Wiley.

Murphy, Peter E. 1985. *Tourism—A Community Approach*. New York: Methuen.

SUGGESTED READINGS

Arbel, Avner, and Abraham Pizam. 1977. "Some Determinants of Urban Hotel Location: The Touristic Inclinations." *Journal of Travel Research* 15(3): 18–22.

Baud-Bovy, Manuel, and Fred Lawson. 1977. *Tourism and Recreation Development*. Boston: CBI.

D'Amore, L. 1983. "Guidelines to Planning Harmony with the Host Community." In *Tourism in Canada: Selected Issues and Options*, ed. P. E. Murphy. Victoria: University of Victoria, Western Geographical Series 21, pp. 135–159.

England, R. 1980. "Architecture for Tourists." *International Social Science Journal* 32: 47–55.

English Tourist Board. 1981. *Planning for Tourism in England*. London: English Tourist Board.

Gearing, Charles E., William W. Swart, and Turgut Var. 1976. *Planning for Tourism Development*. New York: Praeger.

Gee, Chuck Y., Dexter J. L. Choy, and James C. Makens. 1984. *The Travel Industry*. Westport, Conn.: AVI, pp. 88–103.

Gunn, Clare A. 1972. *Vacationscape: Designing Tourist Regions*. Austin: University of Texas, Bureau of Business Research.

Gunn, Clare A. 1979. *Tourism Planning*. New York: Crane Russak.

Hawkins, Donald, Elwood Shafer, and James Rovelstad. 1980. *Tourism Planning and Development Issues*. Washington, D.C.: George Washington University Press.

Kaiser, C., Jr., and L. E. Helber. 1978. *Tourism Planning and Development*. Boston: CBI.

Mathieson, Alister, and Geoffry Wall. 1982. *Tourism: Economic, Physical and Social Impacts*. London: Longmans.

McIntosh, Robert W., and Charles R. Goeldner. 1984. *Tourism: Principles, Practices, Philosophies*. New York: Wiley, pp. 205–220, 225–231, 353–389.

Murphy, P. E. 1985. *Tourism—A Community Approach*. New York: Methuen, pp. 104–115, 153–165, 119–126, 134–151.

Wahab, S. 1975. *Tourism Management*. London: Tourism International Press.

World Tourism Organization. No date. *Presentation and Financing of Tourist Development Projects*. Madrid: WTO.

An Introduction to
Feasibility Studies

In tourism planning for a community, hotels are a prime consideration, in regard to both their size (number of rooms) and their location. Hotels usually are located in commercially zoned areas: Groups of hotels can often be placed reasonably close to one another as long as they are surrounded by natural areas that form a boundary.

For a tourist community that is being planned, it is important to determine the traveling and vacation habits of potential guests so that accommodation and other facilities can be planned accordingly. That is, these facilities will be planned with the community's goals kept in mind.

TOTAL COMMUNITY ACCOMMODATION NEEDS_____

The following equation can be used to determine a community's accommodation needs, assuming initially a 100 percent occupancy of that accommodation and a year-round tourist season:

$$\frac{\text{No. of tourists x Percent staying in hotels x Average length of stay}}{365 \text{ x Average number of persons per room}}$$

For example, assume the following estimates for a community for a year:

Visitors anticipated: 780,000

Percent staying in hotels: 95%

Average length of stay: 7 days

Average number of persons in a room: 1.5

The number of rooms demanded at 100 percent occupancy would be

$$\frac{780,000 \times 0.95 \times 7}{365 \times 1.5} = \frac{5,187,000}{547.5} = 9,474 \text{ rooms demanded}$$

Because hotels do not normally have 100 percent occupancy year-round, the number of rooms demanded will have to be converted to the quantity required at a realistic average year-round occupancy. For example, assuming 70 percent, the actual number of rooms needed will be

$$\frac{9,474}{0.7} = 13,534 \text{ rooms required}$$

Seasonal Situations

If the season were shorter than 365 days, then the lower number of days, representing the actual length of the shorter season, would have to be used in the equation. For example, assume, given the same information, that this were a 150-day seasonal ski resort but that during this season, hotel demand was so high that occupancy was an average 90 percent. The demanded hotel rooms would be

$$\frac{780,000 \times 0.95 \times 7}{150 \times 1.5} = \frac{5,187,000}{225} = 23,053 \text{ rooms demanded}$$

and

$$\frac{23,053}{0.9} = 25,614 \text{ rooms required}$$

Calculating the number of rooms is a critical first step because other tourist supply items (restaurants, shops, attractions, utility supply, and other needs) are based on the number of visitors to be accommodated at any one time.

When a tourist destination already exists, we will then need a calculation of the additional rooms that can be supported by expanding one or more existing hotel properties or by building a new hotel facility. The need for these additional hotel rooms is usually documented in a feasibility study.

FEASIBILITY STUDY

A feasibility study is an in-depth analysis of the marketing and financial feasibility of a property development, rather than a promoter's guess that a new idea will be economically viable: A feasibility study is not designed to prove that a new venture will be profitable. An independent feasibility study prepared by an impartial third party could result in either a positive or a negative recommendation. If it is negative, both the borrower and the lender should be happy that the proposal has gone no further. However, if it is positive, this should not be taken as a guarantee of success. A feasibility study can consider only what is known at present and what may happen in the future. But because the future is impossible to forecast accurately and so many unforeseen factors can come into play, there can be no guarantees. Thus, a feasibility study may reduce the risk of a particular investment, but it cannot eliminate it.

Some feasibility studies seek out the most appropriate location for a new property and continue with the study from there. Others accept a given location without considering the alternatives.

FEASIBILITY STUDY FORMAT

Although the scope of a feasibility study for a suburban motel will differ considerably from that for a major downtown hotel complex, the basic format will be the same. Most feasibility studies have two parts. The first discusses the marketing aspects and justifies the number of new rooms required. The second part covers the financial implications. In the following discussion we shall assume that the feasibility study is for a hotel with food and beverage facilities. (In a feasibility study for a motel with only room facilities, only data relevant to guest rooms would be included.) The format for a hotel feasibility study would probably cover each of the following.

Front Matter

The front matter includes an introduction explaining why the study was made, what property is being evaluated and how this evaluation was conducted, when the study was made and by whom, and a summary of the findings, conclusions, and recommendations.

General Market Characteristics

The general market characteristics include items such as site location, the area's population growth trends, industrial diversification and growth, building permit activity, employment and economic trends, disposable incomes of tourists and/or potential tourists, housing, transportation, attractions, convention facilities, and special factors (for example, is the area's economy highly dependent on its local tourist business, or is it more broadly based, and if so, how stable is this base?). Only those items relevant to the proposed new hotel should be discussed, and both descriptive and statistical data should be included. The information should be concise and primarily related to the demand for rooms (other services offered by a hotel are derived directly from room usage).

Site Evaluation

If the study contains an in-depth section on site location, it would include detailed maps of the location. Whenever possible, those maps should show important sub-centers of activity related to the proposal, such as industrial areas, shopping malls, and convention and sports centers. Transportation routes, including, for example, routes to and from the airport, should be shown, and if auto access methods are important, they should be indicated as well.

This section should give physical information about the site, such as dimensions, existing improvements (buildings) on the site, and adequacy of the site for future expansion. Included as well would be the cost of the site, site preparation costs before construction, and property taxes. Finally, it would contain any other important matters such as zoning restrictions, height restrictions, parking space requirements, future traffic flow changes, and availability of utility services.

Supply and Demand Information

There are three possible reasons for a new hotel: (1) The current demand for rooms is greater than the current supply; (2) the demand from a new market is not being served by the existing supply; and (3) the quality of current supply cannot meet the needs of the current demand or market. It is therefore important that the study analyze the supply–demand situation in order to identify the market for a proposed new property, by looking at the entire local market and then adjusting for anticipated future changes. This information should include the following:

1. Occupancy trends in the local area for the past five years, broken down by class of hotel (see next item) if possible.

2. A list of the hotels currently serving the local market, categorized by class of hotel. Three classes are commonly listed: those that would be the most competitive properties, those that would be somewhat competitive, and those that would be the least competitive. The list should name each hotel, specify the number of rooms each has, and give each hotel's current room rates. This list may also contain additional information such as the facilities they have other than rooms (for example, the number of seats in their restaurants) and the quality of those facilities. The information about the most competitive hotels should include their room occupancy rates, food and beverage facilities usage (for example, seat turnovers and average checks), and the composition of their market for rooms, food, and beverages.

3. The principal sources of demand should be specified. Generally, for a city hotel, the sources of room demand are from business travelers, convention delegates, and tourists or vacationers. For a tourist resort destination hotel, vacation travelers and the convention trade would

probably be more important than regular business travelers. Each category should list relevant data that could indicate the demand for rooms.

For business travelers the relevant data might include growth in local airport traffic and/or growth in local office space occupancies for the past five years, as there is frequently a close correlation between those items and the demand for hotel rooms. Data concerning convention or business meeting delegates are the number of conventions held each year in the area, the types of conventions, their size, the total number of delegates, the average length of delegate stay, and the average conventioner's daily spending. Data concerning vacationers are number of tourists, average length of stay, average daily spending on hotel accommodations and meals, and any change in or extension of the tourist season over the past several years. Any significant demand for hotel accommodations from special sources should be mentioned. For example, sporting events can often be a major source of demand for hotel rooms close to the sporting event's location.

Much of the information necessary for this section of the study can be obtained from local chambers of commerce, convention and visitor bureaus, hotel and motel associations, airport authorities, government agencies, and, in the case of office space occupancies, the local office building owners' association.

Supply and Demand Analysis

Once the supply and demand information has been assembled and tabulated, it must then be analyzed to determine whether additional hotel rooms in the area can be justified. This requires four steps.

Step 1: Calculate the most recent twelve-month average occupancy of the most competitive hotels

Let us assume that there are five competitive hotels and their number of rooms and occupancies are as follows for the most recent year:

Hotel	Rooms in Hotel	Average Occupancy	Average Nightly Demand
1	320	70%	224
2	108	75%	81
3	246	85%	209
4	170	70%	119
5	312	85%	265
Total	1,156		898

For each hotel the number of rooms is multiplied by that hotel's average occupancy percentage to arrive at the average nightly demand. The total average nightly demand here is 898 rooms. The average annual occupancy of the most competitive hotels is then calculated by dividing the total average nightly demand by the total rooms available and multiplying the result by 100:

$$\frac{898}{1,156} \times 100 = 78\%$$

Step 2: Calculate the composite growth rate of demand from the various sources

Let us assume that we have the breakdown figures in percentages for each source and the annual compound growth rates for that source.

Source	Source of Demand	Annual Compound Growth	Composite Growth
Business travelers	75%	8%	6.0%
Convention delegates	10%	5%	0.5%
Vacationers	15%	10%	1.5%
Total	100%		8.0%

The source of demand percentages are multiplied by the annual compound growth rate percentages in the next column to find the composite growth rate figures in the right-hand column (for example, 75% x 8% = 6.0%). The annual compound growth rate figures can be estimated from historic growth rate figures projected into the future. The total overall composite growth rate figure is 8.0 percent.

Step 3: Calculate future rooms demand year by year

This calculation is as follows:

Year	Demand	Composite Growth	Future Demand
1	898	108%	970
2	970	108%	1,048
3	1,048	108%	1,132
4	1,132	108%	1,223
5	1,223	108%	1,321

In year 1 the current average nightly demand for rooms, 898 (calculated in step 1), is multiplied by the composite growth rate, 108 percent (100% + 8% composite growth rate, as calculated in step 2), to arrive at the future demand figure of 970 rooms in year 1. This figure is carried forward into year 2 and is itself multiplied by 108 percent. Similar calculations are made for each of the remaining three years.

Step 4: Calculate the future supply of rooms

We know from step 1 that the current occupancy rate in the competitive area is 78 percent. Let us now assume that a 70 percent occupancy of hotel rooms is "normal" for our competitive area. Normal means that at that occupancy a hotel should be profitable. We therefore know that the local market could support additional rooms right now, as the current occupancy is averaging 78 percent. We can calculate the current need for additional rooms at a 70 percent occupancy rate by dividing the current nightly demand by 70 percent:

$$\frac{898}{70\%} = 1{,}283$$

From this we can conclude that there is currently a "shortage" of 127 rooms (1,283 that the market could support less the 1,156 that the market currently offers). Stated another way, if a new 127-room hotel were built today, given the current demand for rooms, the new overall average occupancy would be 70 percent:

$$\frac{898}{127 + 1{,}156} \times 100 = 70\%$$

Next, the future demand for additional hotel rooms is projected for the next five years, as follows:

Year	Demand for Rooms	Normal Occupancy	Supply Required	Current Supply	New Rooms Required
Current	898	70%	1,283	1,156	127
1	970	70%	1,386	1,156	230
2	1,048	70%	1,497	1,156	341
3	1,132	70%	1,617	1,156	461
4	1,223	70%	1,747	1,156	591
5	1,321	70%	1,887	1,156	731

In this tabulation each of the future demand figures from step 3 has been divided by a 70 percent occupancy rate (as was demonstrated earlier for the current year) to arrive at the figures in the supply required column, and from each year's supply required figure the current supply of rooms (1,156) has been deducted. The end result is a forecast of the number of new rooms that could be supported over each of the next five years, given all of our assumptions. We see that at the end of five years, 731 additional rooms could be supported, with an average occupancy of 70 percent. Note also that the figures for rooms required, in the right-hand column, are cumulative from year to year.

To reduce risk we might want to assume a 75 percent, rather than a 70 percent, occupancy. In that case the year-by-year demand figures would be divided by 75 percent, resulting in fewer additional rooms per year that the market could support.

Before the supply–demand analysis is completed and a recommendation is made about the size of property to be planned, other factors may need to be considered. For example, if any of the existing competitive facilities will be removed from the market (demolished or converted to some other use), the supply figures should be adjusted accordingly. Similarly, if any information is available about other proposed competitive hotels in the area, this should be considered in the future supply figures. Finally, the decision about whether to build should not be based on numbers alone. Frequently, two adjacent, competitive hotels, motels, or restaurants will have vastly different demands for their products. Many nonquantifiable factors can cause this to be so, such as atmosphere, quality of decor, management, and staff training.

Space Recommendations

The feasibility study at this point might include information that the architect requires in order to prepare more detailed plans, such as number of rooms, the number of rooms of various types (singles, doubles, twins), the proportion of space and number of seats recommended for food, beverage, and related facilities like meeting rooms and public space (lobbies), and possibly even suggested themes for bars and restaurants. Back-of-the-house facilities, space requirements (kitchens, storerooms, offices), and parking space requirements may be included. Finally, any recommendations concerning recreation facilities should be covered in this section.

FINANCIAL ASPECTS

Once the feasibility study's marketing aspects have been discussed, the financial aspects must be addressed. A full explanation of the financial aspects of a feasibility study are beyond the scope of this textbook, but in summary they would include at least the following:

1. Capital investment required in total for land, building, furniture and equipment, interest on construction financing, preopening operating expenses, and initial working capital.

2. Breakdown of required investment into a financing plan showing which funds will be from debt (borrowed money) and which from equity (funds to be provided by the business's owners or shareholders).

3. Pro forma income statements showing department by department (for example, rooms, food and beverage) what the revenues and the expenses will be so that the anticipated net profit can be determined. These income statements would be for a minimum of the first five years and preferably for ten or even more years.

4. Conversion of the projected net profit into a cash flow and an evaluation of the returns against the equity investment using a method such as net present value or internal rate of return.

DISCUSSION QUESTIONS

1. State the equation for calculating an entire community's needs for visitor accommodations.

2. In the first question, how is this equation changed for a seasonal situation?

3. Because a feasibility study for a proposed new venture cannot guarantee that the venture will be successful, what value does it have?

4. In a feasibility study for a suburban transient motel, what general market characteristics do you think might be relevant?

5. In preparing a feasibility study for a motor hotel to be located in an area where there are several other motor hotels, what factors would you consider to determine which of the other operations was the most competitive?

6. A resort hotel is to be located in a mountain area near a major highway about 150 miles from the closest town or city. What sources of demand might you consider in a feasibility study for this property?

7. Briefly describe how a composite growth rate of demand for hotel rooms can be calculated.

8. List and briefly discuss the four major financial subsections that would appear in a feasibility study.

PROBLEMS

1. A new tourist destination community estimates that it will have 1.25 million visitors a year and that 90 percent of these will stay in hotels. The average

number of people per room will be 1.6, and the average length of stay will be ten days.

a. Calculate the number of rooms required, assuming a 75 percent occupancy of hotel rooms.

b. How many rooms would be required in this community if it were a seasonal resort with a 180-day season and its hotel room occupancy during this season were 90 percent?

2. Six competitive motor hotels have the following number of rooms and current occupancy rates:

Motor Hotel	Rooms	Occupancy
1	140	85%
2	160	80%
3	84	75%
4	90	70%
5	120	80%
6	144	75%

The demand for rooms in the area where the motor hotels are located is broken down into the following sources and growth rates:

Source	Percent	Growth Rate
Business travelers	50%	5%
Vacation travelers	40%	6%
Others	10%	1%

a. Calculate the current average occupancy of the six motor hotels.

b. Calculate the composite rate of growth in demand.

c. Apply the composite growth rate to the demand figures to obtain the projected demand for each of the next four years.

d. Assume that a 75 percent average room occupancy for the motor hotels in this area would be profitable. Assume also that motor hotel 3 is due to be demolished in year 2 to make way for a new highway. Calculate the future supply of rooms that could be supported for each of the next four years.

SUGGESTED READINGS

Lee, Daniel R. 1984. "A Forecast of Lodging Supply and Demand." *Cornell Hotel and Restaurant Administration Quarterly* 25(2): 27–40.

Pannell Kerr Forster. 1986. *Trends in the Hotel Industry.* Houston: Pannell Kerr Forster.

Pannell Kerr Forster. 1986. *Trends in the Hotel Industry, International Edition.* Houston: Pannell Kerr Forster.

Smith, Stephen L. 1977. "Room for Rooms: A Procedure for the Estimation of Potential Expansion of Tourist Accommodations." *Cornell Hotel and Restaurant Administration Quarterly* 15(4): 26–29.

Waddell, Joseph M. 1977. "Hotel Capacity: How Many Rooms to Build?" *Cornell Hotel and Restaurant Administration Quarterly* 18(2): 35–47.

Marketing

CHAPTER OBJECTIVES

After studying this chapter the reader will be able to

- Differentiate, from a marketing viewpoint, a tourism product from a manufactured product.

- Define and discuss product-oriented marketing, market-oriented marketing, and societally oriented marketing.

- List the four assumptions on which market segmentation is based.

- List and briefly discuss the three ways of segmenting markets.

- Define the term *target marketing*.

- Give three examples of external factors that must be considered when analyzing a marketing plan.

- Define, and give an example of, a marketing objective.

- Discuss the product elements of the marketing mix.

- Discuss the various pricing elements of the marketing mix.

- Discuss the various promotion elements of the marketing mix.

In an earlier chapter on planning, the market-planning process was discussed in reference to a destination community or area. This chapter will discuss the marketing process in more depth. Tourism marketing is

- Determining the needed products and services.
- Taking the steps to provide them.
- Pricing them competitively and in a way that will be profitable.
- Selecting the most appropriate ways to communicate information about them.
- Selling them.

THE TOURISM PRODUCT_____

Tourism is an intangible product, and for that reason it is unique. It sells an experience rather than a physical item of merchandise that a potential customer can inspect before purchasing. In addition, the tourism product cannot be stored. For example, airlines must try to fill all seats on all flights, and hotels, all rooms each night. This is usually impossible, but airlines and hotels must nonetheless make the attempt because an empty seat or an empty hotel room is revenue lost forever. There is also no way to increase the supply of tourism facilities in the short run, as the supply is fixed. That supply is also made up of a combination of resources from a variety of different businesses (airlines, hotels, attractions, restaurants, and others) requiring cooperation and interdependence in marketing.

Tourism products are also often located a fair distance from the customers, which requires intermediaries who can influence both the potential tourists and the tourist suppliers. This is the role played by tour wholesalers and travel agencies. Tourism products have to be sold mostly sight unseen by the purchaser. In other words, he or she must spend both time and money before actually using the product or service. Unfortunately, this difference between the time of decision or purchase and the time of use or consumption has allowed, and perhaps even encouraged, promotional practices that are sometimes less than honest. As Murphy (1985, p. 12) stated:

> The image builders are often marketing or advertising experts who select and arrange "facts" about the destination that will entice would-be visitors. . . . This lack of inherent control for the industry's marketing can lead to advertisements of questionable taste and of a self-destructive nature.

Finally, tourism demand (except for business travel) is mostly highly elastic (that is, an increase in price will decrease the volume of tourists), extremely seasonal, horrendously competitive (vacation tourist demand can be satisfied at a choice of locations), and very subject to fads, fashions, and changes in tourist motivation. The tourism product can be either product or market oriented.

Product Orientation

Product-oriented tourism emphasizes the products and services of tourism supply, based on physical, cultural, historic, or folkloric attributes or a combination of several of them. This approach to tourism marketing does not take into account the desires of the potential tourists, particularly if the marketing is totally product oriented. Theoretically, this marketing approach can be successful if demand exceeds supply, but competition among tourism sellers normally does not allow this.

Market Orientation

A market-oriented approach emphasizes the needs and wants of potential tourists. It asks what will satisfy those needs and wants and when those needs and wants will occur and then tries to fulfill them. This marketing approach runs the risk of ignoring such things as local natural resources and culture and, for that reason, may alienate the local population.

Societal Orientation

Societal orientation, a third approach, combines the best of both product and market orientation. It considers the needs and wants of the tourists but does not ignore the long-term interests of the local population in such matters as economic, environmental, and social/cultural impacts.

MARKET SEGMENTATION

Market segmentation is a generally accepted approach to analyzing tourism demand. It is based on four assumptions. First, it assumes that tourists can be grouped into different market segments. Second, it assumes that people have different vacation/travel needs and preferences depending on their particular market segment. Third, it assumes that a specific destination or tourist experience will appeal to some segments of the market more than others. For example, a sea cruise can probably be sold more easily to the elderly segment rather than to young single people. Fourth, it assumes that tourism suppliers can improve their marketing efforts by developing products and services that appeal to specific market segments.

One example of segmentation is the development of a market that will fill in the shoulder areas of a seasonal resort. Many suppliers (such as hotels) find that the market for these months can be the elderly, who prefer to travel in this quieter tourist season. Note also that once market segments have been identified, the tourism supplier can also segment itself to try to reach more than one segment. For example, some hotel chains (such as Quality Inns and Ramada) have two or more distinct classes or types of hotels, with each class appealing to a different market segment and priced accordingly. Alternatively, some hotels segment themselves within a single property and offer guest rooms that contain more or fewer features at different prices. The airlines also do this on the same plane by offering first class, business class, and economy class seats, often at vastly different prices.

The Market Segmentation Process

The market segmentation process begins by identifying the various segments by any one of three methods or a combination of those methods. The most commonly used method is to identify a segment according to socioeconomic factors. In particular, factors such as age, education, and income are generally successful indicators of people's propensity to travel and differentiate them from other segments who are likely to travel. A second method is to segment people by geography. Contrasting and compatible climates, cultures, and scenery can attract different types of tourists. A third method is to segment the market by psychographic factors. Gathering psychographic information is both difficult and expensive. Psychographics focus on present and future buying behavior, physical needs, life-styles, and values, that is, how purchasers behave. This method is often used to supplement the socioeconomic or geographic methods.

Once certain broad segments have been established, they can then be broken down further. One way of doing this is according to vacation activity preference. A recent study of the potential pleasure travel market for Canada by residents of the United States and prepared for Tourism Canada (1982) identified four pleasure segments and researched the various attributes that were important to all of them as well as those that were important to each of them separately. The results are shown in Figure 22-1. The report also stated that the four attributes common to all segments are critical and must be in place before the other attributes would have any real significance. This type of information is extremely important to planning marketing promotion.

The Target Market

Once the segments have been classified, the marketer must identify which ones a particular destination will use to attract potential tourists. Those selected are commonly referred to as the *target market.*

Target marketing requires analyzing the sales potential of that segment or segments; that is, assessing the number of both current and potential new tourists and their per-person per-diem spending. Target marketing must also consider the competition, the cost of developing a destination for the target market, and the destination's financial and managerial capability of handling or servicing that target market. Note that in this context, the term *destination* can be a general tourist area or a specific enterprise, such as a hotel, in that area.

MARKET PLANNING

Once the target market has been selected and analyzed, marketing can move into the planning mode, which studies the external forces over which the planner has little or no control. These forces may be political (are there restrictions on currency or travel by the target market's country?), economic (is the total price, combined with the length of stay, too high for the target market?), technical (are there enough

Important to all segments:

1. Value for vacation dollar
2. Variety of activities
3. Friendliness of local residents
4. Good service

Important to urban segment:

1. Cultural activities
2. Historic buildings
3. Cosmopolitan atmosphere
4. Shopping
5. Big cities

Important to tourism segment:

1. High-quality restaurants
2. First-class hotels
3. Smaller towns
4. Countryside
5. Cultural activities
6. Historic buildings

Important to resort segment:

1. High-quality restaurants
2. First-class hotels
3. Resort areas
4. Nightlife and entertainment

Important to outdoor segment:

1. Countryside
2. Seaside
3. Lakes and streams
4. Mountains
5. National parks and forests
6. Wilderness

FIGURE 22-1. Important vacation attributes by market segment. (Source: Adapted from "Study of the Potential Pleasure Travel Market for Canada in the United States," prepared for Tourism Canada by Markets Facts of Canada Ltd., March 1982.)

air flights into the destination?), and even cultural (will there be too much conflict between the host community and the target market?).

The planner must also decide whether the marketing strategy proposed fits in with the overall strategy of the destination, or the business if the planning is for an individual business such as a hotel. The product and service must be analyzed to ensure that they are fully compatible with the target market. The competition must also be investigated: What is it likely to do to adapt to the planner's proposed marketing strategy?

Finally, the planner must make sure that the overall proposed marketing strategy is appropriate, considering the strengths and weaknesses of each section.

Marketing Objectives

At this point, marketing objectives can be established to determine the type of tourist or market segment one wishes to attract. For example, tourists could be identified as repeat tourists versus new tourists, high spenders versus low spenders, or elite tourists versus mass tourists.

Some tourists prefer to travel where there are few tourists. Others feel more comfortable when they are surrounded by similar types of people. Switzerland, for example, purposely chose a middle route between these two and has been very successful in creating a matching image of Switzerland. Maintaining this image, unless its tourism begins to decline, is thus important to Switzerland's marketing objectives. As another illustration, Bermuda, because of its relatively small island area, has opted for the top end of the market (and its hotel rates reflect this) and allows no charter or large-group arrivals.

The image, or type of tourist, that a destination wishes to attract must, of course, be compatible with the level or class of products and services offered and also with such matters as whether the products (for example, hotels) must be locally owned or financed by outsiders or foreigners, whose objectives may differ.

Travel Patterns and Marketing

For marketing to work there have to be appropriate travel connections between a destination and its market. In many cases, in which short distances are involved, the automobile provides this link. In other cases the bus or train is suitable. For longer distances there need to be suitable air connections or, in the case of water travel, cruise liner connections or, in some cases, river connections. These connections are only part of the requirement, however. For there to be a profitable traffic flow between two areas, there must also be an appropriate supply for the markets' demands. In other words, supply and demand must complement each other. Areas often complement each other because of contrasting climate. For example, it is not surprising that most of Florida's winter visitors are from the northeastern U.S. states and the provinces of Ontario and Quebec in Canada.

The cost of travel between a supply area and a demand area is also a factor to be considered in marketing. If the distance translates into a long travel time as well as high out-of-pocket costs, then many potential customers may seek a destination closer to home.

Many communities depend on their tourist revenue from nearby, rather than long-distance, visitors. By the same token, many communities depend on domestic tourism rather than international tourism. These considerations seem to imply that nations that are adjacent to each other will have a large flow of international short-distance travel between them, but that is not always the case. For example, consider Austria, a small country whose economy today is highly dependent on tourism. Immediately to the north of Austria is Germany, and the majority of Austria's tourists are from Germany. Immediately to the south of Austria is Italy, but Italy provides very few tourists to Austria. Obviously, the reasons are other than proximity and include language, food habits, culture, commercial associations, political ties, and others. That is, the accessibility of a destination to a potential demand source is not simply a matter of distance and ease of access. Some highly personal decisions are often the motivating force that creates tourism, and so those involved in planning must be aware of these motivators, many of which were discussed in Chapter 4.

Travel flows, once built up, will often stabilize and hold at a certain level. However, marketing experts must be aware of potential competition, as a new development (and even a new method of travel) can intervene in even well-established travel patterns.

Marketing Mix

Once the final target market has been pinpointed and the marketing planning established, the marketing mix must be determined. The correct marketing mix helps ensure that the target market will be attracted.

The various components of the marketing mix are the way that a tourist destination communicates with the type of tourists it wants. For example, a brochure illustrating a sea cruise with young customers dressed casually for dinner implies that it is not oriented to the elite high-priced market. The marketing mix has four elements: product, price, promotion, and distribution.

PRODUCT

Product planning is essential to developing a profitable destination or a profitable enterprise within that destination. It is often stated that to have a profitable product one must achieve the five "rights": the right product, at the right place, at the right time, at the right price, and in the right quantity. To achieve this, traditional marketing theory states that product planning must be approached from the consumer's point of view, keeping in mind consumers' constantly changing needs and desires.

But today, in tourism planning and marketing, that one-sided approach is changing. It still is important that the product or service satisfy the needs and wants of the target market, but tourism is now recognized as a user of resources in an area, and the consumers' needs must be balanced against the community's needs, with particular reference to its economic, environmental, and social/cultural aspects.

Product Considerations

A tourist product or service is unlikely to appeal to all possible market segments, and it probably will not be limited to only one segment. The destination must be able to produce its product. For example, a destination might decide that a new attraction (such as an amusement or theme park) will multiply an area's tourism severalfold. But are the millions of dollars of financing available for such a major enterprise, and even if financing is available, will the product fit environmentally into the area?

Sometimes products are complemented by having a facility that does not, by itself, generate any revenue. For example, expanding the beach area will not directly produce any revenue, but it will indirectly, as more people can enjoy the beach and may be attracted to stay in nearby hotels. For this same reason some governments own airlines that do not make money, for it is politically important to them to have their own national carriers to bring tourists to their tourist destinations. Those tourists will be profitable to the various local tourist enterprises who pay taxes.

In tourism product planning, the life-cycle concept must also be kept in mind. This concept was discussed in Chapter 4. The potential life cycles of tourism products should be of concern to both a tourism area in general and to each supplier in that area.

PRICE

A second factor in the marketing mix is price. Over the long run, price is based on supply and demand. But in the short run other important factors need to be considered.

The Organization's Objectives

Prices must be established with the organization's long-term objectives in mind. A typical objective could be any one of the following: to maximize sales revenue, to maximize the return on the owners' investment, to maximize profitability, to maximize business growth (in a new establishment), or to maintain or increase the market share (for an established business). A clearly thought-out pricing strategy will stem from the business's objective or objectives and will recognize that these objectives may change over the long run.

Besides a long-run pricing strategy, a business also needs short-run or tactical pricing policies to take advantage of daily opportunities. Such policies will consider elasticity of demand, cost structure, the competition, and product differentiation.

Elasticity of Demand

Elasticity of demand pertains to the responsiveness of demand for a product or service when prices are changed. A large change in demand resulting from a small change in prices is referred to as an *elastic demand*. A small change in demand following a large change in prices is referred to as an *inelastic demand*. Perhaps the easiest way to test whether a demand is elastic or inelastic is to note what happens to total revenue when prices are changed. If the demand is elastic, a decline in price will increase the total revenue because, even though a lower price per unit is received, enough additional units are being sold to more than compensate for a lower price.

For example, assume that the average restaurant customer spends $10.00 and that an average of 3,000 customers per week are served. The total revenue per week will be $30,000. If the average food check is reduced by 5 percent to $9.50 and the average weekly customer count goes up 10 percent to 3,300, the total revenue will then be 3,300 × $9.50, or $31,350, which is $1,350 more than before. The demand thus is elastic. A rule of thumb is that if demand is elastic, a change in price will cause the total revenue to change in the opposite direction.

If the demand is inelastic, a price decline will cause the total revenue to fall. The small increase in sales will not be sufficient to offset the decline in revenue per unit. Again, one can say that if the demand is inelastic, a change in price will cause the total revenue to change in the same direction.

One of the factors that influences elasticity of demand is the availability of substitutes. Generally, the hospitality businesses that charge the highest prices are able to do so because little substitution is possible. That is, an elite hotel with little competition can charge higher room rates because its customers expect to pay higher rates, can afford to do so, and probably would not move to a lower-priced, less luxurious hotel if the room rates were increased. The demand is inelastic.

On the other hand, a restaurant that is one of many in a particular neighborhood catering to the family trade would probably lose a lot of business if it raised its menu prices out of line with its competitors. Its trade is very elastic, and its price-conscious customers will simply take their business to another restaurant. In other words, one restaurant can easily be substituted for another. Alternatively, a restaurant with a high average check will probably find less customer resistance to an increase in menu prices. In general, one can say that the lower the income of a business's customers is, the more elastic their demand will be, and vice versa.

Closely related to income levels are the habits of a business's customers. The more habitual the customers are, the less likely they will be to resist some upward change in prices, as customers tend to have "brand" loyalties to hotels and restaurants, just as they have to other products they buy. Enterprises that need repeat business must be aware of the effect that price changes may have on that loyalty. Note also that the demand for a product or service tends to be more elastic the longer the time period under consideration is. Even though customers are creatures of habit and do develop loyalties, those habits and loyalties can change over time.

Each hospitality enterprise must therefore be aware of the elasticity of demand of the market in which it operates and how loyal its customers are. In other words, it must have a market-oriented approach to pricing. This market orientation is particularly important to short-run decision making such as offering reduced weekend and off-season room rates to help increase occupancy, or special food and beverage prices during slow periods. These reduced rates or prices are particularly effective when demand is highly elastic.

A hospitality enterprise manager must also realize that what happens in one part of the industry may affect other parts. For example, the hotel sector cannot act in isolation from other sectors. The effective manager must be alert to changing trends and new developments that may affect elasticity of demand and pricing decisions.

Cost Structure

A business's specific cost structure is also a major factor influencing pricing decisions. Cost structure in this context means the breakdown of costs into fixed and variable. Fixed costs are those that normally do not change in the short run, such as a manager's salary, or insurance expenses. Variable costs are those that increase or decrease depending on sales volume. An example is a restaurant's food costs. As food sales go up and down, food costs also will go up and down.

If a business has high fixed costs relative to variable costs, its profits are likely to be less stable as the volume of sales increases or decreases. In such a situation, having the right prices for the market becomes increasingly important. In the short run, any price in excess of the variable cost will contribute to fixed costs and net income, and the lower the variable costs are, the wider will be the range of possible prices. For example, if the variable, or marginal, costs (such as housekeeping wages, and linen and laundry expense) to sell an extra room are $10.00 and that room normally sells for $40.00, any price between $10.00 and $40.00 will contribute to fixed costs and net income. In such a situation, those who establish prices have at their discretion a wide range of possibilities for imaginative marketing and pricing to bring in extra business and maximize sales and profits. That is, they can take good advantage of tiered pricing.

Note that this concept of variable or marginal costing is valid only in the short run. Over the long run, prices must be established so that all costs (both fixed and variable) will be covered, in order to produce a long-run net income.

A knowledge of fixed and variable costs within an individual business is also useful for calculating that business's break-even level. This was discussed and illustrated in Chapter 13 with reference to hotels.

The Competition

A hospitality enterprise's competitive situation is also critical to pricing. Very few hospitality businesses are in a monopolistic situation (although some are, such as a restaurant operator who has the only concession at an isolated airport or a national government airline that allows no competition from others, as is the case in many European countries).

In a monopolistic, or nearly monopolistic, situation the operator has greater flexibility in determining prices and may, indeed, tend to charge more than is reasonable. However, in such situations the customer still has the freedom to buy or not buy a meal or drink, to stay fewer nights in an accommodation, or to choose rail travel or some other method over air travel. Also, in a monopolistic situation in which high prices prevail, other new entrepreneurs will soon be enticed to offer competition (unless the law prohibits them!).

In a more competitive situation an oligopoly often exists. An oligopoly contains one major or dominant business and several smaller, competitive businesses, with the dominant business often the price leader. Thus when the price leader raises or lowers prices, those of the other businesses are raised or lowered in tandem. An oligopolistic situation could arise in a resort area that has one major resort hotel surrounded by several other motels catering to slightly lower-income customers. And since airline deregulation in the United States, it appears that an oligopolistic situation may have arisen with the major national carriers.

Most hospitality enterprises, however, exist in a purely competitive situation in which the demand for the goods and services of any one establishment is highly sensitive to the prices charged. In such situations there is little to choose, from a price point of view, from one establishment to the next. Competitive situations are most obvious in the accommodation, foodservice, wholesale tour, and travel agency sectors of the industry. When there is close competition, competitive pricing will often prevail without thought to other considerations. For example, an operator practicing competitive pricing may fail to recognize that her particular product or service is superior in some ways to her competitors' and thus could command a higher price without reducing demand.

Product Differentiation

In a highly competitive situation, astute operators will look at the strengths and weaknesses of both their own situation and those of their competitors. In analyzing strengths and weaknesses, operators should try to differentiate themselves and their products and services from their competitors. Typically product differentiation has either an operational or a production orientation. An operational orientation concentrates on the need to sell more tour packages, to fill more hotel rooms, to sell more restaurant meals. A product differentiation marketing strategy will make heavy use of promotion, relying on demographic data to help design promotion methods.

The establishments that are most successful in differentiating then have more freedom in setting their prices. For a hotel, this differentiation can be ambience and atmosphere, decor, location, view, and similar things. Indeed, with differentiation, psychological pricing may be practiced, in which prices are set according to what the customer expects to pay for the "different" goods or services offered. The greater the differentiation is, the higher the prices can be set. For example, this situation prevails in fashionable restaurants and exclusive resorts where a particular market niche has been created, and at this point, a monopolistic or near monopolistic situation may again prevail. Thurow (1983, p. 10) explains:

> But the real world . . . is often marked by non-price forms of competition. In fact, you could say that price competition is too easy. Because no one thinks that he can get a comparative advantage by simply cutting prices, a business tries to focus competition on areas (quality, service, product differentiation) where it may be possible to get a non-duplicable edge. Restaurant owners know that customers may be attracted by posh surroundings and good service rather than cheap food.

PRICING SUMMARY

There is no one method of establishing prices for all hospitality enterprises. Each establishment will have somewhat different long-run pricing strategies for its overall objectives and will adopt appropriate short-run pricing policies depending on its cost structure and market situation. McIntosh and Goeldner (1984, pp. 212–213) list eleven factors that a tourism manager must consider in establishing prices:

- Product quality
- Product distinctiveness
- Extent of competition
- Method of distribution
- Character of market
- Cost of product and/or service
- Cost of distribution
- Profit margin desired
- Seasonality
- Special promotional prices
- Psychological considerations

PROMOTION

The third factor in the marketing mix is promotion. The consumer is able to see and inspect most products before purchasing. But this usually is not the case with the tourism product, although travel and promotion videos or films can give potential customers a preview. Therefore, for most tourism products and services, the challenge is promotion, or advertising, as a means of communication. This communication problem is compounded by the fact that in most cases the vacation/travel decision must be made by the purchaser long beforehand, except for impulse buying for short trips.

Persuasive Communication

Advertising, or promotion, is sometimes referred to as *persuasive communication* and is intended to

- Advise potential new customers of the business and the goods and services it offers.
- Remind current customers of the goods and services offered and their prices.
- Persuade customers that they need a particular good or service now and that they should purchase it from the advertiser.

Planning Advertising

Advertising is an investment rather than an expense, and successful advertising is planned, anywhere from six months to a year ahead. It should answer two important questions:

1. Why is the advertising being done? The reason for advertising should be more than simply to attract new customers. It also should emphasize certain aspects of the product. Will it be the business name, location, and types of products or services? Or will it emphasize that the business is new and has something different to offer? That is, advertising should have a purpose.

2. When should the advertising be done? This question is often answered once the advertising purpose has been determined. For example, a tour wholesaler might want to advertise a new group of tour packages to a new destination. Such advertising must reach the potential market at the time they are beginning to think about their vacation trips. Alternatively, that advertising may need to coincide with a special event, for example, Mother's Day in a restaurant advertisement. On the other

hand, if the advertising is meant to reinforce a business's name, it can be more flexible and less committed to specific times.

Tourism marketing decision makers must know where and when to advertise and promote. It is probably fair to say that millions are spent annually on advertising without the spender's being able to measure the results. Even if the results are known, the trends over time are not necessarily analyzed. Trends can show such things as whether or not the market is growing, which types of tourists are entering or leaving it, and whether or not the tourist mix is changing.

Some advertisers concentrate on advertising in new markets, and others on established ones. For example, an airline opening up a new route must concentrate on new customers. In terms of total advertising (apart from some governments) the airlines are the biggest advertisers, and they can often immediately measure the results of special promotions by the number of additional seats filled at that price. The advertising method actually used will depend on a number of factors.

Promotion Objectives

One of these factors is the promotion or advertising objectives. They should be as specific as possible, be reasonably attainable, be measurable (quantifiable), and be accomplished within a given time period. For example, an airline's objective might be to print a specific number of brochures and distribute them to a stated number of retail travel agencies by a specified time, at a stated cost, with the objective of communicating to a defined target market. Note that it is often preferable to have promotion objectives stated in terms of their communication purposes rather than in more general terms such as the sales to be generated. However, the "before and after" measurement of such quantifiable items as additional sales generated can be used to see whether the communication objectives were achieved.

Message Form

A second factor is the message form and content. It must tell the target market what they need to know to make a decision. Once the advertising message is created, it should be tested before it is actually used, to ensure that the person receiving the message understands what is being communicated.

The effectiveness of the message must be measurable. This can be done by surveying the target market after the message has been sent or distributed to determine how well the message has achieved the promotion's objectives. In some cases the media themselves (for example, a radio station or magazine) can help a business prepare an effective advertising message campaign.

It is important to be careful about any claims made in advertising messages. False, exaggerated, or misleading statements can cause later legal problems with customers. Finally, before they are printed, advertisements should be carefully proofread to eliminate any errors.

Budget Available

Another factor to consider is the budget. Advertising budgets are usually established as a percentage of sales or revenue. Guidelines are available regarding the amount of money that various tourism enterprises spend on their advertising/promotion budgets in relation to their total annual revenue, such as

- Tour wholesalers 10 to 20 percent.
- Travel agencies 4 to 6 percent.
- Airlines 3 to 7 percent.
- Hotels 2 to 5 percent.
- Restaurants 2 to 3 percent.
- Resort destinations 3 to 6 percent.
- Government tourist offices 50 to 80 percent.

These figures do not indicate what a specific enterprise must spend; they only are industry averages. A particular enterprise may have an advertising budget that is within these guidelines, but there is no reason that more cannot be spent in order to meet a certain objective.

Some argue that the budget percentage should increase when sales decline (because at that time the products or services need the advertising) and should decline when sales increase. Regardless of the policy, the objective of advertising is to maximize the benefits of advertising within budget limitations. The advertising budget will generally be higher during peak sales periods, as advertising can be aimed to bring people in during slow sales periods. Advertising during slow periods for the peak season can be ineffective, particularly if the business will be running at 100 percent of capacity during the peak period anyway.

About 20 percent of the total budget will be for developing the advertising message, and about 80 percent will be for the actual cost of running the advertisement using one or more of the available media. Sometimes it is useful to base an advertising budget on past successful efforts, assuming that the results of past marketing efforts will continue in the future. For example, if spending 5 percent of sales last year, rather than a normal 3 percent (a two-percentage-point increase in the advertising budget), produced 10 percent more business, then should not 7 percent next year (another two-percentage-point budget increase) raise sales a further 10 percent? The answer is, not necessarily. For example, last year's 10 percent sales increase may have been achieved by operating at capacity, and so no more business can be accommodated by further advertising. Alternatively, the potential market may be saturated with a 5 percent advertising budget, and so spending more may bring in no further business.

For most tourist enterprises, advertising is an absolute necessity. However, in comparison with a large company, the small tourist business operators (and they form by far the largest sector of the industry) are at a disadvantage in some ways in advertising, as, to be effective, the advertising budget of the small business has to be a relatively larger percentage of the sales dollar. In addition, the typical large business, because of its large advertising budget, can also use advertising agencies that have professional staffs.

Advertising Agencies

An advertising agency can do any or all of the following:

- Use its own and other resources in market analysis and research so that advertising messages can be geared to the best prospects.
- Provide advice on the best media to use to convey the message. (The various media will be discussed later in the chapter.)
- Develop message, or "copy," ideas and message layout using a mixture of words and graphics.
- Establish achievable promotion goals.
- Plan and carry out public relations programs. (Public relations will be covered later in the chapter.)

The small business cannot usually afford this service, as commission costs can amount to as much as 15 percent of the amount spent on advertising, which must be added to the cost of any artwork or photography required.

Preopening Promotion

A rule of thumb for a new business opening is that the advertising budget should be doubled during the first year, and the added amount should be spent within a month or two before the opening. For example, if a new hotel's sales goal were $1.5 million a year and the advertising budget were 4 percent of that, or $60,000 a year, an additional $60,000 might be set aside for advertising in the opening year to provide the potential market with information and/or to encourage business away from competitive hotels.

Established Versus Created Demand

A successful existing business has an established demand for its goods and services, but this established demand needs to be supported by continued advertising. Conversely, increased business for an existing tourist supplier, and new business for a new supplier, must generally depend on created demand: advertising that attracts new customers, or old customers to new goods or services.

Once an advertising strategy has been designed, it should be maintained, although this does not mean that if the need arises, occasional special advertising cannot be added.

Methods of Promotion

Advertising, or sales promotion, can be either direct or indirect.

DIRECT SALES PROMOTION

Direct sales promotion is defined as sending a commercial message to both established and potential customers, with the objective of increasing sales. There are various forms of advertising media that a tourist business can use to send its advertising message to its customers. Whichever medium is selected, the advertising must be

- Within the budget.
- Compatible with the image and product or service being promoted.
- Suitable for the market and geographic area of the business.
- Able to serve the geographic area.

Newspapers

Newspapers are a common and popular advertising vehicle. For example, if a restaurant services only part of a city, then the local community newspaper might be preferable to the large city newspaper and will also cost less. Newspapers offer flexibility (in size of possible advertisements, graphics, and the day(s) on which the business wishes to advertise).

The advertiser must be familiar with the market area that the newspaper serves and obtain its circulation. Newspaper advertising rates are based on circulation: The higher the circulation is, the higher the cost will be. The advertising cost divided by the newspaper's circulation gives a cost per reader for purposes of comparison.

Newspaper space is sold in lines or inches and columns. For example, a two-column, twenty-five-line advertisement would cost the same as fifty lines in one column. Newspapers will also generally offer special contract rates when the advertiser agrees to purchase a specified minimum number of column inches over a year. This can significantly reduce the cost per column inch.

The main disadvantage of newspaper advertising is the newspaper's short life.

Radio

For a restaurant a local radio station can often be a useful form of advertising. Radios can reach a wide range of customers with a short lead time, although repetitive advertising is generally required for it to have any effect. Repetition, however, does cost money.

Radio advertising is usually sold in ten- , fifteen- , thirty- , or sixty-second "spots." The half-minute and one-minute spots are the most popular. Costs vary depending on the time of day, listening-audience size, and the particular radio station. Advertising just before the news and from 7 to 9 A.M. and 4 to 6 P.M. will probably cost more than the same ad halfway through an hour of music.

It is important to find out the cost per thousand listeners. For example, if a spot announcement costs $30.00 and reaches five thousand people, the cost per thousand listeners will be $6.00. The cost per thousand can be compared from station to station and from one time period to the next on each station.

Also, as with newspaper advertising, the cost per thousand will decrease if the business signs a contract to run a specified number of advertisements. Radio advertising is consumer oriented and useful for prompting impulse buying.

Television

Television advertising is very expensive. It does have the advantage of a visual impact that radio does not have, but in addition to the TV station's cost of time, there can be production costs that, even for a thirty-second ad, can run into the tens of thousands of dollars. Television is used on local stations by local restaurants and on national stations by hotels and cruise lines. Governments at various levels involved in tourism often also use television advertising. Television is primarily consumer oriented, and advertising on it is seasonal.

Magazines and Trade Journals

Magazine and trade journal advertising can be expensive but may reach more directly the type of customer who is interested in the tourist products advertised. However, if the business is localized (as it might be in many restaurants), then the expense of advertising in this medium may not be worth the cost, other than in the case of local magazines such as tourist visitor guides.

An advantage of magazine advertising is that unlike radio, television, or newspapers, magazines can last for long periods of time and can be read by a succession of people. However, the small tourist business should advertise in them only with caution and recognize that they may need from two to four months of lead time to prepare and run an advertisement.

Direct Mail

Direct mail can be an effective form of advertising, particularly if it can be selective (for example, a hotel's mailing a brochure to customers previously served). It is relatively inexpensive, and its effectiveness is easy to measure.

Direct mail includes the use of business cards, postcards, coupons, catalogs, letters, circulars, and price lists. The rate of return in direct mail campaigns usually averages about 2 or 3 percent. In other words, if a travel agency sent out ten thousand circulars, it might expect two hundred to three hundred people to respond in some way. Handbills, or general flyers, are a form of direct mail. They are unaddressed sheets that are distributed to a specified geographical area, such as households. Their purpose is to advertise certain products or special sales. Flyers are particularly well suited to the business with a local market (such as a restaurant or travel agency), as the cost of advertising in this way is relatively lower than with most other media. Direct mail flyers, as opposed to general flyers, are addressed to specific households of people who have been, or are likely to be, customers. They can be more effective than general flyers, as they are individually addressed and are therefore less likely to be thrown out immediately.

Direct mail companies can supply names and addresses of potential customers to add to a property's own lists. For example, a hotel can obtain from these specialist companies the names and addresses of credit card holders, airline frequent flyers, professional or other association members, or similar groups so that it can advertise directly to those potential customers.

Brochures and Pamphlets

Brochures and pamphlets are often used by individual hotels, motels, attractions, and by small resort destinations to explain such items as accommodation types available, restaurants, attractions, climate, and maps of the area.

Directories

Directories, particularly a telephone directory's yellow pages, can also be useful for a business whose customers might want to reach it by telephone (for example, a hotel or restaurant for making a reservation). Because telephone directories are usually published annually, their advertising messages have a relatively long life. Another type of directory is that used by an airline or independent package tour or cruise company for listing destinations, schedules, dates, and costs for all the various tours or cruises for an entire season.

Public Transportation

Public transportation (buses, subways, taxis) are another popular way to advertise, although it is difficult to determine their effectiveness.

Highway Billboards

Billboards are still used by many small businesses (for example, restaurants or motels) where they can be strategically located to catch the eye of potential customers. Billboard advertising is relatively expensive, for both the billboard rent and the advertisement production costs. They are also prohibited, or restricted in size and design, in many jurisdictions, for environmental reasons.

Travel Shows and Travel Films

Travel shows and travel films concerning a tourist destination are often used by tourist organizations. For example, a city or resort destination might show a film about its area in order to try and attract a convention group.

INDIRECT SALES PROMOTION

In addition to direct methods of advertising, there are also the following indirect forms of advertising.

Tourism Organizations

Tourism organizations are groups such as visitor and convention bureaus, hotel associations, or even chambers of commerce. One of the main objectives of such groups is to advertise and publicize the destination in an unbiased way in order to attract tourists, including business and convention groups. In other words, the organization makes the sale for the individual tourist business operator.

Tourism organizations often have to advertise two to six months ahead of the actual season, and for conventions the selling job may have to be done years ahead.

For the general tourist, the advertising is usually oriented to prompting inquiries for additional information, and impulse buying is often the result. Government organizations often set up information offices at border-crossing points, highway entrances to destination areas, and even airports. These information offices are usually well stocked with brochures, pamphlets, and other literature about accommodations and attractions in the area, as well as maps, and sometimes even directories of lodging and dining places and attractions. These offices play a key role in tourist promotion. Their job is not just to encourage inquiries but also to establish a positive image of an area as a vacation destination.

Tourist organizations' and group information offices' promotion costs are shared by their many tourist suppliers, which lowers the cost to the individual operator and makes the promotional messages more effective. This is sometimes referred to as *joint marketing*.

Usually a hotel, attraction, or resort destination will have its own independent tourism promotion campaign as well as cooperate in a group organization's efforts for the area as a whole.

Public Relations and Publicity

Public relations is an attitude expressed by placing priority on the public at large when business decisions are made. It is a form of advertising that generally costs only time. Public relations is both an internal and an external opportunity for increasing sales.

Internal public relations includes how customers and employees are treated, as both groups can be goodwill ambassadors for a business. External public relations means letting people know, and generating publicity, about the good things that the business is doing, by releasing "news" items or photographs to local newspapers, radio stations, and even television stations. For example, if a hotel sponsors a sports team, participates in a charitable event, has some celebrity visitors, or is the site for making a film, the local news media might like to know about this. The stories must be newsworthy and not resemble an advertisement in order for them to be acceptable to the news media. Words and pictures go a long way in creating community goodwill that is part of public relations, and this type of advertising can be done for little, if any, cost.

One successful method of publicity is to arrange a special promotion by inviting groups of people such as news media writers and photographers to a reception or the opening of a new restaurant, hotel addition, or attraction. There is a cost attached to this kind of publicity, but the benefits can be long lasting.

DISCUSSION QUESTIONS

1. From a marketing perspective, how does a tourism product differ from a manufactured product?
2. Define product-oriented marketing, and explain whether it is feasible.
3. Define market-oriented marketing, and explain whether it is feasible.
4. Define societal orientation as a marketing approach to developing and selling a tourism product.
5. Market segmentation makes four assumptions. What are they?
6. List and briefly discuss three ways of segmenting markets.
7. What is a target market?
8. In analyzing a marketing plan, there are some external factors that a planner may have no control over but that must be considered. Give an example of three of them.
9. Define marketing objectives, and give an example of one.

10. Briefly discuss "product" as one element of the marketing mix.

11. Discuss elasticity of demand in pricing.

12. Explain how a business's cost structure can affect its pricing.

13. Discuss competition in pricing decision making.

14. Discuss product differentiation in pricing.

15. What are promotion objectives?

16. Discuss message form and its role in promotion.

17. Explain how budgets can affect promotion.

18. Contrast direct sales promotion with indirect sales promotion.

19. Discuss how both radio and television can be used as advertising media.

20. Explain how tourism organizations can be part of an independent supplier's promotional campaign.

21. Explain how public relations can be used in a promotional plan.

22. It has been suggested that tourists are not so much concerned about specific tourist facilities and travel arrangements as they are about having a pleasant total experience. Discuss this tourist characteristic and its implications for a marketing plan to attract visitors to a destination.

PROBLEMS

1. You have been appointed the advertising manager for a "spoke" (that is, regional) airline based in a city located in an agricultural area with a regional population of about 500,000. You know that most people in that regional airline's area have never been on an airplane. The airline has links with both national and international air carriers that can offer a wide variety of destinations and airfares, including package tours with hotels, restaurants, and attractions at sun destinations. Discuss which advertising media you could best use to reach a potential target market of "new" flyers. What incentive messages might you use in the advertising?

2. Obtain an advertising brochure (for example, for a hotel or attraction) from a tourist supplier such as a travel agency or local visitor bureau. Discuss its message content. For example, you might want to analyze the target market for this establishment. Does the brochure make this clear and achieve its communication objectives to reach this market? Does the advertiser make promises it may not be able to keep?

REFERENCES

McIntosh, Robert W., and Charles R. Goeldner. 1984. *Tourism: Principles, Practices, Philosophies.* New York: Wiley.

Murphy, Peter E. 1985. *Tourism—A Community Approach.* New York: Methuen.

Thurow, Lester C. 1983. *Dangerous Currents: The State of Economics.* New York: Random House.

Tourism Canada. 1982. *Study of the Potential Pleasure Travel Market for Canada in the United States.* Ottawa: Tourism Canada.

SUGGESTED READINGS

Archer, Brian H. 1980. "Forecasting Demand: Quantitative and Intuitive Techniques." *International Journal of Tourism Management*, March, pp. 5–12.

Bowen, John. 1986. "Computerized Guest History: A Valuable Marketing Tool." In *The Practice of Hospitality Management II*, ed. Robert C. Lewis, Thomas J. Beggs, Margaret Shaw, and Steven A. Croffoot. Westport, Conn.: AVI, pp. 193–201.

Bryan, Barbara E., and Andrew J. Morrison. 1980. "Travel Market Segmentation and the Implementation of Market Strategies." *Journal of Travel Research* 19(3): 2–8.

Coffman, C. DeWitt. 1980. *Hospitality for Sale.* East Lansing, Mich.: Educational Institute of A.H. & M.A.

DeVito, Richard. 1986. "The Senior Citizen Travel Market: Still in Its Growth Stage." In *The Practice of Hospitality Management II*, ed. Robert C. Lewis, Thomas J. Beggs, Margaret Shaw, and Steven A. Croffoot. Westport, Conn.: AVI, pp. 467–471.

Ferguson, Dennis H. 1987. "Hidden Agendas in Consumer Purchase Decisions. *Cornell Hotel and Restaurant Administration Quarterly* 28(1): 31–38.

Garvey, Joe. 1986. "Outlook and Opportunities in Market Segmentation." In *The Practice of Hospitality Management II*, ed. Robert C. Lewis, Thomas J. Beggs, Margaret Shaw, and Steven A. Croffoot. Westport, Conn.: AVI, pp. 451–455.

Gee, Chuck Y., Dexter J. L. Choy, and James C. Makens. 1984. *The Travel Industry.* Westport, Conn.: AVI, pp. 126–139.

Graham, John E. J., and Geoffrey Wall. 1978. "American Visitors to Canada: A Study in Market Segmentation." *Journal of Travel Research* 16(3): 21–24.

Haywood, Michael K. 1986. "Scouting the Competition for Survival and Success." *Cornell Hotel and Restaurant Administration Quarterly* 27(3): 81–87.

Jarvis, Lance P., and Edward J. Mayo. 1986. "Winning the Market-Share Game." *Cornell Hotel and Restaurant Administration Quarterly* 27(3): 73–79.

Laudadio, Dante M. 1984. "Market Research in the Hospitality Industry." In *Introduction to Hotel and Restaurant Management*, ed. Robert A. Brymer. Dubuque, Ia.: Kendall/Hunt, pp. 164–171.

Lewis, R. C. 1981. "Marketing for Full Service Restaurants—An Analysis of Demographic and Benefit Segmentation." In *Marketing of Services, Proceedings Series*, ed. H. Donnely and R. George. Chicago: American Marketing Association, pp. 43–46.

Lohr, Judi, and Jim Moore. 1986. "Marketing Research: A Practical Application Case Study." In *The Practice of Hospitality Management II*, ed. Robert C. Lewis, Thomas J. Beggs, Margaret Shaw, and Steven A. Croffoot. Westport, Conn.: AVI, pp. 439–448.

Makens, James C. 1986. "Don't Let Your Sales Blitz Go Bust." *Cornell Hotel and Restaurant Administration Quarterly* 27(1): 65–71.

Makens, James C., and Chuck Y. Gee. 1987. "Building Sales Success with Travel Missions." *Cornell Hotel and Restaurant Administration Quarterly* 28(3): 67–73.

McCleary, Ken W. 1984. "Consumer Behavior in the Hospitality Industry." In *Introduction to Hotel and Restaurant Management*, ed. Robert A. Brymer. Dubuque, Ia.: Kendall/Hunt, pp. 171–175.

McIntosh, Robert W., and Charles R. Goeldner. 1984. *Tourism: Principles, Practices, Philosophies*. New York: Wiley, pp. 94–105, 249–262, 267–306, 311–345, 503–518.

Meyer, Robert A. 1987. "Understanding Telemarketing for Hotels." *Cornell Hotel and Restaurant Administration Quarterly* 28(2): 22–26.

Murphy, Peter E. 1985. *Tourism—A Community Approach*. New York: Methuen, pp. 104–115.

Renaghan, Leo M. 1984. "Marketing in the Hospitality Industry." In *Introduction to Hotel and Restaurant Management*, ed. Robert A. Brymer. Dubuque, Ia.: Kendall/Hunt, pp. 155–164.

Smith, Donald L. 1984. "Merchandising: Influencing the Consumer Purchase Decision." In *Introduction to Hotel and Restaurant Management*, ed. Robert A. Brymer. Dubuque, Ia.: Kendall/Hunt, pp. 176–184.

Swinyard, William R., and Kenneth D. Struman. 1986. "Market Segmentation: Finding the Heart of Your Restaurant's Market." *Cornell Hotel and Restaurant Administration Quarterly* 27(1): 89–96.

Troy, David A. 1986. "Marketing a Destination Area." In *The Practice of Hospitality Management II*, ed. Robert C. Lewis, Thomas J. Beggs, Margaret Shaw, and Steven A. Croffoot. Westport, Conn.: AVI, pp. 433–438.

Warren, Peter, and Neil W. Ostergren. 1986. "Trade Advertising: A Crucial Element in Hotel Marketing." *Cornell Hotel and Restaurant Administration Quarterly* 27(1): 56–62.

Witham, Glenn. 1986. "Hotel Advertising in the '80s: Surveying the Field." *Cornell Hotel and Restaurant Administration Quarterly* 27(1): 32–55.

Yesawich, Peter C. 1986. "A Market-based Approach to Forecasting." In *The Practice of Hospitality Management II*, ed. Robert C. Lewis, Thomas J. Beggs, Margaret Shaw, and Steven A. Croffoot. Westport, Conn.: AVI, pp. 419–432.

Yesawich, Peter C. 1987. "Hospitality Marketing for the '90s: Effective Marketing Research." *Cornell Hotel and Restaurant Administration Quarterly* 28(1): 49–57.

Tour Wholesalers and Operators

The complexity of tourism can best be appreciated if we take a look at the vast variety of organizations and firms that might be involved in a tourist's trip:

- Embassies and consulates
- Tour companies
- Travel agents
- Airlines
- Ships
- Railways
- Buses
- Taxis and limousines
- Hotels or other accommodations such as motels or campgrounds
- Restaurants and bars
- Entertainment places such as movies and theaters
- Attractions
- Shops
- Gas stations

- Laundries and dry cleaners
- Advertisers
- Suppliers to all the above

The tourism industry is unlike many others. In most manufacturing industries the product is packaged and shipped out through wholesalers to retailers to be bought by the consumer at a local shop. With tourism, the consumer or tourist has to be brought to the place where the product is "manufactured" before it can be enjoyed.

Some companies do their marketing directly. For example, airlines have ticket offices, and people can telephone or walk in, make reservations, and purchase tickets. Similarly, hotels advertise, and customers can write or telephone (frequently toll free) to make room reservations. In other cases, the marketing is done indirectly through tour wholesalers or, more often, travel agencies that represent airlines, hotels, or tour wholesalers.

TOUR WHOLESALERS

Tour wholesalers are companies that put together packages of tourism experiences for consumers. A tour package consists of at least transportation and accommodation and may also include some or all meals and even entertainment or attraction entrance fees. Sometimes this tour is sold through the wholesaler's own company, or a retail outlet that it owns or controls, or approved retail travel agencies. These packages can be offered to the public at lower prices than the individual tourist could find, because the wholesaler can obtain lower bulk prices from airline and other transportation companies, hotels, restaurants, attractions, and others. The wholesalers can package a wide range of different tours at different prices, with different destination choices, different hotels at each destination, and different lengths of tour.

Tour wholesalers generate a large amount of revenue for the travel industry. Although there are many tour wholesalers, within each country a few major companies seem to predominate. Most of the sales volume generated in each country is with those larger companies, as they can deal more easily with tourist suppliers such as the airlines and the hotels and thus offer the tourist lower prices.

Tour wholesalers have existed since the middle of the nineteenth century but have only more recently become a major component of the tourism business. The tour wholesaler's role expanded considerably when wide-bodied jet aircraft were introduced in the early 1970s and required more people than ever to fill those airline seats and the hotel rooms built to accommodate the airline passengers. In addition, as people learned that tour packages were generally cheaper than if the individual tourist put together and paid for the various parts separately, the consumer demand for these packages increased.

Tour packages have always been particularly popular in Europe. For example, it is estimated that the British spend about $3 billion a year on package holidays to sun countries such as Portugal and Spain.

Airline Wholesalers Versus Independent Wholesalers

Some tour wholesale companies are subsidiaries of airline companies which establish wholesalers in order to help fill the seats on their planes. In other cases the wholesalers are organizations independent of the airlines. Most wholesalers are independent but as a result do not always have the same great financial backing of a large airline. The risks and the mortality rate thus are high among independents. Some large retail agencies also put together their own tour packages. Some independents specialize in a specific destination that they know well; others specialize in particular ethnic groups or other market segments.

Tour Packages

The tour wholesalers work with airlines, shipping companies, hotels, restaurants, entertainment and attraction businesses, auto rental companies, and even with governments to put together attractive packages for potential tourists. The suppliers of all these services like this arrangement because unless a wholesaler is not successful, it guarantees the suppliers revenue they might not otherwise earn. As a result, they can offer price discounts to the wholesaler, who assumes the risk for selling the airline seats, hotel rooms, and other products and/or services.

Wholesalers then market their packages, sometimes directly but, more commonly, through retail travel agencies. About 80 percent of all package tours are sold through retail travel agencies. Some larger retail travel agencies become both wholesalers and retailers, by putting their own packages together. However, wholesalers and retailers usually are independent of each other, even though the success of each may depend on the other. Another arrangement is selling package tours through department store retail travel agencies by direct mail. The large German department store chain Neckermann does this through a direct mail catalog of the tours it handles.

THE WHOLESALER'S ECONOMICS

The tour wholesale business is characterized by its ease of entry. It is not difficult to open a tour wholesale business, as it requires very little cash to start up.

Although there sometimes are government or industry constraints on what constitutes a tour and how long it may last, the wholesaler needs only a local business license to operate and then to abide by airline and/or government constraints on pricing, advertising, bonding, and commissions. The wholesaler contracts with airlines, hotels, and others for a specified number of seats and hotel rooms on which a deposit may be required. This deposit is recovered by the wholesaler fairly rapidly from the deposits paid by customers who buy the package.

The balance of the customer's price is paid before the trip begins, but the wholesaler does not pay the suppliers (such as hotels) the balance owed them until after the trip is over. During this period the wholesaler has the use of these funds, known as *float*. Wholesalers run into trouble when the float from one tour is used to finance their deposits to suppliers on the next one. A rule of thumb is that a tour wholesaler will make money only if more than 85 percent of the packages are sold; that is, 85 percent is the break-even point.

The Wholesaler's Profits

The wholesaler generally makes a profit only on the nontransportation parts of package tours (unless he is also his own retailer), because the commission from the transportation company goes to the retail agent as his revenue, from which his operating costs are deducted to earn a profit. The wholesaler must therefore be sure that the markup on the contracted prices from hotels and other suppliers is high enough to cover all his operating costs, such as office rent, labor, and advertising, in order to provide a profit.

Normally, about 50 percent of the price paid by a tour purchaser is for the nontransportation aspects of a tour. A wholesaler might expect to have as a profit about 3 percent of the total price for a package. That might not sound like much, but it can provide a substantial return on investment, as there is little up-front wholesaler investment required. Typical per-person income, expense, and profit for a wholesaler's tour might be as follows:

Tour revenue:		$1,000
Direct costs:		
Airline	$480	
Hotels and food	220	
Sightseeing	40	
Auto rental	30	
Agent commissions	50	
Other	30	
		850
		$ 150
Fixed costs		120
Profit		$ 30

According to McIntosh and Goeldner (1984, p. 463), a recent tour industry study showed that the direct or variable cost of business was 84 percent of the total business cost. The indirect or fixed cost represented 13 percent, leaving a before-tax profit of 3 percent.

Lead Time Required

One problem that tour wholesalers have is that it can require as much as eighteen months from the start of putting a package together until it is over. During this lead time the wholesaler must do market research, including analyzing the results of past tours, in order to develop any new destinations and services, and decide on each particular tour's specifications.

About a year ahead of the tour, ground services (hotels and other aspects of the tour) and transportation commitments must be made. Subsequently, pricing decisions for the ultimate tour traveler must also be made. Over the next few months advertising brochures must be prepared, a reservation system established, and arrangements made with the travel agencies who will actually handle the tour sales. Once this is done, the brochures must be distributed and any other advertising (newspaper, radio, television) planned. Before the tour actually begins, this cycle of events will have already begun again for the following year's business.

One of the problems that wholesalers have is that as much as a year ahead of a tour, contracts will have been signed committing the wholesaler to pay stipulated prices to foreign suppliers in their local currencies. The wholesaler receives his payments in the currency of the country where the tour is marketed. An unfavorable change in currency exchange rates thus could quickly erode the wholesaler's profit. On the other hand, a favorable change could substantially increase his profits.

TOUR OPERATORS

A tour operator differs from a tour wholesaler by the scale of operations. A tour operator is usually an independent entrepreneur who might put together only a handful of tours per year, with a limited number of travelers (for example, twenty) on each. The operator makes all the arrangements for the travelers, just as the wholesaler does. However, the operator, or his delegate, will accompany each tour and act as a tour leader, making sure that all arrangements are in order for each stage of the tour, acting as a tour guide, and solving any problems as they arise.

GROUND OPERATORS

Ground operators provide the ground services during a package tour customer's trip or at the eventual destination. Ground operators are not directly involved in air or ship transportation but, more commonly, in bus transportation and other land arrangements such as airport-to-hotel transportation and sightseeing trips. Ground operators may also put together their own packages, including hotel accommodations, to "sell" to wholesalers, who add the air or ship transportation for final marketing.

A ground operator might also put together a complete package of hotel, restaurant, ground transportation, and sightseeing services that is sold without any ship or air transportation necessary. For example, a tourist could fly independently from the United States to Europe and then take a package bus tour around Europe that is purchased directly from the ground operator in Europe. In this situation one could say that the ground operator is also a wholesaler. Ground package operators can sell their packages independently, but most often they are marketed through retail travel agencies.

Ground operators who specialize in providing packages or services for incoming foreign visitors are also sometimes known as *receiving agents* or *inbound agents.*

TOUR WHOLESALERS' COMPLAINTS

Over the past few years there have been more and more complaints about some participants in the tour wholesale industry. Generally these complaints have been directed at the less well managed wholesale companies. The tour business has grown rapidly owing to the public's demand for this type of travel arrangement, and many new, inexperienced operators have entered the field. They have made promises they have been unable to keep or made statements in their advertising that are not true. These complaints have surfaced as the consumers/tourists have become more cost conscious and more aware of their rights and the need to receive value for money.

Again, one of the factors that distinguishes travel purchases from the purchases of most other tangible goods is that the customer can rarely inspect the goods in advance. Choices have to be made mainly from advertising brochures or descriptions provided by travel counselors. In order to make a wise choice, the potential traveler must have accurate information. Sometimes a promised beachfront hotel is blocks from the beach, or a sea view can be obtained only by climbing onto the hotel's roof, or flight times are rearranged at the last minute to inappropriate times for the traveler. In some cases even the tour prices are changed.

Sometimes these changes are not the fault of the wholesaler. For example, flight times can be changed by the airline, and price changes can be caused by fluctuations in currency exchange rates. For this reason, in their advertising, most wholesalers make a statement about the limitations of their liability, but some less reputable companies phrase their limitations so narrowly that they exclude themselves from any liability whatsoever.

ORGANIZATIONS

Most tour operators belong to the U.S. Tour Operators Association (USTOA) and the American Society of Travel Agents (ASTA) in the United States, the Association of Canadian Travel Agents (ACTA) in Canada, or the Association of British Travel Agents (ABTA) in Britain, as well as to other organizations such as the Pacific Area Travel Association (PATA), and the Association of Caribbean Tour Operators (ACTO).

DISCUSSION QUESTIONS

1. Explain how the tourist product differs from a manufacturing industry's product.
2. What does a tour package normally contain?
3. Why did the role of the tour wholesaler expand in the 1970s?
4. Why do tourism suppliers such as airlines and hotels like to deal with financially sound wholesalers?
5. Discuss the economics of the tour wholesale business.
6. Why does the tour wholesaler not make a profit on the air portion of a packaged tour?
7. Explain the cycle of events that a tour wholesaler has to go through to arrange a tour, and the time frames involved.
8. Explain why currency exchange rates can be a risk for a wholesaler.
9. How does a tour operator differ from a tour wholesaler?
10. Differentiate between a tour wholesaler and a ground operator.
11. What is a receiving or inbound agent?

PROBLEMS

1. Obtain a tour wholesaler brochure from a local travel agent. Discuss this brochure with particular reference to any descriptive clauses that are vaguely stated and for broadly based liability disclaimers or fine-print disclaimers that are buried at the back. Also state your reaction, with reasons, as positive or negative, concerning whether as a potential client you would want to use this wholesaler's company.
2. To organize a specific tour, a wholesaler has fixed costs of $14,000. The selling price of the tour will be $2,000 per person. The wholesaler's variable costs per person for each tour sold are 95 percent of the per-person revenue. Using the

break-even equation discussed in Chapter 13,

a. Calculate the break-even number of customers required.

b. Assume that the calculated break-even number of customers represents 80 percent of the maximum number of customers that can be accommodated on this tour. Calculate the maximum number of tours that can be sold.

c. Calculate the tour wholesaler's profit, assuming that the maximum number of tours is sold.

REFERENCES

McIntosh, Robert W., and Charles R. Goeldner. 1984. *Tourism: Principles, Practices, Philosophies.* New York: Wiley.

SUGGESTED READINGS

Curran, Patrick, J. T. 1978. *Principles and Procedures of Tour Management.* Boston: CBI.

De Souto, Martha Sarbey. 1988. *Group Travel Operations Manual.* Albany: Delmar.

Gee, Chuck Y., Dexter J. L. Choy, and James C. Makens. 1984. *The Travel Industry.* Westport, Conn.: AVI, pp. 150–152.

Phillips, Ralph G., and Susan Webster. 1983. *Group Travel—Operating Procedures.* Boston: CBI.

Reilly, Robert T. 1988. *Handbook of Professional Tour Management.* Albany: Delmar.

Travel Agencies

The travel agency is probably the most important link in the tourism distribution network. The travel agency is the final contact between those who wish to sell tourism and those who wish to buy it. Travel agents are the main distributors for travel suppliers. They book a greater percentage of airline seats, hotel rooms, and cruise reservations than does any other single type of distributor. Travel agencies have survived in the tourism business longer than some other sectors of the industry have, because they have been able to change with the times and adapt quickly to altered circumstances.

THOMAS COOK, AMERICAN EXPRESS, AND OTHERS_____

The two largest free-enterprise travel agencies in the world are Thomas Cook and American Express.

Thomas Cook

The first travel agent was Thomas Cook. He booked 570 passengers on a train in 1841 for a fifteen-mile ride between the towns of Loughborough and Leicester in England. For his efforts he received a 5 percent commission and then never looked back. By 1851 Cook had booked 165,000 people for trips to London to visit the first World's Exposition at Crystal Palace. In 1855 he arranged a five-day trip from England to the Paris Exposition and soon began conducting tours to Germany's Rhineland and then to Switzerland and Italy. He popularized Switzerland and other mountainous European areas as destination points for English tourists wishing to hike and climb in the mountains. This, in fact, laid the foundation that turned countries such as Switzerland and Austria into the major tourist-receiving countries they are today. In 1867 Cook led the first excursion to the United States and two years later guided a tour through the Holy Land and Egypt. In 1872 Cook had arranged the first round-the-world trip, a journey that took its travelers 222 days. In 1874 he provided travelers with circular notes, accepted by foreign banks and hotels, which were the forerunner of today's travelers' checks. Perhaps one of Cook's most spectacular achievements was the transportation of an entire expeditionary force of 18,000 men up the Nile River in 1884.

Cook recognized what economists refer to as the elasticity of demand of tourism. If prices can be brought down, more people will travel. So to help reduce prices he booked entire trains and blocks of hotel rooms to obtain a discount that he could pass on to his customers. In fact, the Thomas Cook Company chartered an entire Cunard liner in 1923 for an around-the-world cruise.

In 1931, the Thomas Cook Company merged with Wagons Lits, the operators of sleeping and dining cars on continental European express trains. Today, Thomas Cook has about six hundred offices and ten thousand employees around the world. Cook's true significance, according to Burkart and Medlik (1974, p. 15), was his invention of the excursion or holiday as a single transaction or package, rather than his establishment of a retail agency. His concept perfectly complemented the growth of the railways and later passenger shipping and brought organized travel to an increasingly large segment of the public.

American Express

The other major international travel agency is the U.S.-based American Express Company, or Amexco for short. Coincidentally, it was in 1841 (the year that Cook arranged his first rail excursion) that Henry Wells got started in the travel business and created the Wells-Fargo company. Amexco grew out of the Wells-Fargo company in 1850. In the latter half of the nineteenth century Wells-Fargo was primarily in the freight business and not in the people business. Then Wells-Fargo/Amexco introduced money orders in 1882 and travelers' checks in 1891.

Today, Amexco is a travel and financial conglomerate with about fourteen hundred Amexco agencies around the world. Amexco is said to be a major factor in world currencies because of its immense volume of daily financial transactions. Indeed, it has been described as a travel-oriented bank, rather than simply a travel agency.

Float

It is estimated that Amexco at any one time has $2 billion outstanding in travelers' checks, an amount commonly known as *float*, which represents the travelers' checks that people have purchased but not yet used. As long as they do not cash in those checks, then Amexco (and others who sell travelers' checks) have the use of that float for other purposes. It is as if they were given an interest-free loan, and it is no wonder that they encourage people to hang on to uncashed travelers' checks at the end of a vacation until they are needed for the next trip! Amexco has about 50 percent of the worldwide travelers' check business. Amexco also issues credit cards.

Other Travel Agencies

Thomas Cook and Amexco are not the only travel agencies: It is estimated that there are some sixty thousand agencies around the world, and about half of these are in North America. Some of the earliest travel agencies were hotel hall porters or concierges who would sell hotel guests rail and steamship tickets, as well as provide other services, and receive a commission. In those days most hotels were near the railway stations or dock areas at seaports. When the commercial airlines began operating in the 1920s and 1930s, they often located their sales offices in hotels and, because they sold directly to passengers, did not need to pay commissions.

Increase in Air Travel Volume

After World War II the dramatic growth of the airlines meant that they could not provide enough sales outlets of their own. Thus the specialist travel agency began to flourish, selling not only airline tickets but also the rail and ship tickets previously sold by the hotel concierges. Indeed, virtually all cruise ship tickets and about 75 percent of all airline ticket sales today are handled by travel agencies.

TRAVEL AGENCY OPERATIONS

Today's travel agencies provide many other services such as making hotel reservations, counseling customers on alternative vacation choices, handling auto rentals, selling travel insurance, advising on passport and visa requirements, and, in some instances, selling travelers' checks.

Agencies carry no inventory (other than items such as blank tickets and brochures provided free by the tourism suppliers). Generally, agencies are not tied to any particular airline, railway, shipping company, or hotel and can therefore be impartial in their advice.

Computerized Reservations

Today most North American agencies use computerized reservation systems. A variety of different systems are available, most of them developed by the airlines for their special needs. An agency is free to rent whichever system it wishes, but there is concern that each system tends to favor the airline that developed it, even though it can show, on the computer terminal, alternative schedules and fares from competing airlines. Attempts have been made to eliminate bias, but if there are more than two items on any list, one of them has to be listed first, and this immediately creates a bias. When introduced, the airline's computer reservation system first displayed on its screen all its own airline's flights, and if other airlines paid to have their flights displayed also, they were shown afterward. Today, to overcome this kind of bias, the general rule is that the shortest flights are listed first (regardless of airline).

A reputable agency will, of course, ensure that the customer knows all the travel alternatives so that he or she can make the final decision with full information. These computer systems also allow the agent to tie in a trip with hotel and car rental reservations.

Europe

European travel agencies are not now as computerized as North American agencies are. However, United Airlines and three European carriers (British Airways, KLM Royal Dutch Airlines, and Swissair) recently signed a computer system agreement that will provide more information to travel agents in Europe and improve flight service information both in Europe and the United States. United does not currently fly to Europe, but its Apollo reservation system is to be the model for the European system. (Apollo and the Sabre reservation system of American Airlines are considered to be the most advanced systems in the world.) The travel agencies now using Apollo in the United States will have up-to-date information on European flights, fares, seat availability, hotel space, car rentals, and train tickets. United will also benefit, as the three European carriers can steer passengers to United when they make U.S. travel arrangements for their trans-Atlantic flyers. United is obviously expected to reciprocate and favor the three European carriers when U.S. travelers are flying to Europe.

Home Computers

There is a suggestion that customers may one day have direct access through home computers to the airline reservation systems and will be able to make their own reservations, not only for air travel, but also for hotel accommodations and car rentals. In fact, with a microcomputer and telephone modem, one can already access the Source computer data bank in the United States and not only make an airline reservation charged to a credit card but also, given enough advance notice, have the ticket sent to a home or business address.

Satellite Ticket Printers

One of the most recent advances in travel agency operations is the satellite ticket printer (STP). An STP can sit in the office of a corporation and, when activated by a travel agent through a telephone line hookup, print out tickets in the office of the corporation. This will radically change the way corporate travel is handled and eliminate the agency's high cost of delivering tickets. In addition, if a major corporation wants to deal with one travel agency office that has special expertise, it can do so. Distance is no barrier. An STP also will allow a high-volume corporation to receive a single agency report for overall corporate travel analysis and audit.

The major problem with STPs is the concern over the security of blank-ticket stock. Agencies today are fully responsible for the blank tickets in their possession, and so moving that inventory of blank tickets to a corporate office would require some agreement on liability between the agency and the corporation.

Also in use today for the general public are airline ticket–dispensing machines, accessed by a credit card, that are located in banks, supermarkets, or other convenient areas. These same machines may eventually be programmed to issue travelers' checks. It is not likely that automatic ticketing machines will initially take a large share of the market. The reason is that at the moment, the system of routes and airfares is far too complex and would need to be simplified for the average tourist, who has limited time and interest in sorting through a great deal of computer information to find what is wanted. Also, ticketing machines cannot offer the counseling and other services that a complete travel agency can.

Commissions

A travel agency's advertising costs (brochures, posters, schedules) are paid by the suppliers who want to obtain the tourists' business through the travel agency. For generating this business the agency receives about a 10 percent commission on sales, from which it deducts its operating costs (salaries and wages, rent, office supplies, and so forth) to achieve a net profit. Most of the typical travel agency's commissions are earned from selling airline tickets. In some cases an airline will offer an agency an override, which means that the higher the sales are that an agency makes with that airline, the higher the commission rate will be. Some see this as encouraging agencies to favor a particular airline instead of being impartial.

At present, a customer pays no more whether booking directly with an airline or with an agency. But there has been some discussion among travel agencies that commissions may eventually be replaced by service fees. In other words, agencies will buy tickets at full price directly from the airlines and receive no commission. Their income will derive, instead, from charging their clients a service fee, probably based on the length of consulting time. Thus travel agency customers would be paying more for an item such as an airline ticket than they would by buying it directly from the airline. The agencies argue that they provide many more services than the airlines are willing to provide and that their customers should expect to pay for this service.

Discounts

Theoretically and legally airline seats are not allowed to be sold at less than the stated price—or to be discounted. But there are agencies, particularly in Britain, that discount airfares to passengers who are prepared to travel on short notice. That is, they sell these seats (or discount them) at less than the airline's stated price so that the airlines will receive some money for seats that would otherwise go empty. The agencies who do this type of business are commonly referred to as *bucket shops*. Airlines can also undercut their own stated prices by back-door discounting, that is, offering agencies higher-than-normal commissions. This benefits both the airline (through the agencies favoring it) and the agency (with higher commissions).

In North America there are also companies known as *consolidators*, operating with the participation of the airline industry, even though in the United States the Federal Aviation Act makes the practice illegal. The airline sells tickets to the consolidators and gives them a rebate or commission as high as 40 percent. The consolidators in turn distribute the tickets to retail travel agents at commissions that vary from 15 to 35 percent. Note that these consolidators are different from the discount bucket shops in Britain: The bucket shops deal directly with the public and sell only some flights to limited destinations at a highly discounted price. Consolidators, on the other hand, sell most of the flights of a particular airline to travel agents. Their net discount is lower but more widely available. Note too that with bucket shops the consumer gains, as he or she deals directly with the shop, but this is not true with consolidators, unless the customer is prepared to negotiate with the travel agency for a portion of the agency's commission! Indeed, some government agencies, and others who know about this, routinely place demands for rebates into the written agreements they negotiate with the travel agencies handling their air ticket purchases.

Sometimes when last-minute tickets are available, these rebates, or a portion of them—particularly on international tickets—are passed on to the customer who is willing to travel on short notice. The availability of these rebated tickets is detailed in the classified travel section of daily newspapers.

Corporate and Specialist Agencies

Some corporations and governments operate their own travel agencies to handle the travel arrangements of their own employees. The commissions they receive thus reduce their own operating costs, as the commissions do not go to a third party.

Because of the complex nature of today's tourism, there also seems to be a trend toward agency specialization. That is, a specialist agency can become an expert in a particular tourist destination or travel mode, rather than try to be a generalist at everything. For instance, an agency may specialize in cruise travel, or package bus tours, or trips to the South Pacific. Some agencies handle only tour packages, as the commissions on this are considerably higher than on other types of agency sales.

Franchised Agencies

Franchising also occurs in the travel agency business. By joining a franchise organization, an otherwise independent agency can benefit from the franchise organization's expertise, operating system, and national advertising. To join a franchise organization, the individual agency has to pay an initial entrance fee, plus an annual royalty usually expressed as a percentage of sales. A franchise organization is also likely to be able to use its size to negotiate for higher commissions from suppliers such as airlines and hotels. These higher commissions can be shared by the individual franchised agencies. (The subject of franchising is covered in some depth in the Appendix.)

Agency Cooperatives

Some independent agencies who do not wish to join a franchise have formed associations or cooperatives. Two of these are GIANTS (Greater Independent Association of National Travel Services) in the United States and INTRA (INdependent Travel Retailers Associated) in Canada. Members of these cooperatives can also benefit from the higher commissions negotiated by the head office through bulk buying. Agencies also pay an annual membership fee to the head office, but not an ongoing royalty based on sales, as is the case with a franchise. With the continued growth of chain agencies, franchises, and cooperatives, the independent travel agency entrepreneur will find it more and more difficult to survive financially.

Hotels and Agencies

Airlines, tour wholesalers, and cruise ship companies are highly dependent on travel agents. Although they have always dealt in only a limited way with travel agencies, hotels are now beginning to make much more detailed arrangements with them, as the hotel industry recognizes that there are additional profits to be generated by promoting their properties through travel agencies. Another reason is that more and more air travelers are using travel agencies, and it makes sense for them to have the agency book their hotel accommodations at the same time as they reserve their airline tickets.

TRAVEL AGENCY "APPOINTMENTS"

It is not difficult to enter the travel agency business, as the startup costs are relatively low. Money is needed mainly for office rent and furnishings, including a computerized reservation system. In most jurisdictions only a local business license is needed. However, some countries (for example Austria, Belgium, Bulgaria, France, and Italy) do require a government license.

What is difficult for a new independent agency (particularly if the owner has no previous experience) is surviving the first few months. During that period an agency must pay cash to obtain tickets from the carriers. As the tickets are sold the agency receives its cash back from the customer but does not receive any commission.

At the end of these first few months, if the agency has operated in a reputable and businesslike manner, it will receive an "appointment." At that time commissions will be paid to the agency retroactively for those first few months, and the agency will no longer have to pay cash to obtain tickets. From that point on, as tickets are sold, the agency will turn over the cash from the ticket sales to the supplier and hold back the commission earned.

A typical agency will receive appointments from groups such as the IATA (International Air Transport Association) for international airline ticket sales and from the agency's domestic airline association (such as the Air Traffic Conference—ATC —in the United States), as well as from other associations representing shipping and railway companies. These appointments are sometimes referred to as *exclusivity clauses*, as they allow the appointing body (for example, the IATA in the case of international airline tickets) to give travel agencies the exclusive right to write and sell airline tickets. These appointments have traditionally been made to ensure that there was as much professionalism as possible in the distribution and sale of airline tickets and that the customer's money paid for those tickets would be properly safeguarded. Before awarding appointments these supplier associations want to be assured that an agency and its employees have the competence to represent the supplier, have a good location to do a sufficient volume, and have a reasonable financial standing.

TRAVEL AGENCY ASSOCIATIONS_____

As is the case with many other business groups, the travel agencies have formed their own association to represent them as individual operators. The largest travel association in the world was founded in New York in 1931 and is today known as the American Society of Travel Agents (ASTA). Despite its name, ASTA has many members from around the world. These members may be travel agencies, tour wholesalers, travel suppliers, and allied members. Because its membership is so diverse, there is also a group that represents only retail travel agencies: the Association for Retail Travel Agents (ARTA).

Although travel agencies from around the world are members of ASTA, many countries or areas have their own independent association, such as the Association of British Travel Agents (ABTA), the Association of Canadian Travel Agents (ACTA), the Pacific Area Travel Association (PATA), and the Caribbean Tourism Association (CTA). International travel agency organizations include the International Federation of Travel Agencies, the World Association of Travel Agents, and the Universal Federation of Travel Agents Association.

In North America travel agency organizations have as one of their purposes improving the business and professional competence of their members. They do this by offering educational courses and certification. The major certifying body is the Institute of Certified Travel Agents in Washington, D.C. Its program leads to a Certified Travel Counselor (CTC) designation and requires the candidate to pass a qualifying examination and have at least five years of related travel and tourism experience. A similar program is offered in Britain by ABTA through its Institute of Travel Agents.

U.S. Airline Deregulation and Travel Agencies

Airline deregulation in the United States was instituted in order to improve airline productivity, promote competition, and lower rates. Although deregulation did not specifically consider travel agencies, it has had a major impact on them. For example, the ATC (the appointing body between U.S. domestic airlines and travel agencies) and the IATA (the international body) theoretically lost their sole authority to make appointments, that is, to give travel agencies the right to write up and sell airline tickets. Individual airlines thus were free to make appointments independently of groups such as the IATA and ATC, and the agencies themselves became deregulated, making it theoretically much easier for anybody to start up a travel agency.

Another impact of travel agency deregulation is that commission rates between airlines and agencies in the United States are no longer fixed by general agreement among all the participating airlines. A travel agency is now free to negotiate with each airline. As a result, overrides, discounts, and rebates are much more common than they used to be.

One issue not yet decided is whether travel agencies should still have the exclusive right in the United States to sell airline tickets. Some feel that if anyone can sell airline tickets, the distribution system as it has been for decades will be severely disrupted, as any person or organization that an airline considers suitable will be free to write and sell airline tickets. A large corporation could sell tickets to its own employees and even to the public at large, as could a hotel front-desk clerk to guests of the hotel. The agencies feel that these forms of airline ticket distribution will affect the counseling and other services that the agencies now provide.

DISCUSSION QUESTIONS

1. Who started the first travel agency, and when and how?
2. How do large travelers' check–issuing companies make most of their money?
3. What were some of the earliest travel agencies?
4. Apart from selling tickets, what other services do today's agencies normally provide?
5. Why do travel agencies' computerized reservation systems tend to favor particular airlines?
6. What is an STP; how does it operate; and what advantages does it offer?
7. What is an override?
8. Discuss airline ticket price discounting.
9. What is a ticket consolidator? How does a consolidator operate and differ from a bucket shop?
10. What is a corporate travel agency?
11. What is a travel agency appointment? What effect did airline deregulation in the United States have on appointments?
12. Translate the following acronyms: ASTA, ARTA, ABTA, ACTA, PATA, and CTA.
13. Discuss the effects of airline deregulation on U.S. travel agencies.

PROBLEM

You are a travel counselor advising an elderly, recently widowed woman who is somewhat shy but nevertheless anxious to make her first extended vacation trip alone. Using your knowledge gained in earlier chapters in this book about people and their motivation to travel, and assuming you know nothing else about this woman, what kind of trip would you recommend? What questions would you ask her?

REFERENCES

Burkart, A. J., and S. Medlik. 1974. *Tourism: Past, Present, and Future*. London: Heinemann.

SUGGESTED READINGS

Bitner, Mary J., and Bernard H. Booms. 1986. "A Model of the Hotel Selection Process and Preliminary Analysis of the Travel Agent's Influence." In *The Practice of Hospitality Management II*, ed. Robert C. Lewis, Thomas J. Beggs, Margaret Shaw, and Steven A. Croffoot. Westport, Conn.: AVI, pp. 473–487.

Bitner, Mary J., and Bernard H. Booms. 1981. "Deregulation and the Future of the U.S. Travel Agency Industry." *Journal of Travel Research* 20(2): 2–7.

Davidoff, Philip G., and Doris S. Davidoff. 1988. *Financial Management for Travel Agencies*. Albany: Delmar.

Gee, Chuck Y., Dexter J. L. Choy, and James C. Makens. 1984. *The Travel Industry*. Westport, Conn.: AVI, pp. 142–150.

Godwin, Nadine. 1987. *Complete Guide to Travel Agency Automation*. Albany: Delmar.

Lehmann, A. D. 1980. *Travel and Tourism: An Introduction to Travel Agency Operation*. Indianapolis: Bobbs-Merrill.

Lehmann, A. D. 1988. *A Travel Agency Policy and Procedures Manual*. Albany: Delmar.

Miller, J. R. 1987. *Legal Aspects of Travel Agency Operation*. Albany: Delmar.

Pudney, John. 1953. *The Thomas Cook Story*. London: Michael Joseph.

Stevens, Laurence. 1983. *Guide to Starting and Operating a Successful Travel Agency*. Albany: Delmar.

Stevens, Laurence. 1988. *The Travel Agency Personnel Manual*. Albany: Delmar.

Thompson-Smith, Jeanie M. 1988. *Corporate and Business Travel*. Albany: Delmar.

An Introduction to Franchising

About sixty years ago, Howard Johnson operated a small drugstore in the town of Quincy, Massachusetts. He was constantly trying out new methods to improve the quality of his soda fountain ice cream and testing techniques of food processing. His objective was to start up a chain of sandwich and ice-cream stands offering a uniform product and with an outdoor sign easily identifiable and recognizable by passing motorists. He sold his idea and the use of his name and symbol to a Cape Cod restaurant operator and received in return a fee and a contract to supply standardized food and other supplies. He had sold his first franchise. By 1935 there were thirty-five Howard Johnson restaurants in Massachusetts and, by the start of World War II, about one hundred of them along the coast auto routes from New England to Florida. Today, of course, the Howard Johnson name is nationally known, not only for its restaurants, but also for its franchised chain of motor lodges.

The link between tourism and franchising has been a strong one. For example, today about 75 percent of fast-food restaurants are franchised. It was franchising that allowed companies to expand so rapidly (by using the franchisees' capital) in the rapid-growth years of tourism after World War II. This expansion was both national and international, and today we see hotel chains (such as Holiday Inn, Quality Inn, Ramada, Sheraton), motel chains (Days Inn, Travelodge, Treadway, Rodeway), restaurants (McDonald's, Wendy's, Burger King), travel agencies (Travel Network, Fugazy, Empress), auto rental companies (Hertz, Budget, Dollar, National), and campgrounds (Safari, Kampgrounds of America) now offering their services to tourists in many locations around the world.

Franchising as a means for the independent entrepreneur to go into business for himself or herself has been booming for the last twenty years, and no letup is in sight. One only needs to look at business journals and newspaper business sections, or even in the business opportunities section of newspaper classified advertising, to see the many references made to franchised businesses.

Franchising is simply a form of distribution of a good or a service and, because of its high profile in the fast-food industry, has often been identified with that type of business. But there are many other types of franchised tourism operations to which the traveler can be exposed apart from those already mentioned. Some of these are service stations, bus tour operations, convenience-food stores, and drug stores. Even the tourist buying a cola drink from a grocery store is also probably buying a product made locally under a franchise agreement. The tourist's life is touched by franchising at every turn!

WHAT IS FRANCHISING?

There is no commonly accepted definition of franchising that can be applied in all cases, but in general terms it is a method of distribution or marketing in which a company (the franchisor) grants by contract to an individual or another company (the franchisee) the right to carry on a business in a prescribed way in a particular location for a specified period. The franchisee may be allowed to operate only one establishment or may be given an area in which a number of franchised outlets may be operated. That area could be a city, a state or province, a major portion of the country, or indeed the whole country. For example, Wendy's in the United States a few years ago gave a private Canadian company the territorial rights to all of Canada for Wendy's restaurant operations.

Fees and Other Requirements

For the services that it provides, the franchisor receives a fee, or royalty, usually based on gross sales or else a fixed fee (for example, a flat monthly or annual amount, or a fixed fee based on the number of rooms in a hotel or motel franchise). In addition the franchisees usually have to pay their own share of local, regional, or national advertising costs. Again, this advertising cost is usually a percentage of sales revenue. The fees and other costs are generally payable monthly.

For what the franchisees pay, they may receive business advice and counsel, financial aid (direct or indirect), market research, lease negotiation, site evaluation, building plans, training programs, national advertising, an accounting system, and an established and widely recognized name and image.

Although the franchisees must arrange for most of their financing, the franchisor may provide some. In such cases the monthly fee will probably include an extra amount to pay back this franchisor financing, with interest. But even if the franchisee has to arrange for the entire financing, the franchisor's credit strength and reputation can be of help in seeking a loan.

The franchisees usually are required to maintain certain standards established by the franchisor, such as housekeeping standards (in a hotel or motel), pricing, and the requirement to purchase products from the franchisor at prices higher than they can be purchased locally. The individual franchisee may see these standards as an imposition, causing a loss of independence. But on the other hand, the franchisee has to consider the benefits of increased business that national advertising can produce or the advantages of a tie-in with a chain hotel's or motel's national or international reservation system.

A BRIEF HISTORY OF FRANCHISING

Although it is thought that there were some forms of franchising in Europe in the eighteenth century, they did not have any great impact on the way most business was conducted. In fact, franchising's major impact began in the United States when the Singer Sewing Machine Company initiated a manufacturer/retailer distribution franchise system after the Civil War.

At the beginning of the nineteenth century the Industrial Revolution gained momentum in the United States, and the resulting advances in technology, combined with a good transportation system and improved communication, set the stage for mass production and distribution. Manufacturers and producers quickly realized that the distribution of their products to the marketplace was a key to their success as producers.

In the 1920s and 1930s the automobile industry grew rapidly as the public began enjoying the mobility afforded by the automobile and the manufacturers established franchised dealers (retailers) to distribute their product. Similarly, soft drink producers realized that they would have problems shipping bottled soft drinks over great distances and therefore established local franchise producers operating under license. A third major force was the petroleum industry that moved its products to the market through independent franchised service stations.

Boom Period

The period after the second World War saw a tremendous surge in the acceptance of the franchising concept. This period, to about the mid-1960s, is often called the boom period of franchising and is generally attributed to the mobility of the North American traveling public and its heavy demand for tourist services such as roadside accommodations and food services. During this period many new categories of franchising were developed, such as fast-food restaurants, automobile and trailer rentals, motels, and recreation facilities. The franchisor companies' shares on the stock markets became the glamour stocks of this era, and at the time, the sky seemed to be the limit to the franchising phenomenon.

Unfortunately, the stock market boom in these glamour stocks began to fall apart, mainly because of adverse publicity regarding a number of the franchise schemes in the fast-food industry built around famous personalities. Because of these "names," the franchisors were able to charge exorbitantly high initial fees to franchisees, while providing little in return in the way of operating services or training. This, combined with high interest rates, caused the failure of many franchisors. One of the more famous (or infamous) was that of Minnie Pearl (a chicken-based franchise scheme). By the summer of 1969 nearly two thousand franchises had been sold in North America, but fewer than two hundred restaurants actually opened, and none of these survived. Such abuses, and in some cases illegal practices, resulted in court decisions and restrictive regulations that created a slowdown in franchise expansion, particularly in the fast-food restaurant category.

Solid Base

This retrenchment was finally overcome, and since about 1970 the franchising method of distribution of goods and services has built a solid base and expanded into many new areas. The maturity of franchising is now more obvious. Franchising's growth rate is steady, and once again many established companies see it as an attractive way to expand. Franchisors with little to offer are being eliminated, and the ones that remain will be those with experience and management competence.

In particular, the hotel and motel franchising segment has shown solid growth (despite the mounting costs of energy). The computerization of both national and international reservation systems has contributed to this growth. One new segment is the budget motel that offers a minimum of frills but a very low room rate. Franchised campgrounds have also appeared during this period, as have travel agencies, suntan parlors, and other recreation, entertainment, and travel businesses.

A fast-food franchised operation is usually distinctive and easily recognized, frequently offering a limited menu and takeout service. This type of fast-food operation is still a leader in the field, although some types of sit-down restaurants have opened franchised operations. Many of the entrepreneurs who obtained franchises in the early days of fast-food franchising were able to control a particular territory and prospered along with the franchisor. Indeed, in some cases the multiownership of franchises has resulted in chains within chains, with some franchisees now larger in dollar sales strength than their franchisors are. Despite this, many opportunities still exist for prospective franchisors with new, small, expanding chains that can offer a good product to franchisees. The fast-food field runs the whole gamut from hamburgers, hot dogs, french fries, and milkshakes, to pizza, barbecued beef or ribs, fried chicken, steaks, Mexican food, seafood, pancakes and waffles, roast beef sandwiches, and fast-food pies, to name only a few. The trend toward a shorter workweek, longer vacations, more legal holidays, more disposable income, and earlier retirement all have contributed to the growth of leisure and travel business franchises.

ADVANTAGES OF FRANCHISING FOR FRANCHISEES

Some of the major advantages to a franchisee entering a tourist business are

- The possibility of starting up as a generally independent entrepreneur but with the support of an established parent company: the franchisor. The franchisor may provide assistance in such matters as financing, site selection, construction supervision, employee training, and support during the difficult period just after opening.

- The opportunity to buy into an established concept, although this by itself is no guarantee of success. The risk of failure, however, is generally reduced. Statistics show that the independent entrepreneur opening a small tourist business stands a 70 to 80 percent chance of not surviving the first few critical years. As a franchisee, similar statistics show an 80 percent chance of success.

- The ongoing support of the franchisor, who can provide assistance and help solve problems, as it can afford to hire specialists in the head office in such areas as cost control, marketing and sales, and research and development.

- The potential for local, regional, national, or even international advertising campaigns successfully developed by the franchisor.
- Access to credit that might not otherwise be available. Banks and similar lending institutions are usually more willing to lend money to an entrepreneur who has the backing of a successful franchisor than they would to an independent entrepreneur.
- The opportunity to purchase supplies at a reduced cost, as the franchisor can purchase in bulk and pass on the savings to the franchisees (as much as 3 to 6 percent on costs may be saved in this way).
- An opportunity to take over a turnkey franchise operation. A turnkey operation is one in which the franchisor provides a complete franchise, performing services such as assistance in obtaining financing, site evaluation, selection and acquisition, construction and equipping of premises, training of staff, "startup" assistance, initial inventory, management and accounting reporting systems, advertising, public relations and marketing services, and, after opening, supervision and guidance. In other words, about all the franchisee has to do is turn the key in the door and start in business.
- Finally, franchising offers many of the advantages of an integrated chain business (without some of the disadvantages) because of the voluntary nature of the contract rather than central ownership.

DISADVANTAGES OF FRANCHISING FOR FRANCHISEES

Just as there are advantages to the franchised form of business, so are there some disadvantages:

- The cost of the services provided by the franchisor come off the top of sales revenue and can add up to 10 percent or more of that revenue.
- Even though the franchise arrangement allows the franchisee to start a business that he or she might otherwise be able to begin only with difficulty, there will be some loss of freedom, as the franchisor's standards must be maintained, and there may be few opportunities for individual personal initiative.
- In some cases the franchisor's markup on the products that must be purchased from it can increase operating costs, particularly if an equally good product can be purchased locally at a lower cost.

- Experience shows that the franchisee runs some risk of not achieving the sales potential, and thus the profit, that the franchisor stated was possible when selling the franchise.
- If the franchisor operates from a jurisdiction other than the one in which the franchisee operates, and its obligations are not fulfilled, it can be difficult, if not impossible, to seek redress.

THE FRANCHISOR'S CONTROLS

A prospective franchisee needs to find out what controls the franchisor plans to exercise. Controls, or standardization, are what holds together many franchise systems. Most franchisors exercise this control in order to influence their own eventual profits. However, the franchisor's success is dependent on the image of the franchise system as perceived by the franchise's customers. If the system does not have a product or service that is consistent in appearance, quality, service, or price, many of the franchise system's advantages will be lost. That is, the market image is essential to the franchise concept.

The controls that a franchisor may use include any or all of the following:

- Architectural design and layout of the franchise outlet.
- Insurance requirements.
- The source of equipment and furnishings required.
- Where the product, or the ingredients in the product, to be sold must be purchased.
- The product quality and/or service.
- The selling price(s) of the product or service.
- Hours of operation.
- Parking space requirements.
- Advertising and promotion delivery methods for the product or service.
- Training requirements for each new employee.
- Accounting procedures and required reports (and possibly even the franchisor's access to the franchisee's accounting and banking records).
- The right of the franchisor to have the last word in any disagreements between the franchisor and the franchisee.

Controls are usually instituted for the good of all franchisees (and obviously for the good of the franchisor!). But sometimes, unfortunately, controls are imposed for the sole benefit of the franchisor. For example, there have been cases of franchisees' following controls to the letter, building up the business, and then finding that the franchisor can terminate the agreement and continue to reap the profits. Similarly, franchisees have found that their "exclusive" territorial rights are not sufficiently protected in the contract to ensure that the franchisor does not open up a competitive operation on the other side of the street.

CONTINUED MANAGEMENT ASSISTANCE

A prospective franchisee should ask questions about various key areas. For example, a franchisee will probably be better off with a franchisor who can show evidence of continued management assistance after opening. This may include ongoing management or employee training, new merchandising ideas, and new products. Management assistance should also include visits by the franchisor's representative to the franchisee's premises. A potential franchisee should find out the frequency of these visits. Is there any assurance that head office personnel will be available for consultation when problems arise? This should be provided, as the franchisee should be able to look to the head office in the same way as a chain hotel or restaurant manager can look to the head office. What kind of backup management help does the franchisor have in its head office? Are there specialists who have worked in the field themselves? Are there accounting and finance experts, as well as specialists in areas such as site selection, construction supervision, marketing, advertising and promotion, personnel and training, operations, real estate, and research and development? Only a larger franchisor will be able to afford specialists in each of these areas. If a franchisee is going with a smaller, newer franchise concept, he or she may still want to ensure that there has been some general experience with the concept. For example, if it is a new motel franchise, at least one of the franchisor's principals should have had experience in operating motels.

THE CONTRACT

The backbone of any franchisor–franchisee relationship is the contract or agreement signed by both parties. The franchise agreement differs from the usual contract in that it contains restrictive clauses exclusive to the franchising relationship. These restrictive clauses limit the franchisee's rights and powers in the conduct of the business. Sad to say, too many franchisees probably read their copy of the contract with their eyes shut, and even if they do read it with their eyes open, they do not bother checking it out with a lawyer who could explain some of the more complex clauses.

The franchisee should not be talked into making any deposit or down payment to "demonstrate good faith" or "hold a contract open" or "put you at the head of the waiting list" while he or she studies the contract and goes over it with a lawyer. Reputable franchisors do not practice this kind of high-pressure salesmanship. If a franchisee does make a deposit with the franchisor because he or she is not sure about proceeding, the franchisee should insist that the deposit be held in trust and that this is so stated in the contract. An honest franchisor will agree to this.

If any promises are made about the franchisor–franchisee relationship that are not in the contract, the franchisee should insist that they be added before it is signed, because if any item is later disputed, the courts will generally recognize only what is in the contract.

The franchisee should not be afraid to negotiate more favorable terms in the contract. Most ethical franchisors understand that sometimes special conditions are necessary for a particular franchisee and may agree to these as long as the franchisor still maintains its return on investment and its integrity in terms of quality control. However, an ethical franchisor will not negotiate away essential major points that will violate the franchise system. To do so would mean that there is no reason to have them in the contract in the first place. If any franchisor is willing to concede such major points, such as erosion of quality standards in order to obtain fees, this should warn the prospective franchisee to turn to other franchisors.

The Franchisor's Obligations

There is no such thing as a standard franchise contract. Each contract differs in some way(s) from all others, although most contracts contain clauses or sections covering the restrictions and obligations of both the franchisor and the franchisee. The franchisor's obligations may include any or all of the following:

- Financial assistance.
- Site selection and layout.
- Plans and specifications for buildings and other site improvements.
- Specifications for any necessary equipment and furniture.
- Promotional and advertising material.
- Employee hiring assistance.
- Franchisee and staff training.
- Business opening assistance.
- Business operations manuals.
- A bookkeeping/accounting system.
- Product supply assurance.
- Ongoing support in such things as consultation, visits to the premises, and staff retraining.

The Franchisee's Obligations

The franchisee's obligations might include any or all of the following:

- Construction according to plans and specifications provided.
- Maintenance of construction and opening schedules.
- Adherence to lease commitments.
- Purchase of required insurance.
- Completion of required training.
- Adequate working capital.
- Full-time effort.
- Purchase of products and other items from the franchisor or from an approved supplier.
- Agreement to abide by the operations manual.
- Proper repair and maintenance of the building and site.
- Financial reporting and prompt payment of amounts due.
- Proper use of trademark.
- Participation in regional or national cooperative advertising.

In addition there will probably be clauses regarding bankruptcy, transfer of the business, renewal of the contract, provisions for fee and royalty payments, trademark usage, facilities design, purchase and sale of the products or services, inventory, pricing, advertising, operating procedures, and accounting methods.

FRANCHISE COSTS AND ROYALTIES

One of the first items mentioned in the contract will be the cost of getting started. This amount can vary from thousands to hundreds of thousands of dollars, depending on the type of business involved, who owns what assets, and the services provided by the franchisor.

Although service franchisors (such as a travel agency organization) might charge a franchise fee for the use of their name and operating methods and forms, this amount is generally relatively nominal. In addition, there may be no ongoing fee or royalty. If there is, for services such as advertising, it will be a percentage of gross sales or revenue. In some cases there may be no initial fee nor a continuing percent of revenue. The franchisor leases the premises to the franchisee who must purchase supplies from the franchisor (which, along with the rent payments, is where the franchisor makes its profits). At the other end of the scale is the restaurant or motel franchise for which the initial and ongoing fees can be quite sizable, depending on who owns the land, building, equipment, and furnishings. The initial franchise fee includes the right to use the franchisor's trade name, licenses, and operating procedures, as well as any initial and ongoing training, and possibly even assistance in site selection. In some rare instances this initial fee is refundable when the business is on its feet and is making a return on its investment. Some franchisors also charge an additional site evaluation fee.

The contract should state when the franchise fee is payable and when it is fully earned. Normally the fee is payable on signing and is nonrefundable on termination of the agreement for any reason. The contract will usually state that the fee is fully earned by the franchisor on the signing of the agreement or, in some situations, when the building plans and specifications have been provided by the franchisor or when the operations manual has been turned over to the franchisee. In some contracts the franchisor may require the franchisee to put up a certain amount of working capital, in addition to the initial franchise fee, to cover operating costs until the business is making a profit.

Royalties

In addition to the initial franchise costs, the franchisor is typically paid a royalty, ranging from 2 to 6 percent of gross sales revenue, depending on the services provided. These services include accounting records, inventory control, management counseling, product research, and, in the case of businesses such as hotels, motels, or campgrounds, a reservation and referral service. A major item in this royalty cost is advertising.

If the franchisee's participation in advertising campaigns is not tied to a percentage of sales, he or she should find out the cost of any advertising and have this stated in the contract. If he or she wishes to do any local advertising at his or her own cost, does it have to be approved in advance by the franchisor if no advertising materials are provided? Does the advertising royalty have to be paid when sales are not adequate, and if so, what is the sales level that is considered inadequate? The franchisor might also increase its revenue by supplementing the royalty payment with interest charges on any financing provided, markups on supplies or equipment to be purchased from it, or higher-than-normal rent payments (if the franchisor is also the landlord). The facts in each case should be in the contract.

TERRITORY

The contract should be carefully checked for matters such as territorial restrictions and territory exclusivity. Ambiguities are common in this area. The word *exclusive* may imply that the franchisor will not operate, nor franchise out to others to operate, a business from a location within the same specified territory. There is nothing wrong with a nonexclusive territory (in fact it can be advantageous if the market supports it) as long as the franchisee knows about it in advance and agrees to it. Nonexclusivity may provide a reduced sales base, but it can also offer sales benefits by keeping the name of the franchise in front of the public.

Some questions about territory that the franchisee should have answered in the contract are

- Exactly what are the geographic boundaries of the territory, and is it marked on a map as part of the contract?
- Does the franchisee have a choice of other territories?
- What direct competition is there currently in the territory chosen, and how many more franchises does the franchisor expect to sell in that area in the next five years? In other words, how much time does the franchisee have to build a solid base of customer goodwill?
- If the territory is an "exclusive" one, what are the guarantees of this exclusivity?
- Even with these guarantees, will the franchisee be permitted to open another franchise in the same territory? Alternatively, is the guarantee valid only if the franchisee agrees to start up one or more franchises in the same territory in a given number of years?
- Can the franchisor reduce the territory at any time?
- Has the franchisor prepared a market survey of the territory? If so, it should be reviewed.
- Has the specific site within the territory been decided? If not, how will this be done?

TRAINING

Because tourist businesses are usually service businesses, employee training is critical. Most franchise contracts include one or more sections concerning the training provided for a new franchise outlet. Training may last anywhere from a few hours to several weeks, sometimes at the franchisor's head office. For example, McDonald's operates a Hamburger University at its corporate headquarters and offers a degree in hamburgerology!

The contract should spell out exactly what training is offered and its duration, who pays for it, whether transportation and lodging (if involved) are paid by the franchisee or the franchisor, and whether the franchisee and any staff involved will be paid a salary or stipend during any extended training period. In addition, the franchisee should check to see whether the training program includes working in a successful operating unit of the franchise company for a certain period of time. Some franchise contracts require the completion of training as a prerequisite to becoming a franchisee. If the contract has such a provision, the franchisee should determine what the criteria are for the successful completion of the training, and whether the initial franchise fee is refundable should the franchisee or any of his or her employees fail to complete the training satisfactorily.

Because the franchisor–franchisee relationship does not terminate at the end of the training period, the contract should spell out any on-the-job training that will be offered by company representatives, supervisors, or franchisee coordinators, particularly when new employees are hired. Are any company newsletters, film-strips, or tapes provided that will keep the franchisee and his or her employees updated on new products or sales methods? If franchisees are expected to attend refresher courses from time to time, is this spelled out, and who will pay the costs?

OPERATIONS

Most franchisors want fairly tight control over day-to-day operations. This is usu-ally achieved by giving the franchisee a copyrighted operations manual that spells out, procedure by procedure, the ways in which the franchisee is expected to run the business. It includes the franchisor's policies and procedures and covers such details as the hours the business must remain open, record-keeping methods, pro-cedures for hiring employees, and (in a restaurant operation) such matters as reci-pes, portion sizes, food storage and handling procedures, menu mix, and selling prices. The franchisee should inspect the manual, if possible, before signing the franchise agreement to be sure that its requirements are practical.

The franchisor's operating policies and procedures are an area that can cause considerable franchisee dissatisfaction once a new business has been successfully established, particularly if they force the franchisee to follow inefficient or unprof-itable methods or preclude him or her from taking advantage of local suppliers' discounted product prices that are lower than the franchisor's.

If the franchisee is required to purchase products and/or supplies from the fran-chisor or approved suppliers (this is referred to as "tied" selling), he or she should consider the suppliers' locations, as this will dictate shipping costs and distances as well as the timing of deliveries which may be important in the case of perishable supplies. The contract should ensure that the franchisee can select the supplier if circumstances permit.

Does the contract call for a minimum purchase quota (a form of hidden cost)? If the franchisor requires that the franchisee purchase only from it, how will the price of the products and/or supplies be established? What assurances are there that the prices will be reasonable or competitive? Does the contract prohibit the franchisee from purchasing from other sources from which he or she could buy identical or similar supplies at a lower cost? Finally, is there a contracted right to the franchi-sor's latest innovations or products? Does the contract require any additional fee for this right?

SUGGESTED READINGS

Adams, John, and K. V. Pritchard Jones. *Franchising—Practices and Precedents in Business Format Franchising*. London: Butterworths.

Friedlander, Mark, Jr., and Gene Gurney. 1981. *Handbook of Successful Franchising*. New York: Van Nostrand Reinhold.

Seltz, David D. 1982. *The Complete Book of Franchising*. Reading, Mass.: Addison-Wesley.

Siegel, William Laird. 1983. *Franchising*. New York: Wiley.

Index